Across
the Cimarron

By JAMES D. HORAN

BONANZA BOOKS • New York

To Gary and Danny, once the littlest cowboys.

Printed in the United States of America

Contents

An Author's Search into
the Life of a Frontiersman

ONE APRIL day in 1953, Sylvester Vigilante, then of the New York Public Library staff, called to ask if I would like to meet one of the last of the frontier deputies. He had lived in Dodge City, Vig said, when Wyatt Earp, Bill Tilghman and other lawmen were taming the wild West. "He's the real thing," he assured me. "I've documented some of the things he has told me."

"Where is he, Vig?" I asked, impressed. "Wyoming?"

"Fifteen minutes from Times Square by the West Side subway," Vigilante replied. His name was George Bolds. One of the last frontiersmen here in New York City! Now I was *really* interested.

I found a tall, soft-spoken white-haired man, with a wry sense of humor and an incredible memory. Although he was almost ninety, he was still a handsome figure. His eyesight was almost gone—he saw me as a shadow—but at eighty he had taught himself to type. I have many of his typed letters and memoirs; they are almost without an error.

The first time we met, George was not particularly eager to talk, but Vig, whom he knew and respected as one of the finest students of the old West, was able to thaw his reserve. The next time George was more affable; someone had read to him a piece I'd written about Clay Allison. That night he talked of Dodge City in the days when he had first ridden into town, "green as a gourd."

Both Vig and I tested his tales by deliberately substituting false names and dates. "When the Earps left Dodge in 1882 (1879), George . . ." or "It was then that Bat Masterson killed Sergeant Queen (King), wasn't it?"

But George was both patient and modest. He didn't profess to know every date of every Western incident. He didn't claim undying friendship with the Earps or Doc Holliday, nor did he insist that he had killed countless numbers of men. He was even reluctant to discuss the fatal shootings in which he had taken part. "I killed two, possibly three men in my lifetime, Jim," he said. "No intelligent man brags of taking human life."

As we listened we found gradually emerging a vivid picture of life on the frontier, as it was lived by an educated young hellion who had a keen eye and a remarkable memory. This man was among the last living links with the Wild West. I wanted to preserve his stories and I suggested bringing along a tape recorder on our next visit. George was dubious, but said he thought it would be all right "if you can get the damn thing through the door."

The first time George held the mike he almost got buck fever, but after several attempts he began to relax. As the months passed my pile of tapes grew high. In the intervals between our recording sessions, George wrote me long letters, apologizing for his failure to recall a certain incident or date, then adding as many as twenty pages of single-spaced copy to augment the last tape.

When I approached George about doing a book on his life, he snorted, "Who the hell wants to read an old coot's memoirs?" But George agreed to think over my suggestion. "Jim," he said, some weeks later, "If you're fool enough to try and make an old man's memories readable, well, I'll help all I can."

We started at the very beginning—the day his father came home from the Civil War. As the weeks passed, a moving love story began to emerge; a love story of a wanderer and a firm-minded young woman, tested by gunfire, violence and great distances. "Adda was not only the prettiest but the wisest woman I ever met. I wish you could have met her." I wish so, too.

He had a real flair for spinning a yarn. As I sat in his tiny apartment his clear, steady voice took me along the rutted streets of Dodge City, across the empty Kansas prairie, into the blazing guns of Cimarron at the side of a fiercely independent youth, searching through the West to quell the restlessness in his heart.

But after months of reliving the old days with me, George began to fail. He became completely blind and his legs grew unsteady. The tapes at this period are marked by a deep, racking heart cough. We deliberately stayed away for fear that we were wearing thin his failing strength. But there was always a cheerful note from George. At this writing I am reading: "Waited for you kids until 9 P.M., then had a couple of drinks and went to bed. Give me a shout next week. I'm here—where the hell can I go?—if you want me. . . ."

We went back. George kept on until he grew too feeble. Death, it seemed, waited impatiently outside his door, but somehow the keen mind and tough old body, toughened by blizzards, winds and long hours in the saddle, refused to surrender. Heart and brain remained alert until almost the very end. Then one night he slipped away, to join his beloved Adda and the host of shadows wearing wide-brimmed hats and carrying guns that he had summoned back for us.

He had many other things to tell me. Among his papers was a note: "Tell Jim about fight on Salt Fork. . . ." He had left some notes on Doc Holliday. He had promised a story on Buffalo Jones and the day the buffalo ran wild in Kansas City.

He had written to a ninety-year-old gentleman in Kansas who was to have supplied me with a good story about himself.

The pressure of another project—a book I was writing on the Civil War—interrupted my further examination of George's papers. One night I switched on a western on TV and just as quickly shut it off. It was incredibly juvenile. I removed the stack of tape recordings from my files and brought out the tape recorder.

"Want to hear a real western?" I told my son. "This is the way it really was."

"Turn it on," he said warily.

George Bolds' voice soon filled the room. Strong men died, county-seat wars flared up. We could see the vast empty prairies, the miles of campfires along the Oklahoma line winking like yellow cats' eyes in the blackness. We saw dusty Dodge City and shared the bitter hours of a lonely boy with a restless heart.

"He really *was* there," my son said admiringly. I began to write this book that night.

When I began to check George Bolds' story I found that he had been amazingly accurate. Of course, he had a few first names wrong and his spelling in a few instances was wrong. But he was close—Wilson for Watson and Hawkins for Horton, for example.

He had remarked that some newspapers had listed his name among the wounded at the Battle of Cimarron. A search of the New York papers of that month produced a column-long story, with Bolds listed among the wounded. He recalled having been at the bar with the New York *Herald's* correspondent who'd covered a bullfight in Dodge, and my search of the *Herald's* files produced such an account.

That Bill Tilghman liked the restless young wanderer is evident in what Mrs. Zoe Tilghman, his widow, herself an author and historian, in her letter to me, recalled, "Bill spoke many times of George Bolds and held him in high respect."

And a ninety-year-old Kansan recalled just before he died two years ago, "George was out here when the country was young. He was handy with both a gun and a surveying rod. I don't recall the killings, but I do know that paved highways now follow where he set down his rods."

In rounding out and checking the life and times of George Bolds, I have had the help of several individuals—some of whom I have met only through the mail—and a number of historical societies.

The first is Mr. Sylvester Vigilante, now of the New York Historical Society, who realized the importance of preserving the old gentleman's memoirs, and Mr. Homer Croy, that timeless Missourian, who turned over to me notes of interviews he'd had with George Bolds; Mr. Jay Bolds, who searched for his father's papers in New York and Indiana and turned them over to me, along with his own memories of what his mother had told him; Mr. and Mrs. Kenneth Bolds, for their memories; Mr. Forrest Luther, of Cimarron, Kansas, who wrote me of his memories of George, and Mrs. Luther, who searched for pictures of those long forgotten days; the staff of the American History Room of the New York Public Library; the invaluable Mr. James Heslin and the staff of the Library of the New York Historical Society; the staff of the Newspaper Room of the Library of Congress; Mrs. Zoe Tilghman, Bill Tilghman's widow; and Miss Ina T. Aulls, of the Western History department of Denver's great Public Library. I am indebted to Miss Helen Staeuble and Miss Joan Duhigg for their fine editorial assistance.

There is ancient authority that the last shall be first, and in this case it is Gertrude, whose assistance was vital to this book.

I would also like to thank the two Joes—Mr. Joseph Dorrity and Mr. Joseph Estrada—who solved the difficulty of getting a tape recorder wired for DC to work, when we had only AC current.

JAMES D. HORAN

Horan's Boondocks
April 1, 1956

The Return of "The Brave"

MY WORLD in the sweet month of May, 1865, was the front yard of our log cabin in the heart of Adams County, Indiana. There was a spreading apple tree whose blossoms showered down like gentle snowflakes when I shook the lower branches. In the yard was a chopping block, chickens which were eternally scratching and clucking and a rooster—my deadly enemy.

Beyond the split rail fence was the forest and still farther away was the black swamp. Across a rutted dusty road was a pasture, fragrant with clover and dotted with daisies. There our plow horses fought the deer flies with their tails and cropped the grass. This was my world, where I lived with my mother, my sister and my brother.

My father was away at war. He had enlisted with the 2nd Indiana Regiment and we had had no word from him for almost two years except from a neighbor who had seen him briefly in a hospital before he had been moved out.

As I send my thoughts back almost a century to that afternoon I can catch only far-off glimpses of a woman in a long dress, bending over a tub, but I can almost sense the warm sun and smell the apple blossoms and feel the dust under my bare feet.

As always, I was chasing the rooster. Mother had just scolded me and I was sitting on a stump looking out across the pasture. Suddenly I called out, "Mama . . . Mama . . . Joe is coming."

I ran to the fence and peered through the rails. I had seen Cousin Joe Pine on his half-broken bronc, which only he could ride, skimming the fences like a great hunter. Now we could hear his faint shouts.

Mother gathered me up and ran to the gate. I kept fighting to get down, but Mother paid me no heed. Later, she told me her heart had whispered that *he* was home.

Cousin Joe cleared the last fence and galloped up the road. At our gate he pulled back hard on his reins. "They're coming from the railroad, Aunt Leah . . . they're coming!"

Now we could see two horsemen riding slowly toward us. Cousin Joe raced up to them, then wheeled about and returned to us, shouting to my mother. She only hugged me tighter and walked through the front gate out into the middle of the road. At last they were before us and both weary riders slid out of their saddles.

One of them came toward us. Suddenly smothered by a man in a rough blue coat, I twisted frantically and screamed. I recall standing on the ground, Mother's face next to me and a gaunt man with a grizzled beard kissing me. The beard scratched my face and the man was crying. So was Mother.

Father was home from the war—with an empty blue sleeve. He had left his left arm at the battle of Nashville and a good part of his health in the mud and filth of a front-line hospital and prison. Years later he told us how he had chewed on a minié ball when the surgeon removed his arm. "I swear my teeth met when that saw went through the bone. But I considered myself lucky that I didn't land in the dead men's tent with some undertaker pumping embalming fluid into me." The other man was his brother-in-law, John Van Deening, who had married one of my aunts.

I remember running in the yard the rest of the morning, watching neighbors arriving in wagons and on horseback, hurrying across the yard and into our house. I didn't care; I was chasing the red rooster and there wasn't anyone to tell me to stop.

The log cabin had been the home of Leah, my mother, and Alexander, my father, since their marriage in 1855. Father had been out in the wilderness since he was ten, when his father had left the rockbound hills of upper New York State for Medina County, Indiana. When my father was about sixteen a cholera plague swept across the wilderness. He buried his mother in the morning and his father that night. For a week he lay in his bed, heartbroken and sick. Gradually he crawled to the kitchen to eat some fruit. The next few days were a haze as he went on about his farm chores automatically.

It was the back-breaking work of caring for the farm that turned his grief into a dull ache in his heart, which stayed there until he left Medina County. His sisters brought him back with them to their home in Adams County. The old farm was sold for fifty cents an acre. Father was given the four horses and wagon and farm implements. But living with his in-laws was not to his liking, so he began roaming the wilderness, searching for good land and a suitable wife. He found both the land and the girl at a local barn-raising.

One night, as Mother told me when I asked about her childhood memories, her Pennsylvania Dutch father had called a council of his large family back in Lancaster, Ohio. He was ready to start for Indiana within a week and wanted to hear their comments. Though Leah's older sister had gained a beau, she was overruled. In the wilderness of Adams County, fifty miles south of Fort Wayne, he bought several tracts of land at $1.50 an acre. A tireless man, he cleared the land, which he divided into sections, one for each child.

Mother received her tract of land as a marriage gift and on it my father built a two-room log cabin with split log floors. They were made simply by splitting a log, putting the beveled part down and hewing the other part off with an ax. Father still had his wagon and horses, so it didn't cost them much to take up housekeeping. In their first year of married life my mother received a share of her grandfather's estate. Father hired some hands and, by working dawn to dusk, within a few years had forty acres under cultivation.

Father loved books, but he loved the wilderness first. About six foot tall, he had thick black curly hair and gray eyes that turned to slate when he was angry. He was a splendid woodsman and a superb shot. When a turkey shoot took place, he invariably took first prize.

Mother was small, but brave and as tough as rawhide. It wasn't unusual for her to work shoulder to shoulder with Father in the field or clearing the brush. She disliked firearms, but she was a good shot. I can recall her shattering a bottle at a distance of twenty-five feet and walking away, head up. There were few men left to protect the small frontier community of ten families when the Civil War came, but the women valiantly managed the farms alone.

My brother, with me tagging along, would help with the sheep. Wolves and foxes were still fairly plentiful and fences had to be mended and watched. The sheep were washed and shorn by hand and the wool picked clean of burrs and knots. When it was combed it was put on the spinning wheel and made into yarn. I can still hear Mother telling us a story against the steady click of the wheel. Like other frontier women Mother also set out flax. When that was dried she would beat out the seeds and save them, because they were as good as money. We used a hackle—a piece of lumber with sharpened pikes—to pull the lint from the tough stalks. The lint, or tow, was used to make linen.

Especially during the war years the families lived off the land. I still sleep under blankets Mother made and they are as firm and pliable as if they had been made yesterday. Mother also made our suits and even soled our shoes. This was in addition to her farm chores, putting out the crops, milking the cows, feeding the hogs, even taking a turn at the forge if necessary. And with all this she could sing—in the fields, in the barn or working the bellows, her sweet face cherry red from the heat.

But the sweet songs died away as the months crept by and there was no news of my father. At night she would sit and rock, staring into the fire or endlessly spinning, the even clicking of the wheel going on far into the hours of the morning, after the fire had sunk into gray ashes and the edge of the cold crept into the room.

Years later Mother recalled for me the night she had received word that Father had been wounded. I remember a little of that night, when a neighbor girl rode up and knocked on our door. She stayed the night with my mother and my brother took me up to his bed in the loft. He told me he'd throw me in the black swamp the next day if I didn't keep quiet. As Mother said in her soft voice, the whole world had suddenly collapsed about her. Stunned, she barely remembered what she said or what she did.

For those next few days she was a robot, automatically tending to the chores, scolding us when we made too much noise, babying me when I stumbled or fell, dully preparing the meals. It was about a week before her head was clear. It was late fall then, cold and gray. At night she would read the Bible by the open fireplace while the wind wailed about the corners of the log cabin or shook the dead limbs of the trees in violent fury.

Later, when she heard officially that Father was still alive, she said she walked back into the woods where we couldn't see her and, falling down on the frozen ground, wept.

But, now—in blossoming May, 1865, the long dark days were over for all of us. My father was home again.

"We'll stay on the farm and we'll suffer no loss,
For the stone that keeps rolling will gather no moss."

—FRONTIER BALLAD

"Cimarron" George Bolds

"Oh, I was a fresh-faced kid all right. But I was going out West."

Son of the Frontier

DAY AFTER day the men of the community who had been away almost since I could remember started to drift in from the war—cousins, uncles and other kinfolk. Like my father, most of them had been released from Confederate prisons or federal hospitals. There was a great deal of sorrow in some of the log cabins where the menfolk didn't come home. Mother and the other neighbor women would go over and sit with the widow or mother, while the circuit preacher was sent for to say a few words of comfort.

After the first surge of joy was over the discharged soldiers were anxious to get back to the plow and the scythe. Although Uncle John Van Deening and my father had been badly wounded, in the end they were doing more work than the able-bodied men.

Mother was a stickler for education and as our family kept increasing she kept nagging Father and Uncle John until they finally called a meeting of the families living nearby. It was agreed that all the men would pitch in to build a log schoolhouse. After Father donated a section of the north pasture the menfolk gathered to cut down the logs, hew a floor, put on a roof and build a small corral for the teacher's horse. Later a well was dug and a stove installed. It was a great Sunday when the schoolhouse went up. The women had baked and cooked for days and the tables groaned with wonderful food. The menfolk played horseshoes, ran footraces, wrestled and shot at marks.

Even though he had only one arm, my father was still a fine shot. I can recall how he kept practicing at bits of wood stuck in the top rail of our fence. I can still see him in my mind's eye—a tall, powerfully built man with a full spade beard, the empty sleeve of his shirt tucked inside his belt, the rifle held in the crotch of his right arm, which gradually became as powerful as a sledgehammer as the muscles tackled the increased farm work. A careful sighting, then the sharp crack. "George, get the mark," he would shout. I would run to find the slab, which would have been knocked down or bored by the slug. "You hit it," I would cry as I ran back to him with the target. "Put it up again, boy, and let's have another try," he would say. At the shooting matches he always came away with a prize. For the next few days he would go about whistling or singing some frontier ballad. Or he would make Lady, our mare, clear the top rail of the pasture fence—to my mother's displeasure.

Our first teacher was Will Sheppard, who owned a farm near us. He was an excellent story-teller and we all sat engrossed, sharing a piece of cake from his lunch box, listening to his tales of George Rogers Clark and Simon Girty, the renegade.

I can never forget the tall stranger who taught us next. With his thick black beard and smoldering black eyes, he looked more like a river pirate than a schoolteacher. He had a cavernous voice and rode a mule that had seen its best days.

That first week was a living hell for all of us. Smith was a born tyrant. Among adults he was a soft-spoken, seemingly well-educated gentleman with a real love of youngsters, but behind the closed doors of that little schoolhouse he was a demon. He threatened us and swung his long hickory poles over our heads so often I think we were all nearly ready to run away.

The second Monday he was there, a cold spell froze the small pond near the schoolhouse where we played shinny—what they call hockey today. The bell rang, but by the time I got my skates off I was one of four pupils who walked in late.

Smith didn't say anything. He just motioned us over to the wall, then stood up slowly, took off his long black threadbare coat and rolled up his sleeves. He took one of the poles, swished it a few times and motioned for the first boy to come to him.

"You're not going to hit *me*," the boy shouted and rushed out the door. I, the smallest, wasn't fast enough. Smith grabbed me by the pinfeathers and hauled me inside. He didn't say a word, just threw me across his desk.

I heard the swish of that pole. Then it seemed as if a white-hot iron rod had been laid across my bottom. I put my fist in my mouth and told myself I would die before I would let old Smith see me cry. Again the swish, again the searing flash. He was in such a fury that when he broke one pole he picked up the second.

Suddenly I heard someone shout, "You hit George again, you old bag of bones, and I'll cut your guts open."

I managed to turn my head and there was my cousin Joe Pine with his pig-sticker open in one hand. He carefully honed the blade on his tight pants leg. Smith put the pole aside, picked me up by the scruff of my neck and marched me back to my seat.

That night I started to bed early. I was usually a heller after school and for me to volunteer for the loft was a sign that I was not right. Mother came up as I was undressing and gasped when she held up the lamp and saw my criss-crossed back and bottom. Mother called in Father, who listened to my account and looked at my back. Without a word he went out.

That night, after making a call on Smith and knocking him down, Father rounded up the school board and told them what had happened. They gave Smith until the next day to get out of town. I think Joe Pine took it upon himself to see that he did.

The last heard of Smith was from Joe. He said he watched the tall lanky man ride down the road astride the old mule. Joe cut back to his house, got his father's rifle and took a short-cut through the woods so he would be ahead of Smith. When the teacher rode up, he started firing in the air. Then he jumped out into the middle of the road, slashing the air with his long knife, striking like a madman.

Smith gave one look—so did the mule—and they were last seen racing down the road in a cloud of dust.

The next teacher was a kind, quiet man who played chess with my father and read thick leather-bound books as he lounged in the shade during recess. When he left, another one took his place but we never had a man like Smith again.

As I grew older Father assigned me more and more tasks about the farm. I chopped wood, repaired fences, took care of the horses and milked the cows. The chickens were Mother's pride and she took care of them herself.

Like most of the farm families of those days, we lived mostly off the land. Flour was about all we bought in town. We had corn, but it was some time before we could raise wheat because there were too many stumps. For sugar we tapped a sugar maple and boiled down the sap. Mother bought green coffee and browned it at home.

Father, my brother and I brought in the meat—deer, wild hogs and turkeys. After the fields were cleared and the wheat was planted, the wild turkeys came to scratch up the seed. That was my most important job—to keep those turkeys out of the wheat. One day I asked my father to give me his old Army musket to do two jobs at one time: scare them off and also kill a turkey or two. He allowed it was a good idea, loaded the rifle and turned it over to me.

The first afternoon the turkeys just roosted in the trees beyond the wheat but wouldn't come down. But as soon as I left they scratched away to their hearts' content. The following day I found an old chalk line. It gave me an idea. I secured the musket on a stump, attached the line to the trigger and retreated as far as the string would allow. Then I hid behind a stump. My old hound dog lay down beside me and we waited. Then, when everything seemed safe, they started to feed. I sighted one big turkey cock and pulled the trigger. The birds flew upward into the trees. The cock was badly shattered, but at least we had won a victory—which lasted for about two days.

My hunting days were linked with a strange and wonderful old man—I can't recall his name—who came by our place after the war. He was anywhere from fifty to seventy and one of the last of the early frontiersmen. Every spring he would vanish, but back he would come in the fall to "help around," dressed in a dirty, greasy buckskin jacket, a faded wool shirt, an old Army greatcoat and Indian moccasins fastened with lengths of rawhide. To us he was the most fascinating personage in our drab winter days. He could talk Sioux, had lived with the Indians and had hunted "buffer." He told us wondrous tales of the great West and of his trapping days.

The old man would take me and my brother Dan and my father out hunting and this would set Mother off. But she would always make sure that we had warm shawls and boots and plenty of food when the day came. We would go out for a few days, never failing to return with deer, rabbit, 'coon and what-not. In town, the old man was a tired-looking old fellow, but in the woods he was a king. He knew a thousand woodland signs.

My brother, who was more of a businessman, didn't care too much for the woods, except when he could sell the hides of the animals we trapped. I took more after my father. The question of what lay over the next hill was to intrigue me for the rest of my long life.

Once the three of us set out together in midwinter. We walked countless miles, plodded through frozen swamps, even ice-fished in the river. At night we slept in a shed made of saplings, rolled up warmly in our blankets, with our feet to the fire. The old man would always repeat the old Indian saying, "White man build big fire and freeze—Indian build little fire and keep warm."

I remember watching the two men squatting over the fire, dragging on their pipes, a jug between them, the light of the fire etching dark shadows on their bearded faces. Then, exhausted, I sank into a deep safe sleep, the sound of their voices growing dimmer and dimmer.

In the winters that followed the old man and my father taught me much. I was a wild, ungovernable boy with a quick temper. I liked nothing more than to pick up my rifle, whistle for my hound and walk five miles through the forest, only to squat, daydreaming, at a clear stream, watching the water rush by. Needless to say, in those daydreams I was always the hero gunfighter, the outlaw leader, the trail-breaker of the West.

The old man taught me a great deal, not only about the woods, but of the world outside our little community. I had already had my share of rough-and-ready fights, but the old man told me I had best be prepared and taught me all the dirty tricks of brawling, kneeing and eye-gouging. I would one day have to use every trick the old man knew to save my own life.

He was like a shaggy old dog. As the years passed his hair grew as tangled as a magpie's nest and his step somewhat slower. One day when we were out alone he took a dirty tobacco pouch from inside his greasy jacket and from it removed a dirty, wrinkled scrap of paper.

"Hit's from my brother's wife," he said. "I lost my spectacles and can't read hit. . . ."

It was barely a scrawl. Almost a century has passed, but I recall it said something about his brother dying and that he was needed to help run the ranch in Montana or the Dakotas, I don't remember which. Scrawled at the bottom was a woman's name.

He thanked me and we started walking. I knew that Indian-like he would talk when he felt like it. But that afternoon we hunted in silence.

After supper he broke his silence; he said he had to leave us. Father just nodded and offered him money for the cars. The old man thought a while and said he'd be grateful if Father would go with him to buy a ticket. He insisted he had lost his spectacles. I was puzzled; I had never seen the old man with glasses.

The last Father ever saw of him, the old man was sitting ramrod stiff in his railway coach, his iron black hair shoulder-length, wearing an old coat of Father's and a borrowed shirt, with a basket of food Mother had prepared for him in his lap. He didn't turn or wave goodbye.

We never saw him again. But the next year Father received a letter. "The old man won't be with us this winter, Mother," he said quietly. "He has taken over his brother's ranch and is helping his widow and her five children."

I was furious at the thought of our old man staying with someone else. Now *their* boys would be with him in the woods. So I searched for something cruel to say.

"What good would he be?" I said scornfully. "He's so blind he can't even read a letter right in front of his face."

"It's not that he has bad eyes, George," my father said gently, "The old man never learned how to read."

The first winter the old man didn't come I set out my first traps. I was then about ten or eleven. Dan helped me skin the pelts, but I did the actual trapping and hunting. For deer skins, well cured, we received a dollar and a half; for red fox pelts, a dollar and a quarter; for muskrats, ten cents. Gray fox skins drew anywhere from seventy-five cents to a dollar. Muskrats were as plentiful as crows; you could catch as many as you had traps in that old swamp. Once or twice we caught beavers. I also discovered that selling nuts could be profitable, so Dan and I gathered hickory, hazel and beech nuts by the sack and sold them around the community.

Our community schoolhouse soon needed an extension. The school board even hired two lady teachers and the hickory sticks were finally dispensed with altogether. It wasn't long before I knew about all there was in those schoolbooks. I wasn't a bad scholar, except in the spring just before school let out. Then, with the smell of the earth awakening and the buds just bursting and the swamp beginning to move with life, I became restless. All of us boys were, but I guess I was more so.

With the coming of the Grand Rapids and Indiana Railroad the town of Geneva—about four and a half miles away from our cabin through the forest—grew bigger. I attended the school there, walking both ways. When we arrived home at night Dan and I had to do the farm chores. Most of our lessons were done in front of the fireplace, and it's a wonder I didn't need glasses until I was nearly sixty.

To get the mail, either my brother or I had to saddle up our old mare and ride sixteen miles to Bluffton and back again. Thirty-two miles for a letter! But it was worth the trouble when the letters were opened and we all gathered around the fireplace, the boys on the floor, Father rocking and smoking his pipe and Mother reading aloud the contents in her soft, sweet voice, with my young sisters gathered on each side of her. Letters were our link with the outside world. We heard of the strange places beyond the big swamp, of the Union Pacific creeping across the continent, of night riders and lynchings, of births, deaths and fortunes won and lost.

A sawmill came into our county one year and Father decided it was time to build a new house. It was one of the finest frame houses in that part of the country. Father also built a real old-fashioned Lancaster bank barn. Painted a bright red, it became one of the sights to see in those parts. My father threw aside tradition and built the house first. "I certainly don't want to freeze my butt off," he told one farmer, "while my cows are as warm as their milk."

After I had finished the courses offered at the school in Geneva I was sent to Valparaiso College. But I couldn't stand the confinement. I was homesick for the woods and the family.

I was about sixteen when Mr. Curry, the county surveyor, came to our house one day to inform my father and our neighbors that he had been ordered by the county commissioners to survey or open all section lines in the township for new roads.

Farmers had begun to fence in their lands and by doing so had closed off sections of the old roads. There had been some shootings over fence rights and the county officials thought it was high time to bring some order.

Mr. Curry had a horse and a buckboard loaded down with surveyor's instruments, charts and maps. When he asked me if I would like to help him I accepted readily.

"Bolds," he told Father at dusk after our day together, "if you can spare George I'll pay him fifty dollars a month for six months and teach him surveying into the bargain. With the new territories opening up out West now, it will be a good profession for him to follow."

Father had asked me several times if I wanted to farm. His lips had become tight and his eyes cold when I told him I didn't care for feeding hogs all my life.

He turned to me now. "Well, George?"

"Yes, sir," I said, "I believe I *would* like to survey." This was something I could love: new lands, wild lands, travel. . . .

Father was satisfied, but Dan went up in the air. He was usually a mild-mannered fellow, but I thought he would toss me over the barn.

"I'm the oldest," he stormed, "and *I* should get the job. If you go, it will mean I'll be working like a slave. . . ."

Father, a fair man, nodded. "That's right, George. Dan will have to do your jobs."

But already I had it worked out in my mind. I knew Dan's best friend John Coyle, who lived three miles from us, was looking for summer work at fifteen dollars a month and his keep. I hired John and he came over the next day. The surveyor was already packed and ready to go and Mother had my gear on Lady. I was ready to set out on my first adventure: living at various homesteads and farmhouses or in the woods. If we needed food, I was to supply it. The surveyor, who didn't do much hunting, had given me custody of his rifle.

Fifteen dollars for John Coyle from fifty still left me thirty-five—a small fortune in those days—and no farm chores! "Mr. Curry," I said, "I think I'm going to like surveying."

We were out all that summer. I thought I knew the county fairly well, but we found places in the forest which I never knew existed. It was exacting work and Mr. Curry had a temper which matched his fiery red hair. Several times he made my head spin with a box across the side of the head when I ruined a survey with my carelessness. I soon found out that surveying was not all play but exhausting work.

The weeks sped past. I seemed to sprout right out of my pants I grew so fast. The summer sun burned my body black and made Curry as red as a lobster. He was an educated man, deeply devoted to Irish history and literature and possessed a native story-telling talent. At night around the fire he made the little people and the dead kings come alive for me. The night he recited from "Hamlet," taking all the parts himself, was unforgettable.

Mr. Curry made it a strict practice to give me instruction in surveying theory at least three nights a week and in September he took one whole day to examine me on what I had learned. Back home, he told Father, "You now have an excellent surveyor, Bolds. He knows as much as I do."

When he left he promised to send me some books and charts from Geneva and sure enough, by October I received a large box from him. I spent many a winter night poring over them before the fire.

Father was impressed with my energy. One day when he went

in to Geneva for some supplies he returned home with a large box. "A present, George," he said.

It was my first surveying equipment.

The next winter a French Canadian passed through, examining lands along the Wabash for white oak and timber for shipbuilding. He liked what he saw on our land and paid us a visit. With Father acting as his guide, he selected several large tracts of land which offered choice ship timber. Father decided he might as well buy these sections.

In the spring the Frenchman returned with a crew of some ten loggers. They were the wildest, merriest bunch of men I'd ever seen, always a-singing and calling out to each other just for the hell of it any time things got quiet in the woods. And how they could swing an axe! Farmers came from all over to see them handle the blades. The stayed at our house, some of them sleeping in the barn, and they were the biggest eaters I ever saw. One or two had accordions and other instruments and the dance they held on a Saturday night was the talk of the county for the next week. I can still remember how one of them took his long knife from his belt, balanced it and, in a swift snap of his wrist, sent it through the air. It plunked into a tree, quivering like a tuning fork.

The Canadians paid by the cubic foot for their ship timber and when they settled up Father found he had made about eight hundred dollars' profit beyond what he had paid the people who had sold him the land. He was so pleased that he deeded me a tract of 120 acres, my older brother 80 acres and my younger brother a smaller tract. My oldest sister, of course, got the home place.

That winter we fenced in the 120 acres and I split more rails with Dan than Abe Lincoln ever saw. It was an eight-rail fence, so that's sixteen rails to a rod. Multiply 120 acres by sixteen and you'll know how many rails my brother and I cut, dragged and trimmed.

Mother had forbidden me to do any skunk trapping, but one day, while exploring my tract, I ran across an old upturned tree and from the skunk trace I knew I'd located a family. I didn't say anything to the folks but waited until Mother and Father and the rest of the family went off to visit Cousin Joe Pine's family.

As soon as the wagon was out of sight I grabbed my gun and a grub hoe and whistled for my hound dog. Rambler knew what I was doing and he tried to warn me by whining, but I just told him to shut up and mind his job. I dug down in that old decayed stump and hit the first skunk. He came past me like a streak, big as all creation. Rambler grabbed him as I lunged for my rifle and he let go—half over me and half over Rambler. Rambler killed him and then stood there in the snow looking up as if to say, "You damn fool. What now?"

Well, there was just too much profit in that stump to give up, so I dug again. Within a short while I had seven skunk pelts, all worth a dollar and a half apiece. I had skinned and dressed the pelts and mounted them on boards by the time the family returned. They advanced, holding their noses, from as far as where our road met the dirt highway.

Mother ordered me to a small shed and she and Father got bundles of straw and started a fire, with Mother sprinkling handfuls of corn meal on the flames to try to kill the smell.

"Young man, you and that dog stay out here until that smell is gone," Mother said and stamped inside. Then she came out with some old sheets and worn blankets and gave them to me. That cold night Rambler and I slept alone and, to tell the truth, the smell was so bad I had to keep the door open.

The next day bucket after bucket of boiling water was brought in and I was scrubbed with everything from coal oil to pumice stone. But before she would help me, Mother made me give Rambler a bath. I swear I bathed that hound ten times that day before she would lay a hand on me. But the smell stayed.

Four days later Mother let us in the house but only in the loft. That cured me. I decided that money wasn't that important.

After the skunk episode my brother and I decided to go in business with our father's blessing. With the money I had saved from my trapping business and nut selling we bought cattle and horses in the fall when it was a buyers' market and sold them at a nice profit in the spring. We built a rough corral for the horses and let the sheep and cattle roam in the tract. They were all right as long as we had feed, which we bought from Father with the promise to pay in the spring when we gathered our profits.

One day I bought a beautiful black mare. Along with being a superb animal she had the added attraction of supposedly having belonged to an outlaw who had stolen her somewhere in Missouri. When she was sold at auction in Bluffton I bid the highest to get her. I guess I was the proudest kid in the county. She was fast and a fine jumper. It was just part of my wildness, I guess; I just had to live with danger and jumping was the closest I could get.

About a week after I had bought the mare my brother came home with a pure black stallion he'd bought from a farmer just north of us. I just had to have that horse.

"Like him, George?" he would call out while I tried to outdo him on my mare. If he would only sell me that horse I could have a fine black team. Dan would only shake his head and pat his horse.

One day I drew out a large part of my profits from our cattle and sheep sales and offered it to Dan. It was so much that it shook Dan and he sold him to me.

I was walking on air. I proudly led both my horses to the watering trough and, after they had had their fill, slapped them and sent them to their stalls. My mare went to hers, but the horse Dan had just sold me walked right into the side of the barn!

When he did it again the next day I felt my heart drop. I examined the stallion and found he was a moon-eyed horse, totally blind in one eye. I was ready to hit my brother with the first thing that came to my hand, but he brought Father out into the barnyard and told him the whole story.

Mother tried to make Dan give me back some of my money, but Father wouldn't let him. "George is stuck with his bargain," he said. "Let him make the best of it."

In time Dan and I laughed about it. I don't think there were any two brothers in the whole county closer than we were. It was just that Dan had more Yankee in him than I had.

The Big Year

SUDDENLY I was seventeen—the big year in my life. Our cattle and sheep business was booming, I fell in love, I went to my first dance and I left home.

The year turned on a violent snowstorm which buried the entire countryside in many feet of snow. My brother and I were up before dawn and to bed late, both of us bone-weary. But despite the bitterly cold weather and the snow, we saved our cattle and sheep. By the looks of it we would have a windfall of profits in the spring when we disposed of our holdings.

As I can recall, it was about midwinter when a fellow by the name of Phil Sill met me in Bluffton when I was getting the mail and invited me to attend a square dance. "Now don't forget, George, there'll be some fine lookers on hand...." Without thinking, I accepted.

I waved goodbye, went in and got our mail, all the while wondering what had made me say I would go. Both my father and mother were strict Methodists, attended church regularly and made sure we went along with them. To them, going to a dance was the first step to hell. Father would beat the tar out of me and Mother—soft-hearted though she was—would not stop him.

However, I was beginning to feel my oats and with spring just over the hill, I was getting restless again. Deep in my heart I knew another spring would surely find me wandering across the West. At first it had been only a dream spun as I lay in the loft at night, listening to my brother's steady breathing. I knew it would be a reality.

By the time I reached home I had a plan. At the back of our house was a large cherry tree. The branches were so near our window Dan or I usually had to cut them back or they would poke right into our bedroom. The nearest limb, I recalled, was quite thick. I could shinny out on it and down the trunk. Father and Mother went to bed with the chickens and a lamp rarely burned in our house after nine o'clock.

That night I crept out of bed, slowly opened the window, dropped my boots and shinnied out across the limb and down the trunk. I retrieved my boots, put them on and ran to the barn. Lady was certainly surprised to see me. She shied away at first, doubting her own nose, but after I patted her and whispered in her ear, she was raring to go.

The night was cold and dark. I could almost taste the snow that lay in the swollen clouds which hid the moon. For a moment I hesitated. Would I be likely to be caught in a snowstorm? But the thought of those pretty girls and the gay music awaiting me conquered all my fears and I was off. The road was frozen, the ruts like iron. Lady felt full of life. She galloped down that road as if her life depended on it. I gave her full rein and kept down near her head, feeling her powerful flanks move under me.

Sometimes the moon slid out of the clouds, momentarily lighting the sparkling snow, the stark trees, dark farmhouses and an occasional frozen pond. The cold air brought tears to my eyes and a flush to my cheeks. I don't think I shall ever forget that night.

At last I could see the lights in the barn like a beacon in the off-shore darkness. As I drew near I could hear the fiddles and the stomping of many boots. I hitched Lady with the other horses at the hitching post and went inside. The first one I saw was Phil, who introduced me to his wife, a pretty young girl of about twenty. Then I saw Cousin Joe Pine, his cheeks flushed and his black hair slicked down. His eyes were dancing as he came toward me.

"Will we get it when they find out!" he whispered, then added, "But damn it, it'll be worth the hiding. You know how to dance, George?"

"Sure," I lied.

"Well, grab yourself a chicken," he said. "I'm after the heifer with the cornsilk hair."

He nodded toward a husky girl, who blushed furiously when Joe winked and waved to her. I noticed that near her was a very pretty, dark-haired girl, the center of a group of boys who were preening themselves nervously, fidgeting and rubbing their boots slyly on the back of their pants.

"I'll take that one," I said.

Joe whistled. "That's Adda Weldon. Her father owns the Merchants' Hotel in Portland."

Portland! I studied her with awe. Suddenly I said to myself that if I was going to make a fool of myself I might as well do it over the prettiest girl in the room.

"I'm going to dance with her," I said.

Joe eyed me suspiciously. "Have you been drinking hard jack, George?"

I shook my head.

The walk across the floor seemed a thousand miles long. At last I was standing in front of this girl, who regarded me quietly with soft brown eyes.

"May I have the honor of this dance, ma'am?" I asked. One of the fellows grunted contemptuously, but I stared him down.

My heart was pounding like a rabbit thumping a warning on a hollow log. At last she nodded. I held out my arm and she took it. We walked to the middle of the floor. When she looked up at me with a gentle smile, I grinned down at her.

"I don't know how to dance," I said.

"Just hold me and make believe you do," she said. "My name is Adda."

I put my arm around her waist and started to shuffle around. I caught Joe watching me with amazement, which made me feel proud as a peacock. I stepped on her foot several times and kept mumbling apologies. I felt her shake with laughter and I found myself joining her.

I danced, if you can call it that, and sat with her and drank punch for the rest of the night. I learned she was visiting kinfolk nearby and was leaving on Saturday. I asked and received permission to see her, come Sunday, in Portland. One of the boys came into the barn just then from outside, shaking snowflakes from his shoulders.

"It's snowing," I said, with the authority of a man announcing a fabulous event.

"Isn't that nice?" said Adda. "Now we can go sledding."

I suddenly remembered that I had left the window open at home!

"Pardon me, Miss Adda," I said, and raced across the floor. Joe grabbed me at the door.

"Where are you going, George?"

I explained hurriedly.

"Dan will close it, George," Joe said.

"Dan wouldn't wake up if the house fell in on him," I said. "But Mother checks every window when it snows or rains."

"Oh," said Joe.

"Please explain to Adda that my folks are sick, or our house burned down, or anything," I said, "and tell her I'll see her, come Sunday."

"I'll tell her, George. Good luck," said Joe as I slipped out the door.

The wind was up, the beginning of a blizzard, when I started home. The cold was numbing, the snow, driven by a high wind, blinded me. I gave Lady the reins and let her take me home. A frigid eternity passed before we turned up the road to the house. I was exhausted from battling the wind and cold and was certainly glad to see the house. In the barn I rubbed down the mare and tossed her some hay. By this time I was feeling just dandy. The blood was running warm again in my veins and I was on top of the world; I was going to see Adda on Sunday. All I had to do now was shinny back up the tree and get in bed.

Climbing up that tree was easier said than done. The trunk was sheeted with ice, giving me a devil of a time. The window was closed and I blessed old Dan. I inched out on the limb and started to open the window. It wouldn't budge. I strained and strained. It was no use—Mother had evidently locked the window. Obviously I would have to spend the night in the barn. I lay down in the stall beside Lady and tried to sleep. When I heard my father crunching his way through the snow, I jumped up and began feeding the stock. He was surprised to see me.

"Why, George," he said, "what are you doing up so early? First time you've beaten me. . . ."

"You've been working too hard, Father," I said, with the piety of a saint, "I feel I should do more."

He looked suspicious, but I kept tossing hay. At breakfast I eyed Mother warily, but she didn't let on what she had in mind. I tried to slip away after a cup of coffee, but she stopped me.

"George," she asked "why weren't you in your bed last night?"

"Couldn't get in, Mother," I said.

"How did you get out?" she asked.

"Shinnied down the cherry tree," I replied. There was no lying in our house, even if it meant a whipping.

"Where were you, boy?" Father snapped.

"Over to Phil Sill's for a dance," I said.

"Why didn't you tell us you were going?" Mother asked.

"Because I knew you don't approve of dancing and wouldn't let me go," I said.

"We would never stop you, George," Father said. "We would tell you we did not approve, but it's about time that you made up your own mind about the principles which must govern your life. You are the master of your own soul and of your fate, and may God be with you in every decision."

Dan, with a smirk, intoned, "Amen." Out of the corner of my eye I could see my sister ready to burst out laughing at my red face.

Suddenly I made up my mind in a second what I had been pondering over for months.

"Father," I said, "I'm going West."

They all stared at me. "You're going to leave, George?" he asked finally.

"Yes, sir," I said. "I have a hankering to see what that country looks like."

"We'll talk about it later," he said. "Now let's get to the chores."

We worked all that day in silence. At night around the fireplace, while Mother rocked and knitted and Dan and my sister listened, Father asked me exactly what I wanted to do. I poured out my heart. I told him I was restless. I wanted to see new places, new faces and new things. I wanted to see what was over the hill.

"When do you figure on leaving, George?" he asked.

The day leaped into my brain with the flash of light. "Sunday."

My mother dropped her knitting. Dan stared at me. Father just nodded and my sister gasped.

"So you figure you want to see what's over the hill, George?" he asked.

"Yes, sir," I said.

"You're nothing but a boy," Mother said.

"Well, Mother, I was like that, too, when I first came out here," Father said. "Always wandering about, footloose and fancy-free, with no one to tell me what to do." He shook his head. "I crossed a lot of hills." He turned to me. "Do you know what I found, George?"

I shook my head.

"Another hill," he said.

He stood up, wound his big watch and said he was ready for bed. Mother put her knitting in the little wooden box Father had made for her years ago and leaned over to kiss all of us good-night. Then they slowly walked upstairs. I noticed for the first time the frost in their hair.

The days, the hours and the minutes flew that week. Before I knew it, Friday night was at hand. The word had gone out that I was leaving so Cousin Joe and some of the boys had ridden in for a farewell feast. Afterward, we sang songs and ate popcorn and home-made taffy. Finally it was time to go.

As always, Cousin Joe danced his crazy mare, whooping like a drunken Comanche. This started them all off. They galloped down the road, whooping and shrieking, the shoes of their horses striking off sparks when they hit stone. I stayed outside, listening to their shouts become fainter and fainter.

Then suddenly I was shivering. For the first time in my life I felt lonely.

It was decided that I would leave Saturday night for Portland. I had subtly suggested that I stay overnight at the Merchants' Hotel there and Father approved. On Saturday Dan and I split our profits. I put some cash in the money belt wrapped around my stomach under my shirt. Mother pinned other small rolls of money inside my long underwear.

Saturday was one of the saddest days in my life. Mother acted as though it were my funeral. My sister was weeping, and my brother—well, he was sorry to see me go because we had always been close and he was also a bit envious.

As for me, I had a mixed feeling of high adventure, sadness and conspiracy. I had managed things to be in Portland on Sunday and still leave home. I could eat my cake and have it, too.

Mother kissed me, whispered to me to watch myself and act always as a Christian. Father gripped my hand and said little. My sister gave me a kiss with the tears welling in her eyes. Dan slapped my back and forced a smile. I tried to wave and shout a happy goodbye, but the words stuck in my throat. All I could do was wheel Lady around in the road and wave. I wasn't as tough as I thought. I still had to wipe away real tears.

I was in Portland by nightfall, stopping first at the livery stable. After explaining that Dan would pick up Lady in a week, I asked the location of the Merchants' Hotel.

I tried to carry off my registration with a flourish as though I stayed at luxurious hotels every day. However, my hand trembled and I could scarcely sign my name. The clerk spun the ledger, examined my name, made a "hmmmm" sound, then asked, "Much snow this winter, sir?"

I launched into a vivid description of the snowfall and he listened respectfully. When he had the bellboy show me to my room I felt so proud I was temped to buy a cigar.

In the room I flung myself on the bed with my boots on. But discipline was too strong. I had an uncanny feeling Mother was standing there frowning. I sighed and took off my boots. Later I put out the light and sat by the window watching the people and the wagons pass. Then I decided to go out.

Passing the desk, I asked the clerk, "Is Miss Adda Weldon here?"

"Yes, sir," he said. "The Weldons have a suite on the third floor. Are you a friend . . . ?"

"Yes," I said, "I know Miss Adda."

"May I send up a message?" he asked.

"Please inform her that George Bolds of Adams County will call tomorrow at two," I replied loftily.

"Very well, Mr. Bolds, I will deliver your message," the clerk said.

Outside, I walked on air. Portland was the first large town I had ever been in. To me it was the most beautiful, the most bustling metropolis in the world. I walked up and down the main street, scanned hungrily all the store windows, studied the houses and drank in the town and its overtones of what I thought was sophistication.

At two o'clock the next afternoon I knocked on the door of

the Weldons' suit. The Weldons greeted me warmly and summoned Adda. We sat in the parlor, talking of crops, the weather and the back country. After about half an hour passed, I dramatically pulled out my watch and announced it was time to go.

"Oh, you must stay and have dinner with us, Mr. Bolds," Mrs. Weldon said.

"I'm sorry, ma'am, but I'm catching the five o'clock for Fort Wayne," I said, with what I hoped was a great deal of nonchalance.

"Fort Wayne!" they exclaimed.

"Yes, ma'am, I'm going West," I said proudly.

"How far West, George?" Mr. Weldon asked.

I was stumped. All this time I was talking about going West, but I did not have a particular state or town in mind. It was just West.

"Quite far, sir," I said vaguely.

"Going to homestead, George?" he asked.

"I have been thinking of homesteading," I said.

"The Indians are still hostile, aren't they?" his wife asked.

"I can take care of myself," I assured her.

"I'm sure you can, George," Mr. Weldon said. "Well, can I drive you to the station?"

I thanked him. He left to hitch up his team and after shaking my hand, Mrs. Weldon left also. Only Adda and I were left.

"You didn't tell me you were leaving, George," she reproached me.

"I reckon I should have," I said. I hoped she recognized I was already using Western lingo.

"I thought we could go for a ride," she said.

"I'll be back and take you for a ride, Adda," I said. And I meant it.

"I'll be waiting," she said. And I knew she meant it because she leaned over and kissed me on the cheek. I was so flustered I almost tripped over my own feet when I followed her father out to the carriage.

We picked up my baggage and drove to the depot. He waited until the train came in and then shook hands with me and said, "Be sure to come and see us, young fellow, when you come back."

I was 'way ahead of him. I'd already planned to make his hotel my first stop and his daughter would be the first one I would want to see.

With a last wave I took my seat. The conductor came along, punched my ticket and grinned down at me.

"Going West to shoot Injuns, kid?" he said.

"No," I said, "I'm going to sell Bibles. Yes, sir, from all the stories I've heard, those terrible people out there need to know God's word. Yes, sir, they certainly need the Good Word...."

I gave him a baby-faced stare as he gave me a long hard look. Then he turned away and continued up the aisle.

Oh, I was a fresh-faced kid, all right. But I was going out West.

"And yet for forty years an infinite drama has been going on in those wide spaces of the West— a drama that is as thrilling, as full of heart and hope and battle as any that ever surrounded any man; a life that was unlike any ever seen on the earth and which should have produced its characteristic literature, its native art chronicle."

HAMLIN GARLAND

First Time Out

WHEN I reached Fort Wayne, I went into the first depot I saw and asked the ticket-seller for a passage to Kansas City.

"We don't sell tickets to Kansas City, sonny," he said. "You'll have to go to the Wabash."

"What in hell do I want to do at the Wabash, Mister?" I said. "I just came from there."

He looked out at me through the grillwork. "The railroad, sonny, not the river." He pointed out the door. Across the tracks I saw another depot.

"Thanks," I said in a small voice.

I started to cross the tracks, but a brakeman shouted at me. "Hey, kid, where are you going?"

"To the Wabash," I said.

"Then go the right way," he said. "Go down the stairway if you want the Wabash."

"Thanks," I said, in a still smaller voice.

"First time out, sonny?" he called out.

"Yes, sir," I said. At the Wabash depot I bought a ticket to Kansas City. With my carpetbag between my knees I waited for the train.

Train after train kept coming in and each time I asked, "Is this the train to Kansas City?" The answer was always, "No, sonny, the next one."

When I finally got on a train I noticed two cars in the middle of the train that reminded me of the hearses back home. I wondered who was dead. Probably a general, I thought, for the railroad to take so much trouble.

After about three stops I thought we should be in Kansas City, but the conductor said, "Not yet, sonny, sit tight." We rode all that day and the next night. The following morning we made a stop and I thought sure this was Kansas City. But it was only St. Louis, not even halfway to where I was going.

I was hungry, so I bought some apples from the newsboy and then settled down. The porter did come up the aisle calling out that "luncheon" was being served in the dining car. I didn't know what he meant, so I bought some more apples. In the evening the same porter came back and called out that "dinner" was now being served in the dining car. The dining car? I puzzled over that.

"Why, that's a place to eat," he said. "A few cars back." I remembered those two hearses.

"Is this your first time out?" he chuckled.

I told him it was and asked him what they had to eat back there. He said, "Anything. If you're damn hungry you can get a good meal for a dollar and a half."

"A dollar and a half?" I said. "Why, that's all a schoolteacher pays back where I come from for room and board for a week."

I bought three more apples and that was dinner.

We made a stop somewhere about fifty miles from Kansas City. There seemed to be an unusual number of people milling about the depot. When some of the passengers hurried out I followed them. Glorious crashing music filled the air—the first circus parade I had ever seen. There were prancing clowns and a calliope, cages of wild animals and ladies riding beautiful white horses, elephants, giraffes with necks ten feet tall and pacing tigers.

A fellow came along selling balloons. "What do you say, kid, how about a balloon? Just two bits." I'd never seen a balloon before, so I handed him a dollar and he gave me the balloon and said, "Stay right here, kid. I'll be back in a minute with your change."

The last elephant was clean out of sight and I was still standing there, waiting for the fellow to bring me my six bits' change.

When I returned to the depot, the train was gone. I said to the ticket man, "Where's that train I came in on?" I showed my piece of pasteboard.

He shook his head. "Nope, that's no good here. 'Bout fifty miles from here by now. Damn near Kansas City, I expect."

"But I've got to get to Kansas City," I said.

"Well, sonny," he said. "There are just two ways to get to Kansas City—buy a ticket or walk. And I don't give a damn which one you do."

I bought a ticket.

When I arrived at the Kansas City depot there were Indians there selling blankets and trinkets. I thought it would be fine to send some of it back home to the folks in Indiana. I went to the express office with the bundle of stuff I bought and waited until the express man came in.

"What's in this package?" he said. I told him.

"How much did you pay for it, sonny?" he asked.

"Twenty dollars."

"That's fifteen dollars too much," he said. "You've been skinned. First trip out?"

I gave him a weary nod. I must be green all over, I told myself.

I decided to hunt up a restaurant. "Do you have any ham and eggs?" I asked the fellow behind the counter.

"Sure," he said, "all you want."

"How much?" I asked.

"A dollar and a quarter," he said, "and with that you get potatoes, bread and coffee."

I ordered up and quickly cleaned the plate. But I was still hollow so I ordered another plate of the same.

He whistled. "First time out, sonny?"

He winked and I winked back.

After polishing that plate off, I went back into the station, found an empty bench and stretched out, pulling my hat down over my eyes. Some time later a policeman came along with a stick and joggled one of my feet. "Get along there," he said. "This is a depot, not a hotel."

"I just came in from St. Louis," I protested.

"St. Louis, hell. You've been here all day and all night sleeping. Where are you going?"

"Out West."

"Where out West?"

"The biggest and toughest town—I don't care where."

Then he took me to the ticket window and said to the ticket-seller, "Joe, here's a kid who wants to buy a ticket West."

"What town, kid?" the agent asked.

"He wants the biggest and toughest town in the West," the officer said.

The ticket-seller reached up, took a pasteboard ticket from its niche, stamped it and slid it through the window. "That'll be eight dollars and fifty cents."

I counted out the money and pushed it across the counter.

"Where are you going, kid?" the policeman asked.

I looked at the ticket in my hand. "Dodge City."

"Come on now," said the policeman. "There's a train due pretty soon and I'm going to put you on it."

As we walked together to the train gate he warned me, "Now you want to be careful out there. I had a brother who went out there and came back."

"Didn't he like it?" I asked.

"They shipped him home in a box," he said.

What they did on that train to Dodge was to wire ahead and order as many meals as were paid for, so you turned in your ticket and received your meal. I was sitting in a smoker waiting for my food when a fellow came along and sat down next to me with a suitcase on his knees. Then he took out three shells and a ball and kept hiding the ball under the different shells. In about five minutes another fellow came along and looked down.

The fellow with the shells looked up at him and said, "I'll bet you five dollars you can't guess which shell the ball is under."

The other fellow said, "I'll bet I can."

He put down the five dollars and pointed to the shell on the left. The fellow with the suitcase lifted the shell and there was the little ball.

"Well, you win, Mister," he said and handed the fellow the five dollars.

"That's damn decent of you," the winner said and took the five dollars and walked away. A few minutes passed and another fellow came along and did the same thing. Only this time the fellow bet ten dollars.

After he had walked away with the money the fellow with

the suitcase turned to me and said, "I guess this is my bad day. I'll go broke if they keep this up."

I said scornfully, "Any damn fool can figure that out," as I watched him moving the ball.

"Think *you* can guess which one it's under?" he asked.

"Sure," I said.

"What will you bet?"

"I'll bet you ten dollars on the one in the middle."

"No, it's got to be more than that," he said. "I lost a lot of money today. Let's make it twenty."

"All right," I said, "let's make it twenty."

I peeled off the bills and laid them on the suitcase. I pointed to the middle shell. The ball wasn't there. He asked me to try again, but I declined with thanks. I wasn't that green.

We were about seventy-five miles from Dodge when a drunken cowboy came aboard with his saddle and blanket-roll. He took out a six-shooter from his holster and let a shot down through the floor and another through the roof. Then he walked up the aisle, let one go through the door and began howling, "Bury me not on the lone prairie, where the coyotes and the outlaws roam. . . ." Every few words were punctuated with a shot.

All I wanted was to get out of the car, but I was afraid to pass by him. Finally, the conductor, armed with a shotgun, came in with a brakeman and they disarmed him. At the next stop they put him off and the conductor gave the cowhand his gun back.

When the conductor started to climb up the steps of the car the cowhand pointed his gun at him. I expected to see the man shot down in cold blood right before my eyes. The conductor ignored the cowpuncher and walked up the last few steps. I watched the cowhand's trigger finger pull back the trigger. But there was no sharp crack. He kept pulling the trigger and I had to laugh at the bewildered expression on his face.

The conductor entered our car as the train started. "I thought sure you were a dead one, Joe," someone called out.

"I emptied his gun," the conductor replied calmly. "It's a good thing I did—the damn fool might have killed me."

I was out West now all right.

Dodge

DODGE CITY was a bitter disappointment. It looked dirty, makeshift. Near the depot, towering piles of sun-bleached bones were as high as the top of the freight cars. Don't they even have a cemetery in this town? I thought. I didn't know they were buffalo bones. The dreary collection of clapboard houses, low and flat under a gray and cheerless sky, and the grisly pile of bones gave me an overpowering feeling of loneliness. I transferred my carpetbag to my other hand and was wondering when the next train back left when someone nudged me.

A bearded man with a bulbous red nose, shaggy hair and a torn jacket was standing behind me.

"Just come in on the train, kid?" he asked.

I nodded and he rubbed his beard. "My, that's a lucky thing for you," he said.

"How is that?" I asked.

"Well, now, if you're a stranger, you must be in need of a job," he said.

"Maybe," I said.

"No maybe about it, sonny," he said. "You need a job and I

have one for you. I have twenty dollars coming to me for working on the sulphur ranch south of Dodge. You give me the twenty dollars and I'll give you a slip for it. That way you'll get your twenty back and a job."

"Why don't you want the job?" I asked.

He shook his head and looked sad as a hound dog. "My mother died yesterday," he said. "I've got to get back to Kansas City for the funeral."

I was ready to give him fifty. I reached inside my jacket to get the money Mother had pinned to my underwear. But when I looked up he was walking away. I called out, but he didn't turn around. In fact, he started to run.

"What did he want from you, kid?" a quiet voice behind me said.

I turned around. A slender man, dressed in a dark coat and an embroidered vest and wearing a hard hat, was studying me.

"That man offered me a job in the sulphur mines if I would give him twenty dollars," I said.

"There are no mines around here," he said.

"He said his mother had just died in Kansas City," I said.

"*No* woman would own up to be his mother," he said. "Now where are you from?"

"Adams County, Indiana," I said.

"That's nice country," he said. "What are you doing in Dodge?"

"I wanted to come West," I said.

"What's your name, kid?" he asked.

"George Bolds," I said.

"The Dodge House is the place for you," he said. "I'll show you the way."

He didn't say a word while we walked down the street. When we came up to the Dodge House the clerk was standing outside talking to another man. He called out a greeting and I thought he said "Bat."

"Here's a customer for you from Indiana," my new friend said. He waved to me. "Don't take any more jobs in sulphur mines."

I followed the clerk inside and signed the register.

"I don't think there is anyone in Number Three," the clerk said, handing me the key. "No one will disturb you, kid."

I was starting for the stairs when I suddenly remembered what he had called the man whom I had met at the depot.

"What did you call that fellow who walked me from the depot, Mister?" I asked.

"Bat," the clerk said. "That's Bat Masterson." I wondered who he was in Dodge.

I found Number Three; the door was wide open. I locked the door, stripped to my underwear, made sure Mother's pins were secure and rolled into bed. My bones were sore and I had a crick in my back from those wooden seats, but I fell asleep instantly.

It seemed to me I had been asleep only a minute when there was a loud banging on my door. Half asleep, I got out of bed and unlocked the door.

There was an old man wearing a Prince Albert coat with two guns strapped around his waist. Behind him was the biggest Negro I had ever seen. The old man said, "Son, the clerk downstairs said all the rooms were full except this one. He thought maybe you wouldn't mind if we shared your quarters."

"Come right in," I said.

The old man took off his Prince Albert coat, hung it on the back of the chair and then took off his gunbelt. The Negro spread a blanket on the floor. I noticed he carried a large paper parcel.

"Now you don't mind Zeke," the old man said. "He's my handyman down at the ranch. I brought him along to guard that parcel."

"What's in it?" I asked.

"Five thousand dollars wrapped in that paper. Going to buy a load of breeders tomorrow when they come in."

From his position on the floor Zeke pulled a long, ugly knife from inside his shirt and stuck it into the jamb of the door. Then he took another pig-sticker and jabbed it into the floor alongside the blanket.

" 'Night, Massa Draper."

"Goodnight, Zeke. Put out the lamp, sonny."

I snuffed out the lamp and crept into bed. Like Zeke, he was asleep in a matter of seconds. Between them, they made more noise than a chorus of bullfrogs in the swamp back home. I was afraid to close my eyes for fear that giant Negro would cut my throat before I could wake up. Finally I dozed off.

It was just sunup when the old man shook me. "Come on, boy," he said. "Breakfast is ready."

I dressed as Zeke carefully stowed his knives away, one inside his shirt, the other in his belt.

"I'll fetch the wagons, Massa Draper," he said, and went out.

"Will you join me, young man?" the colonel asked.

So I had my first breakfast in Dodge as the guest of a Texas ranch owner in Dog Kelley's saloon adjacent to the Dodge House. The colonel seemed to be well known and gave everyone a booming "Good morning." I just trailed along, nodding when he said, "My young friend, George Bolds, from—where in the hell did you say you came from, kid?"

"Adams County, Indiana, Colonel," I said.

"That's right—Adams County, Indiana. Nicest folks I know."

I knew he had never been in Adams County, but it made breakfast taste better. He stood me a drink in Peacock's saloon before he left. I had all I could do to swallow my jigger in one gulp. It was the first time I had tasted whiskey. The shot hit the pit of my stomach, bringing tears to my eyes.

The colonel slapped me on the back. "Goodbye, kid, look me up when you get to Texas."

We shook hands. In my befuddled state I didn't realize until he was out the door that he'd left a five-dollar gold piece in my hand. My head was still fuzzy and my legs a little rubbery, so I thought I had better go back to the Dodge House and lie down for a while. Back at the Dodge House the clerk gave me my key. As I turned, my eye caught the sign over his head. For the first time I read the legend:

This house is strictly intemperate.

None but the brave deserve the fare.

No shooting in this house unless in self-defense.

Persons owing bills for board will be bored for bills.

Boarders who do not wish to pay in advance are requested to advance the pay.

Sheets will be changed nightly, once in six months—oftener if necessary.

When you return, if not able to remove your boots, take off your spurs, it's hard on the sheets.

Beds, with or without bugs. All monies are left with the clerk as he is not responsible."

While I was reading the sign a man tapped me on the shoulder and said, "Mr. Bolds?"

I turned and saw a fellow not much older than myself. He was wearing a dark coat and was hatless.

"I'm Joe Clark of the Dodge City *Times*," he said. "I see from the register you're from Indiana."

"Adams County," I said.

He made a note. "Nice country, Indiana," he said.

"Have you ever been there?" I asked.

"No," he said, "but folks say it's nice. You going to stay in Dodge long, Bolds?"

"I have no immediate plans," I said.

He smiled. "Well, keep out of trouble," he said.

"I don't aim to look for it," I said.

"Maybe those clothes of yours are going to lead you to it," he said.

I looked down. I thought my dark suit and bowler were fine.

"Those are dude clothes," he said, "and the cowhands don't like dudes. You had better go down to Bob Wright's and get another outfit."

We said goodbye and I left him, wondering who the hell Bob Wright was.

After lunch I had walked clear through the town and was starting back when two cowhands rode past. They pulled up and stared at me.

"I'll be damned!" one of them said loudly, "the circus is in town."

I didn't hear any music and there was no parade in sight. "I don't see any circus," I said.

"He *talks*!" one fellow shouted. The other punchers lounging in front of the store began to grin.

"Does he dance?" one of them asked.

"We'll soon find out," said one of the men. My heart almost stopped when I saw him draw out his six-shooter.

"Hold on, boys, none of that now," someone called out. We turned around and Bat Masterson and another man were crossing the street. "He's just come in from Indiana."

"He certainly is a dude," the man with Bat said, smiling.

"Well, we'll change that," Bat said. "How long are you staying out here, boy?" he asked me.

"For a spell, I think."

"Well, you had better get some different clothes, then," Bat said. "Have you any money?"

"Yes," I said.

"We'll go to Bob Wright's and get you fitted out properly," Bat said. He nodded to his companion. "This is Ben Daniels." This was my introduction to Ben, one of the true great lawmen of the West.

When we arrived at the store Bat looked at me. "Get out your money, kid," he said.

I hesitated. I actually started to sweat. Bat studied me.

"Haven't you got any, kid?" he asked.

"Yes," I mumbled. Then, wishing that the ground would open under my feet, I blurted out that the money was pinned all over my person, including my drawers. They both laughed until they were beet-red in the face. Finally Bat slapped me on the back and went to find Bob Wright, leaving Ben sitting on a bag of feed, still chuckling.

"We'll take care of you, young fellow," Bob Wright told me and sure enough, he brought me pants, boots and a woolen shirt.

"Count your money and give it to Bob," Bat said.

I counted my money and handed it over to Bob. He told me he would put it in a sack with my name on it. I could take what I wanted from time to time or charge my purchases to ar. account. Green as I was, I knew it would have been dangerous to question their honesty.

When I was dressing, Bat found the .22 short pistol I had bought in Bluffton before I'd left home. He broke the gun, threw the shells out the window and smashed the barrel on the edge of a counter.

"What are you doing that for?" I cried. "That gun cost me seven dollars back in Indiana."

"I'm saving your life, kid," Bat Masterson said.

"Saving my life?" I said. "That's what I bought it for, to save my life."

"If you shot anybody out here with that," he said, "it would make them madder than hell."

Back at the hotel, the clerk didn't even recognize me at first. I felt lost, though, without a gun. I said to Bat, "Everybody's been telling me to watch out not to get hurt. What am I going to do for a gun?"

"When you know how to handle a gun and not before, I'll see that you get one," Bat said.

Ben Daniels nodded. "Out here, kid, when you wear a gun a man assumes you know how to use it. If you don't, God help you."

The Bat Who Wore Guns

I'VE always believed that William Barclay "Bat" Masterson's picturesque nickname had a great deal to do with his winning the public's fancy. I don't think I ever once asked Bat how he got it. In the early days of the West that was asking for trouble. If you were lucky, trouble could be just a kick in the groin instead of a bullet in the heart.

But I wanted to know more about the man who'd befriended me, so I asked around and listened to any story I heard about him. Evidently plenty had happened to Bat Masterson in Dodge before I came on the scene.

Like myself, Bat was a child of the frontier. He knew the forest and its animals and could shoot before he was in his teens. Young Bat and his brothers used to go hunting back in Illinois with an old Army musket which some blacksmith had converted into a straightbore. The musket was so big and heavy the boys took turns carrying it across their shoulders, like a water yoke. A few years after the Civil War the Mastersons moved from Fairfield, Illinois, to Missouri, near St. Louis. It didn't work out there, so the family pushed on to Wichita, Kansas.

Bat was a strapping young fellow by this time, blue-eyed and black-haired, a regular hell-raiser, who loved practical jokes more than anything. The brothers got jobs with a contractor building the Atchison, Topeka and Santa Fe Railroad, only to be stranded in Dodge City when the contractor went broke. Bat stayed on after he met Billy Dixon, one of the great scouts of the West.

Bat joined Billy and became a buffalo hunter as far south as the Texas Panhandle and north into Oklahoma. On June 27, 1874, Bat and his fellow hunters were attacked at Adobe Walls by a large party of Indians on the warpath. For five days the braves charged the tiny trading post, only to be shot out of their saddles by the sharpshooting hunters. On the fifth day, after the Indians broke off their attack, Bat and the other hunters went back to Dodge City.

Later Bat headed a score of civilian scouts who worked for General Nelson Miles, forcing the hostile tribes to make peace treaties. In 1875 Bat killed his first man in a Sweetwater saloon gunfight over a girl. When word came that Bat had been wounded two of Miles' scouts rode to the nearby fort for an Army surgeon and forced him to accompany them to Sweetwater. The surgeon operated in a trading post on a rough table and removed a slug from Bat's hip. The wound, which didn't close, drained for some time, giving Bat no end of trouble in rainy weather or when he jumped down from a horse. I don't think it was popular knowledge that he always walked with a slight limp. But he would rather ride than walk, even for a few blocks.

After service with Miles, Bat served in Dodge City as a deputy under Wyatt Earp. When he was about twenty-two he joined the goldseekers in the Black Hills, stopped off at Cheyenne to clean up at faro, then returned to Dodge City to campaign for the sheriff's job of Ford County.

Dodge in those days was a rough cow town, with plenty of gunfire and tough characters passing through, but Bat was one of its most powerful and respected citizens. He wasn't a killer, but he wasn't a man to be buffaloed either. If you got him to the point where his blue eyes hardened to the color of ice, then you had better leave—or be carried out.

He may have won the Ford County election by only three votes, but now he was Ford County's tin star. In 1878, the year he took office formally, Bat and Prairie Dog Morrow chased and captured a quartet of bank robbers in a cow camp south of Dodge. The year before I arrived, Bat's brother Ed had been killed trying to arrest Jack Wagner, a wild young Texas cowhand who had been in trouble before. The shooting took place at a dance-hall. I heard it this way from Ham Bell, one of Dodge's first citizens.

"Wagner was a troublesome young kid," Ham said, "and seemed to delight in hurrahing the town, shooting at the Lone Star Dance Hall sign and the windowpanes. He was warned several times, but he still kept doing it. One night Ed Masterson took away his gun when he and some of the other cowhands started to disturb the peace.

"I was down in Peacock's saloon," Bell said. "I guess Wagner was pretty upset. Later, he and another cowhand named Walker saw Ed Masterson and Nat Haywood outside the dance-hall. Wagner was drunk and carrying a gun. When Ed saw it, he tried to take it away from him, but Wagner managed to pull the gun free and he shot Ed.

"Just about this time Bat and some other fellows were walking toward the dance-hall and as Wagner and Walker started to run, Bat opened fire.

"I heard the firing, all right," Ham went on, "but I considered it would be pretty silly to put my head outside and maybe get it shot off. I just sat tight at the bar with some of the other fellows. It wasn't long, either. Suddenly the door opened and Wagner stumbled in. He staggered toward the bar and mumbled something about dying. I certainly couldn't help him any though, he just nodded, took a few steps and fell down dead."

Ham paused and shook his head. He was a kindly man and the remembrance of such unnecessary death saddened him.

"Then Walker ran in," he continued, "waving his gun. He kept shouting he didn't want it and someone said, 'If you don't want it, throw it away.' " And Ham said, "Damn if he *didn't* throw that gun on the floor."

"He ran out then, but he was dying. He got about fifty feet before he collapsed. Some men came out of the Peacock and carried him to Bob Wright's, where he died."

It seemed that all this time, Ed Masterson was dying in Bat's room, in great agony. The bullet had been fired at such close range that his coat was charred. Bat just held his brother's hand. Ed never woke up, just slipped away. Someone held a mirror to his nose and after a few minutes said to Bat, "He's gone, Bat."

Bat didn't say a word. He crossed his brother's hands on his chest, closed the dead eyes and walked out of the room. Men who saw him said his face was like stone. He walked up to the livery stable and rode out of town. He never told anyone where he was going, but I think he must have gone out on the prairie to weep.

When he came back, in the early hours of the morning, some of his friends had fixed Ed up the best they could and were sitting around with a bottle. Bat sent a telegram to Wichita to inform his parents of Ed's death.

At that time Dodge had no cemetery outside of Boot Hill,

where the men who had died violently and who were nameless had been buried. The next day Ed's body was placed in a plain pine box and loaded on a wagon and taken out to Fort Dodge for burial. Bat and two or three friends who rode alongside were the only mourners.

Jim Masterson joined his brother Bat as a law officer that year. Bat served as sheriff of Ford County until 1880. Bat as a U. S. deputy marshal had to take an armed posse from Ford County to Canyon City, Colorado, where there was some kind of labor trouble brewing. Neal Brown, another great lawman of the West and my friend for years, told me the boys from Dodge City carried enough artillery on that trip to fight a war. Once Bat was almost murdered by three hired gunfighters who came from the Jesse James country in Missouri. Wyatt Earp was still around then and he and Bat took care of them. When they rode out of Dodge City at sunup they were a terrible sight. Bat and Wyatt had pistol-whipped them with their own guns after they refused to draw. Their own mothers would have had a hard job picking out their own sons.

Jim Masterson was made marshal of Dodge City in the fall of 1879, a few months after I arrived. I can still shut my eyes and see him walking down the street, six-shooter under his coat, hat tilted to one side, a cigar in the corner of his mouth and his face as impassive as an Indian's. I maintain he was the most deadly man with a gun outside of Harvey Logan, the executioner of the Wild Bunch in Wyoming. If Jim Masterson had ever met either Logan or that buck-toothed little Billy the Kid, my chips would have been on Jim.

But when I came to Dodge Bat Masterson's name was on every man's lips. One story, which is not very well known, concerns Bat and a young cowpuncher. This puncher who pictured himself as a tough hombre wore his gun tied gunfighter style, a black shirt and a black sombrero. Once in Dodge he played the part; he cursed everybody, challenged everyone who wore a gun and cursed and reviled the girls and all who crossed his path.

Finally, he wore everyone's nerves thin. Bat took away his gun, slapped him sober and told him to ride south of the river, where his camp was. He warned the kid if he came back he would be flung into jail and fined heavily.

About six or eight months later a tall, rangy cowhand came into Dodge, wearing all his belly hardware as if he were searching for trouble. He hitched his horse and slapped his hat on his knee, sending the dust flying—indicating he'd come a long way. Then he walked across the street to the Long Branch saloon, where Bat happened to be standing.

"Stranger," he said, "where is Bat Masterson?"

"Haven't seen him since sunup," Bat said. "Heard he was out after a prisoner."

"Well, tell him Tom Donaldson is in town and wants to see him."

"Sure," said Bat. "Can I ask your business?"

"Well, he beat up my brother some months back, and if you beat up one Donaldson you have to beat them all," the cowhand said.

"Well, maybe I'd better tell you that I'm looking for that bastard myself," said Bat.

"You got business with him, too, stranger?"

"Mister, I'm going to kill him," Bat announced solemnly.

"I reckon we'll have to toss then," the Texan said.

Bat took out a quarter and tossed it.

"Heads," said the Texan.

"Tails," said Bat.

It was tails. The Texan swore a bit, but said he might get a shot at Bat if the first shot missed.

"Let's go get him," Bat said.

As they walked down Front Street, Bat asked what Bat Masterson had done to the Texan's brother. The puncher told him the boy had come home from Dodge saying Masterson had beaten him up and had taken his gun away from him.

"Why, yes," Bat said, "I think I remember that. But frankly, Mister, Masterson saved your brother's life." Then he went on to tell how the Texan's brother was sassing people and swearing to kill Wyatt Earp and had pushed one or two tough hombres aside in the Long Branch. It was Bat Masterson's interference, he said, that had saved the boy.

The Texan began to look uncomfortable. Finally he blurted out, "Well, maybe I was mistaken about that Masterson."

"Mister, you owe him an apology," Bat said.

"How come you know all these things about my brother?" the Texan said.

"Because *I'm* Bat Masterson," Bat said, "and the best thing you can do for your brother is to take his gun away. He's a hot-headed drunken fool who'll wind up in a slicker in Boot Hill."

The Texan shook his head. "Well, I guess you're right, Masterson. My brother is certainly hot-headed and I guess he just forgot to tell me why you beat him up. Well, at least I can buy you a drink."

Bat asked the man if he wanted a job and got him one at Colonel Harvester's ranch. A few months later a cattle drive came up north, with the Texan's brother riding drag. He was fit to kill a hog when he came into Dodge. But his older brother Tom was there to meet him. When he put on a brag about what he was going to do to Bat, Tom slapped him silly and took his gun away. The next day, when he was sober, Tom Donaldson told his brother off and apparently tamed the boy down. The next thing that happened Colonel Harvester had another new hand—thanks to Bat Masterson. They were still working there when I left the country.

My Tenderfoot Days

THE first weeks I spent in Dodge I had nothing much to do, so I hired a horse and became acquainted with the surrounding country. That country burned itself in my memory: the wild, open sky, the quiet prairie, the keening winds, the land so empty there wasn't a speck between me, my horse and the pencil line of the far horizon. I rode at a quiet pace, keeping in check my desire to race like the wind. I knew that if my horse slipped in a prairie dog hole at a gallop I would really go home in a pine box.

In those first wonderful days I roamed far west and north of Dodge. I got to know the prairie and the occasional horsemen coming in from the ranches. I once passed a man in town whom I had met out on the prairie, and I heard him mutter to his companion that I was the "kid from Indiana who rides around the country."

Sunset was the best part of the afternoon. Sometimes it seemed to fall out of the sky with a strange, savage beauty—all gold, all scarlet, all burning incandescence on the horizon, the sun half a golden pie, then a quarter, then a glowing rim. Then the soft twilight, blessed with the tender, wistful piping of the prairie larks. This was the time to turn home. I would arrive in Dodge hungry as a bear and eager to tell the Dodge House clerk what I'd seen.

Bat Masterson made good his promise about a gun and brought me to Wright's place, where I bought a Colt .44 and a gunbelt. It was a beautiful weapon, but I didn't have it long.

That afternoon Bat took me up to the flats above Dodge where there was an old dugout and had me shoot at some marks. He gave me a demonstration, never missing once. I fired several shots and I was pleased when Bat called me a fairly good shot. He told me to fire twenty or thirty shots a day at a mark and he'd see about allowing me to *carry* a gun.

When I look back at it now, I wonder what made Bat Masterson so solicitous of a green young kid. Perhaps Bat saw in me something of himself, a kid fresh from the backwoods who had come out West to Dodge to become Billy Dixon's best buffalo hunter. By putting me out of harm's reach on the flats afternoon after afternoon, Bat also managed to keep a curious kid from getting in his way.

About a week after Bat had given me my first shooting lesson I was walking back from just north of Dodge. I noticed a couple of fellows on horseback looking at the sky. I stopped and also looked. There in the sky, at what seemed to be level with the horizon, was a beautiful city. It shimmered and wavered in the sun.

"Howdy," I said to the men.

"Howdy, kid."

"What's the name of that town?" I asked, pointing.

They looked at each other, then at me. "Mee-rage," they said and began to laugh.

"The ticket-seller at Kansas City said Dodge was the biggest town in the West," I said, "but it looks like he sure fooled me. How far is Mee-rage?"

"A hell of a way," one of them said and they both rode off, laughing heartily.

I was determined to see that city, so I hurried back to Dodge to hire a horse. I rode for about an hour, but I didn't seem to be getting anywhere near it. The prairie was flat and lonely. I was wishing for some company when a jackrabbit bounced in front of me.

I thought a jackrabbit would be nice to send back home as a pet. I ground-tied the horse and started off after that jackrabbit. He seemed to be limping and I felt sure I'd have him in a very few minutes. After about half a mile I realized it wasn't going to be so easy. I picked up a buffalo chip and threw it at him. The jackrabbit just stood up on his hind legs, gave me the last laugh and took off.

The next morning Bat Masterson was having breakfast at Dog Kelley's saloon when I came in and he said, "Where were you yesterday afternoon, kid? I missed you."

"I set out to find Mee-rage," I said, "but I never found it."

I told him what I had seen. "That's what the fellows called the city," I said.

He explained that on clear days it wasn't unusual to see cities and towns and cattle and horses loom up on the prairie just beyond the horizon. He made me promise not to chase after any more fool things like mirages.

The next afternoon I returned to the dugout to resume polishing up my marksmanship. I had fired about five shots when I noticed, far across the prairie, a horseman. He seemed to be in a hurry, so I sat down and waited until he drew up.

He was riding a fine pony and he talked with a twang. "Want to buy a good horse, kid," he asked.

I went up and ran my hands over the horse. He had been ridden hard, but obviously he was a fine animal.

"How much?" I asked.

"Twenty dollars—with that gun," he said.

He began talking fast. "I'm the foreman over at Betson's antelope ranch, but I had to leave sudden like to catch the next train East out of Dodge."

"Your mother die in Kansas City or something like that?" I asked.

"Hell, no," he said. "My brother killed the sheriff in Kansas City and I got to hire a lawyer for him."

Somehow he looked as if he might have a sheriff-killing brother. I dug down, gave him the money and turned over the gun with what bullets I had.

He stuck the gun in his belt and pointed off to the left. "You ride until you reach an old buffalo wallow. It's five miles west of the ranch. When I came by there, there was an old buck by the wallow guarding his harem."

"What do I want to go there for?" I asked.

"You want to get used to your pony, don't you?" he said, in such a way that I felt like a fool. I swung up and started off. When I looked back he was heading for Dodge on foot.

That pony was really a beauty. I was soon feeling that I was just about the smartest young fellow in Kansas.

As the man had said, I came upon an antelope or two at the wallow. They scattered, with me after them. But it was like chasing the wind. They soon outdistanced me, leaving me and my pony alone on the prairie.

I stopped a while to catch my breath, wondering how near the antelope ranch was, when suddenly I noticed some horsemen in the distance. From the dust they were raising I knew they were riding hard.

Five riders came up and surrounded me. One of them shouted, "That's my horse and that's the fellow who stole it."

I said, "I didn't steal any horse—I bought it a little while ago."

The fellow who'd accused me said, "There's no tree around here to hang him and it's getting dark, so we'll take him to Dodge and hang him in the morning."

One of the fellows put a rope around my neck and tied it to the saddle horn, and another fellow threw a loop over my horse's head to lead it. Then we began moving across the prairie in a procession to Dodge.

It was twilight by the time we rode into Dodge. Fortunately, Bob and Ben Daniels were standing outside Bob Wright's store. Ben stepped down and held up his hand.

"What's wrong here?" he asked.

"We caught a horse-thief," one man said.

"This kid's new in Dodge," Ben said. "He's no horse-thief. Hell, he's got money right here with Bob Wright."

"That's right," Bob called out. "I think there's a mistake here, boys."

"I know my own horse," the man said.

"What happened, George?" Ben said.

I told them exactly what had happened. Bat Masterson came up as I was finishing my story.

"What did this man look like?" Bat said.

After I described him Bat turned to Ben. "Fred Singer arrested him at the depot. He was threatening one of the brakemen. He's in jail right now."

"That's your horse-thief," Ben said. "Let's go down and talk to him."

They took the rope from my neck and I got down. The

owner of the horse was still grumbling. "Next time get a bill of ownership, kid," he said, shaking his fist at me.

Later that night Bat came by the Dodge House and gave me twenty dollars and my gun.

"Now listen to me and listen good," he said. "I haven't got time to wet-nurse a young greenhorn. Don't give your gun away to anyone no matter *what* they offer you. Now, if you don't take some good advice you'll have to go back home."

"What advice is that?" I asked.

"Stop being such a damn fool," he said and walked out.

The nights were getting shorter and so was my cash in Bob Wright's sack. I skipped a few days' practice shooting and did some odd jobs for Bob Wright, then went back to the river, where I practiced my marksmanship on driftwood. I had cut down on my shells and was on my fifth bullet, aiming at the branch of a dead tree stuck along the bank, when I heard a horse snorting.

The horseman was a good-looking Mex about thirty-five. He was dark-complexioned, with the whitest teeth I'd ever seen. He wore a velvet vest and a wide Mexican hat.

"That's nice shooting, keed." He pulled up alongside me and I admired his fine silver saddle. "That was first-class shooting. What kind of a gun is that?"

"Colt," I said, flattered.

"Let's see it," he said and, without thinking, I handed him the Colt. He touched his spurs to his horse and splashed across the ford—it was about three feet deep—and up on the opposite bank.

I ran after him, shouting, "Hey there, give me back my gun."

Of course he never looked around. Within a few minutes he

was gone. I just stood there, refusing to believe that I had been a damn fool again.

I walked back to Dodge, avoiding the main street. But as luck would have it, the first man I met when I entered the Dodge House was Bat.

"Well, kid," he said, "still practicing down at the river?"

"Yes," I said, glumly.

He looked down at my waist. "Where's your gun, kid?"

"Well, I guess I lost it," I said.

Bat groaned. "Not again?"

I nodded and told the story. He listened in silence. "Well, that's the limit," he said. "Earp took that Mex's gun and knife away this afternoon. Now he's got yours."

"Maybe I had better go back East," I said. I meant it.

"Maybe," Bat said. "Well, anyway, we had better go down to Wright's and get you another gun."

I felt as low as a skunk, not saying much as we walked to Bob Wright's place. After Bat told him the story they both looked at me solemnly.

"George," Bob Wright said, "you're as green as a gourd."

I bought myself another gun.

THE TWO-GUN MAN

The Two-Gun Man walked through the town,
    And found the sidewalk clear;
He looked around, with ugly frown,
    But not a soul was near.
The streets were silent. Loud and shrill,
    No cowboy raised a shout;
Like panther bent upon the kill,
    The Two-Gun Man walked out.

The Two-Gun Man was small and quick;
    His eyes were narrow slits;
He didn't hail from Battle Creek,
    Nor shoot the town to bits;
He drank, alone, deep draughts of sin,
    Then pushed away his glass
And silenced was each dance hall's din,
    When by the door he'd pass.

One day, rode forth this man of wrath,
    Upon a distant plain,
And ne'er did he retrace his path,
    Nor was he seen again;
The cow town fell into decay;
    No spurred heels pressed its walks;
But through its grass-grown ways, they say
    The Two-Gun Man still stalks.

—From the Denver *Republican*

The Law of Dodge City

A S MY first days in Dodge City passed I got to know many of its more famous citizens: Ham Bell, the Mastersons, Bill Tilghman, Wyatt Earp, Neal Brown, Fred Singer, Ben Daniels, Billy Ainsworth and Doc Holliday.

I don't mean to pretend that Wyatt Earp or Doc Holliday were particularly close friends of mine. They were far from that. Not only was I a green kid who had nothing in common with them, but also Earp and Holliday were not the friendly type.

The longest conversation I ever had with Holliday was on the street in 1879 before he left Dodge with Earp. Bat Masterson called to me as I passed and introduced me.

Holliday, a slim man with ash blond hair and the mark of tuberculosis on his gaunt face, barely nodded.

"How old are you, kid?" he asked me in a hoarse voice.

When I told him, he said, "I'm just ten years older."

I said goodbye and not long afterward, Doc left town.

The men I really knew were Jim and Bat Masterson. Jim rode with me into the Battle of Cimarron, as did Neal Brown and Fred Singer, who were to become my closest friends. And Ben Daniels and Billy Ainsworth were friends with whom I corresponded for many years after I left Kansas.

Of them all, the man I consider it an honor to have known and to have ridden with was Bill Tilghman. It has always been a mystery to me why Wyatt Earp has been made into the great hero of the frontier. Personally, I think Bill Tilghman's contributions were far more important to our history than Earp's. Bill Tilghman was bringing law and order to a wild and ruthless frontier when Earp was searching for gold in Alaska.

Tilghman was a warm, kindly man in contrast to Wyatt Earp, whose manner was cold and impersonal. Wyatt Earp was a great Western marshal, but to my mind, Bill Tilghman was greater, both in character and in deeds.

To most of these fearless men of Dodge, I was just another green kid seeking adventure. Suddenly, one day it all changed. I saved the life of one of their friends at the risk of my own.

I was standing in front of a dance-hall—I think it was Harding's—when Ben Daniels came walking up the opposite side of the street. He had a Mex in tow. I could see he had his gun out and kept prodding the greaser, who seemed to be either groggy or drunk. I assumed they were on the way to the lockup.

Prisoners being marched up the street to the jail weren't any extraordinary sight in Dodge in 1879-1880, but something made me watch them. As Ben passed I waved. I started to cross the street when someone darted out from an alley. It was another Mex and he was tiptoeing toward Ben. In his hand he held a stiletto. He was going to stab Ben in the back!

I rushed across the street. The sound of my boots made the Mex turn. He gave one wild shout and flung his knife. I ducked and heard it whistle over my head. He tried to run, but I caught him. He twisted out of my hands and when he jumped back he had a gun in his hand.

"Look out, kid!" someone shouted. I dropped as a gun roared—inches, it seemed, from my back. When I looked up, Ben was looking down at me, the smoking gun still in his hand.

"Thanks, kid," he said. Without another look he continued walking to the jail. I stood up, brushing the dirt from my clothes. The Mex who had had the knife was sprawled out, unseeing eyes staring up, blood pouring out of the hole in his face. For a moment I thought I was going to be sick.

The firing had brought men from the saloon on the run and they stood around to stare down at the dead man.

"Who shot him, kid?" someone asked me.

"Ben Daniels," I said. "The Mex tried to bushwhack him."

They stared down for a few minutes, then, one my one, drifted back into the saloon. I was alone with the dead man. What does one do? I asked myself. After a few minutes I also walked away.

When I looked back, a dog was sniffing at the corpse, while a man—a bartender, from his apron—was coming out of a saloon with a newspaper. Probably bad for business, I told myself.

Ben spread the word around about what I had done. Jim Masterson said to me quietly, "Nice work, George," while Bat slapped me on the back.

Bill Tilghman bought me breakfast the next day. For all his soft-spoken way, I think Bill Tilghman knew more than anyone else about me while I stayed in Dodge. He inquired about my folks and our home place and he always listened.

A few days later Bill and Bat found me at the Dodge House and asked me if I wanted to ride with them to the Harvester ranch. I think it was to pick up the foreman, who had been involved in a shooting of a dance-hall girl.

"I have to go to another ranch below there," Bat said, "and maybe you can ride back with the foreman and Bill."

I realized, of course, that I wasn't being invited along because Bill Tilghman needed a green kid to help him; this was sort of an accolade for helping Ben Daniels.

I almost ran to the stable and saddled up. We rode out of town in a leisurely fashion and in an hour or two reached the ranch. Bat went on ahead.

Old Colonel Harvester listened to what Bill said about the foreman and the charge against him.

"Maybe I'd better tell him to come up to the house," Harvester said.

"Never mind, Colonel," Bill replied. "We'll go down and get him."

"The boys won't like it," the colonel said, "but go ahead if you want to."

We rode over to the bunkhouse and, sure enough, some of the hands were waiting, their hands near their guns. Bill ignored them as the foreman came out.

"I know what you're after," he said. "I'm sorry it had to happen. I'll go back to Dodge with you."

"I have to go join Masterson down at another ranch," Bill said. "Suppose you ride in with Bolds."

"Hell, I'm not going to ride in with a kid," the foreman said, "I'll ride in by myself."

Bill nodded. "All right. I'll see you in the morning. Come on, George."

Tilghman and I rode to the other ranch and joined Bat. I don't know what business it was he had there, but he seemed to think it was important. All the way down to join Bat I kept telling Bill what a fool he was to let the foreman go free and to take the word of a cowhand.

"Here's a man who shot a woman, Bill," I said, "and you take his word he will be sitting on the steps of the jail waiting for you to show up. I think that's a lot of nonsense."

All Bill would say was, "He'll be there, George."

The next day I rode into Dodge with Bat and Bill, and I'll be damned if that fellow wasn't standing in the sun outside the jail.

Later that day Bill talked with the foreman, who told him several times that the shooting of the young dance-hall girl was purely an accident.

We went down to the Long Branch and Bill talked to the girl. She was a pretty young thing, dressed in a bright red kimono, with her leg bandaged and resting on a cushion. The bullet had passed through the calf of her right leg, but hadn't touched the bone.

"Marshal," she said to Bill, "I just don't know how that gun went off. We were dancing and fooling around and suddenly I heard the shot and felt the sting in my leg. Now I always liked this fellow and we got along fine every time he came into Dodge. In fact," she said, "I like him enough to marry him."

"We'll be back in a minute," Bill said. "Come on, George."

Then we went out, with me wondering where we were going.

Bill went down to the jail and told the cowboy what she had said and he said, "That suits me."

Bill made the preparations for them to get hitched that afternoon. Later I heard he became the manager of a large ranch in Texas. That gives you an example of the kind of a man Bill Tilghman was. For all his exploits with a gun, he was a peace-loving fellow.

His word was his bond—whether to outlaws, killers, gamblers or whores. As Bill said that day, "He knows me."

Wyatt Earp, on the other hand, was a great believer in the art of the bluff, whether at the card table, or in a gunfight. Earp was a great one for making a man think he was going to draw. He would slash out instead, quick as a snake, and knock the fellow out.

He had a healthy respect for the barrel of his six-shooter, especially his Buntline. Facing that barrel was fearsome. You struck at a man's face and instinctively he forgot the gun at his hip. He put up his arms to shield himself. A terrible blow administered with that barrel could demoralize any man and knock out his courage. For the marshal, it meant one less life taken.

Earp, in those frontier days, is portrayed as a deadly defender of law and order in the old West. Earp was all of that. Of course, there are periods in his life that will be the subject of debate as long as any two students of the old West meet.

Despite the Earp legends, as far as I'm concerned Jim Masterson could outdraw his brother Bat and Wyatt Earp and could match them in courage. I've seen him bash a man in the face who had a gun turned on him and take that same gun and break the barrel on the bar. I've seen him in Dodge buffaloing a bunch of drunken, hooting cowhands by simply walking up, staring at them coldly and ordering them out of town. We were to ride together into the guns at Cimarron, where, with his brother, he held off an entire town while treed on top of an iron safe. Right after the shooting, when they were cutting the lead out of my body, Jim walked in as nonchalantly as if he were returning from a fair. I can still hear his quiet voice, "I nicked a few of them for you, George," and he had.

One December morning I met Bat near the Dodge House. "Going home for Christmas, George?" he asked.

"I've been thinking of it, Bat," I said. The truth was, my first months in Dodge had slipped away so fast December had stolen upon me before I knew it.

"Jim and I are leaving for Wichita tomorrow," he said. "A kid like you should be home at this time of year."

They left and in a few days I followed them, to arrive home in Indiana a few days before Christmas. The farm was the same. Dan, a little heavier, was still keeping up the tract we had. Mother smothered me with kisses, but Father just looked me up and down. His look was as dark as night.

"You're carrying a gun, George," he said. "There's no one here to harm you."

The six-shooter at my hip suddenly felt like a millstone. I took it off and never said a word. On the frontier, a man was conspicuous without a gun; in Adams County, a man was conspicuous with one.

I left Adams County in the winter of 1880 with Portland my next stop. Adda was as beautiful as she had been in my dreams. The night I left Portland for Dodge I kissed her in the carriage that took us to the depot.

That night I almost turned in my ticket, but I still had the West in my blood.

When I got back to Dodge it was soon apparent even to me that the Earps, the Mastersons and Bill Tilghman had taken some of the wildness out of Dodge. Now they were all leaving for Tombstone, Arizona.

"George," Bat said in the Long Branch the night before he left, "do one thing for me, will you?"

"Sure, Bat," I said, "what is it?"

"Don't give your gun to anyone while I'm gone," he said.

I thought the whole damn bar would go into convulsions.

"Cimarron" George

THAT SPRING in 1880 I earned the nickname of "Cimarron" George, which stayed with me as long as I remained in the West. It began one night in Dodge when a girl was shot by her pi, as they called pimps in Dodge, and Ben Daniels and Bill Tilghman set out after him. Since the time I had saved Ben Daniels' life, Ben and I had been rather close. So when he and Bill rode past the Long Branch saloon, where I was standing, wondering how to spend the day, they called, "Want to ride out with us, George?"

"Sure," I said.

I got my horse and joined them. Ben told me they were heading for the Nations to pick up the trail of the pimp.

There had been heavy rains in Colorado that week and the Cimarron River was on a rampage. It was running high and filled with driftwood and brush. Bill and Ben crossed without any trouble, but my horse was a jughead and I had a devil of a time getting him to go in. Finally I spurred him and he reluctantly entered the swirling river.

The first few feet were fine, but suddenly his legs got tangled up in some brush or branches and down he went. That's the last I recall. I woke up hanging over Ben's horse with Ben and Bill working my arms up and down. I thought I would strangle to death. I kept retching until I thought my stomach would coil out of my mouth like a snake. Later back in Dodge, when he was telling the story, Ben would say, "I swear the Cimarron rose a foot after we got all the sand and water out of George."

Finally I was able to stand, although I was dizzy and weak. My cow pony had had to be shot.

"Liberal isn't far," Bill said. "Maybe we can rent George a horse there."

We set out, me up behind Ben and wishing I had never left Dodge.

When we rode into Liberal I noticed a small general-hardware store with the name "Martin's" painted on the sign above the porch.

Bill and Ben went inside and I drooped on the top step of the porch. I had lost my horse, my Winchester and my six-shooter, and I was soaking wet. Fate had destined that either a stranger or a river would claim my firearms. As I remember, I put my head on my arms, which were crossed over my knees, and closed my eyes.

Suddenly a small voice said, "What's the matter, Mister? Fall in the Cimarron?"

I looked up. A small boy about six or eight, with sun-bleached hair, barefooted and wearing a wash-worn pair of overalls, was studying me.

"My, sonny, with that brain of yours you're bound to be somebody yet," I said sarcastically.

The small boy looked at me gravely. "That's what my papa says. He says I have a head on my shoulders ... can you swim?"

"Sure I can," I said. "My horse slipped."

He came over and sat down beside me. "You had better stay away from the Cimarron, Mister," he said. "A man drowned in it last month."

"It was an accident," I protested. "I didn't just fall in."

I wondered why I was explaining to this child. But he seemed so grown-up I felt I couldn't ignore him.

"We're going to move away," he said.

"Where?" I asked.

"Salina," he said. "Papa says they have a school there."

"Your papa's very smart," I said. "Little boys should go to school."

"My papa is the smartest man in the world," he said.

As I rode back to Dodge I couldn't help but chuckle every time I recalled the little tow-headed boy who soberly warned me that the Cimarron was dangerous. The boy was to become Glenn Martin, head of the Glenn Martin Aircraft Company.

MARRIAGES.

Alexander Bolds and
Leah Bolds Was
Marred August the 14
In the year of our lord 1856

george Bolds Was Born
uvember the 13 1823

"Son of the Frontier."
—Adams County, Indiana

"I bought a ticket in Kansas City for the biggest and toughest town in the West . . . Dodge City was a bitter disappointment. Near the depot, towering piles of buffalo hides and sun-bleached bones were as high as the top of the freight cars. Don't they even have a cemetery in this town? I didn't know they were buffalo bones. The dreary collection of clapboard houses, low and flat under a gray and cheerless sky, and the grisly pile of bones gave me an overpowering feeling of loneliness."

"My first friend in Dodge was Bat Masterson, the 'bat who wore guns.'"

" 'George,' Bat said in the Long Branch saloon *(shown below)* one night,
one thing for me, will you? Don't give your gun to anyone while I'm gone.
thought the whole damn bar would go into convulsions."

"I had my first breakfast in Dodge as the guest of a Texas ranch owner in Dog Kelley's saloon adjacent to the Dodge House."

" 'We'll take care of you, young fellow,' Bob Wright told me. And sure enough, he brought me pants, boots and a woolen shirt from his shelves. I counted my money and handed it over to Bob. He told me he would put it in a sack with my name on it. I could take what I wanted from time to time or charge my purchases to an account."

"As my first days in Dodge City passed I got to know many of its more famous citizens. To most of them I was just another green kid seeking adventure. Some of 'the boys' of Dodge shown above are: front row *(left to right)* Charles Bassett, Wyatt Earp, M. C. Clark and Neal Brown; back row *(left to right)* W. H. Harris, Luke Short and Bat Masterson."

"For all his exploits with a gun, Bill Tilghman *(left)* was a peace-loving fellow. His word was his bond—whether to outlaws, killers, gamblers or whores."

"The Girl I Left Behind"

"Adda Weldon was as beautiful as she had been in my dreams. The night I left Portland to go back to Dodge, I kissed her in the carriage that took us to the depot. That night I almost turned in my ticket, but I still had the West in my blood."

"Whenever we had a parade, above all rose the most dreadful clash of metal on metal and wailing horns and the thump-thump of a bass drum ever heard in the West—Chalk Beeson's band."

"Buffalo chips were plentiful on the prairie."

"In the Long Branch saloon someone mentioned that Dave Morrow, with his pointed, nicked ears, looked like a prairie dog, and the nickname stuck."

"That country burned itself in my memory: the wild, open sky, the quiet prairie, the keening winds, the land so empty there wasn't a speck between me, my horse and the pencil line of the far horizon—maybe a buffalo wallow now and then."

"My old friend P. C. J. 'Buffalo' Jones *(right)* used to drive this rig into Garden City from his ranch."

"I'll never forget the time Prairie Dog Morrow's pet buffalo almost wrecked a tent show that had come to Dodge."

"Across the empty plains of buffalo grass west of Dodge ran the ruts of the Santa Fe Trail. The arrow shows where the Trail on my land crossed the Arkansas River."

"The Dodge City *Times* used to boast in its columns that Dodge City was 'the biggest little town in the West.'"

" 'I've only started doing things for you people,' Asa Soule, the Hop Bitters King, told us. One of his gifts was a college in Dodge City for the people of the county."

"The spring made the prairie an enchanted place, but summer transformed it into a miserable hell by a burning sun and hot winds that seemed to drain very bit of moisture from a man's skin. But still the sod-busters came."

The  World.

"Two county seat war-riors, Drew and William Evans."

WITH FIRE AND THE BULLET

The Cimarron, Kan., Mob Threatened to Annihilate Ingalls and Its People.

BUT THE COUNTY SEAT WAR IS OVER

A Sheriff Saved the Imprisoned Deputies Whom the Cimarron Men Had Vowed to Lynch—Ingalls Guarded Last Night to Prevent Its Destruction—More Bloodshed Feared in the Near Future.

The county seat war between Cimarron and Ingalls, Kan., is over for the present. A Sheriff and posse saved the Ingalls deputies who were besieged Saturday night, and whom the Cimarron men had vowed to lynch. The Cimarron men are as ugly as ever, however, but made no further trouble after threatening to burn up the rival town and kill all its inhabitants.

[SPECIAL TO THE WORLD.]

WICHITA, Kan., Jan. 13.—The trouble between the towns of Ingalls and Cimarron over

ditches, the besieged returning the fire from windows and doors. Three of the deputies had been wounded at the first volley, George W. Bold having received a ball in his leg; E. D. Brooks, a shot in the arm

"The streets of Cimarron were deserted that bright, cold morning of January 12, 1889, when our wagon pulled up in front of the two-story brick building in which the office of the county clerk was located."

"Bill Tilghman and another U. S. marshal at the opening of the Cherokee Strip in Oklahoma. I never saw Bill again. I had climbed my last hill . . . I was going home."

"The Fisk Restaurant and Bon Ton Gambling House in Guthrie, Oklahoma, June, 1889. Somehow it all seemed as if everything had happened before."

"Adda and I were married in September, 1891, and I hung up my six-shoo
This is the way she looked the time we went to a fancy-dress party in Gene

e old home place back in Adams
nty, Indiana. My sister is still
ning it."

"I raised pure-blooded Duroc hogs in
Louisiana. Breeders came to the farm
from as far north as Iowa and as far
east as Kentucky."

A steamboat passing the Bolds' Livestock Farm in Plaquemine, Louisiana."

"Our golden wedding day—I guess sort of ate my cake and had it, too."

This is BOOT HILL
famous BURIAL GROUND & MUSEUM
also VISIT BEESON MUSEUM
4000 AUTHENTIC RELICS OF EARLY DODGE CITY (5 ROOMS *of* AUTHENTIC RELICS)
3 blocks east, South across bridge, then across track to first road, turn right ¼ Mi.

"I had to shut my eyes and travel back down through the years in my memory to picture the old Dodge. I took my family to Chalk Beeson's museum there and caught some of the flavor of the town I once knew. But I bet Chalk was probably chuckling to see 'Cimarron' George Bolds walking through his museum like a damned tourist, gawking like I'd never been west of Washington, D. C."

"I remember Adda asking me on one of my trips back home from the West, 'George, what is it that keeps you out there?' Adventure? Even that paled. Perhaps it was the sense of walking with the last. . . ."

"Prairie Dog" Morrow and "Chalk" Beeson

TOMBSTONE is remembered for Wyatt Earp and the battle in the O. K. Corral; Mobeetie for its evil and Dodge City for its colorful individualists, like Prairie Dog Morrow and Chalk Beeson.

Back in the seventies before he settled down, if you can call it that, Dave Morrow was an old buffalo-hunter. He was a sort of deputy in Dodge. In those days you didn't have to have a tin star or a formal certificate hanging up on your wall. It was just a case of strapping on your gun when they said, "Come on." Morrow was always ready to ride. He was a fine shot and had an enormous amount of physical stamina.

There's quite a story connected with his nickname. It seems Morrow decided to ship the stock on his ranch to Kansas City and take their value in better steers. He told his ranch hands to meet him in Dodge. The stock would arrive the following morning, he said, and they were to bring the cattle down to the ranch. He would go on ahead.

Somewhere along the trail he fell in with two fellows who looked as if they had been riding hard. Suddenly one of them pulled a six-shooter and the other a knife. They demanded that Dave turn over the money he'd received for the cattle. Dave kept insisting he had taken only cattle in exchange and that he didn't have a dime on him. Finally, to make him talk, one of the men nicked one ear and then the other.

"If you don't believe me," Dave said, "be at the depot tomorrow morning and you'll see my stock come in."

Blood streaming down from his cut ears, Dave went home to his ranch, treated the cuts and came back to Dodge, blood in his eye and with his Winchester and six-shooter ready. He swore he was going to scalp those two buzzards when they showed up at the depot. He would have, too, but of course they never showed up.

In the Long Branch saloon that night someone mentioned that Dave, with his pointed, nicked ears, looked like a prairie dog, and the nickname stuck. That's the way most nicknames were born—they got the fancy of the boys in the saloon and no matter what you did or how much you threatened, there was no changing it. Like Calamity Jane—*that* name had a nice dangerous ring to it.

Dave had only a few hands on his ranch because his spread was a small one, and most of the time he stayed in Dodge. It was he who shot a white buffalo, one of the few authentic ones in the West, adored by some tribes as a god, and sold it to Bob Wright. Bob sent it around to fairs and exhibitions where it was quite an attraction.

Dave also found a yearling buffalo and brought it back to Dodge one time, nursing it along one winter to make a pet of it. In the spring some of the boys made a corral and soon the buffalo was eating out of anybody's hand. When the days became warmer they would let him loose and he would wander about the town, as friendly a critter as anyone could find. Some of the ladies protested, because the buffalo, who was very near-sighted and depended mostly on scent, would come up behind them and nose them with his snout, sending them skyhigh.

I'll never forget the time Dave's buffalo almost wrecked a tent show that had come to Dodge. It was about ten o'clock and the parade started down Front Street, the men with the horns blaring away and the man with the big bass drum hitting that skin with a sound like a buffalo gun.

Suddenly, up the block came the buffalo. He just squinted with his weak eyes, pawed the ground for a moment, then charged. The parade scattered and the fellow with the bass drum let go the drum to dive for the nearest building.

The buffalo smashed into that drum and shook it to pieces that hung about his neck. It took a devil of a lot of coaxing to get him back in the corral. When the parade started again—without the bass drum—that buffalo almost tore down the corral, so eager was he to charge this strange combination of strange noises.

I was in the Long Branch, drinking with Jim Masterson, when he said, "Come on, George, let's go and see that show."

I agreed and we went over to the tent. On the way we met Dave. He was going too, so he joined up with us. Inside, there was quite a crowd and we pushed our way to the back. But Dave was disgusted.

"I can't hear 'way back here." he said, "I'm going down front."

"No seats down there, Dave," Jim said.

"Then I'll sit on the ground," he said, and pushed his way through. After about a half-hour of serenading, the play started. It was a romance south of the border, about a white cattleman, a Spanish don and his beautiful daughter. There was also a Mex who kept slinking around with his hand on the handle of his dagger.

"Damned if I like that breed," Jim said.

The play went along smoothly, with interest mounting. At one point the cattleman was making love to the don's daughter and the Mex came on the stage, knife in hand. When he started toward the white man Dave jumped up and roared, "You damn Mex! Don't you stick that man!"

More startled than anything, the actor fled into the wings. The white man and the actress, startled, went on with their lovemaking. Out of the wings ventured the Mex and again Dave roared out his warning. Again the actor escaped into the wings and the other actors, now annoyed, went back over their lines.

The third time Dave shouted, the Mex actor ignored him. He raised his dagger and Dave's gun barked. Blood spattered over the man and woman. Women screamed and men shouted. The tent was thrown into pandemonium.

"That damn fool killed those people!" Jim shouted and pushed down the aisle. I followed him.

Dave dived under the tent and rode as if the devil were reaching for his coat-tails, for his ranch. There, his hands later said, he walked the floor all night. In the morning, haggard and red-eyed, he came into Dodge to see the sheriff.

"I want to surrender," he said.

"What for, Dave?" asked the sheriff, who was in on the joke.

"Why, for killing those two people last night. I guess I just lost my head," Dave said. "I never want to see another show."

"Why, you didn't kill those people, Dave," the sheriff said. "That was a rubber knife filled with red ink. It was supposed to open and pour out this stuff all over the actor and the lady. . . ."

"Well, I'll be damned," Dave said, and he just stood there, rubbing the stubble on his chin.

"The manager of the show wants to see you, Dave," the sheriff said. "Wait, and I'll bring him in."

The sheriff sent a deputy to bring back the manager of the show. He began pumping Dave's hand.

"Greatest bit I ever saw," the manager said. "It made the show. Mister, I'll give you twenty dollars a night to do the same thing."

"Not me," Dave replied, "not me. I've had all the play-acting I'm ever going to want."

No matter how much the manager argued, Dave just shook his head. The manager was disappointed but Dave's shot had caused so much talk around the county that instead of playing one night, the show played for two weeks!

About a year or so after the hold-up that gave Dave his Prairie Dog nickname, one of his hands, Billy Brooks, went home to Texas to see his folks.

After his visit there, Billy tried to join up with an outfit coming north with a drive. He finally found a berth in San Antonio where another cowhand, who had once worked with Billy on Dave's ranch, introduced him to the boss of the outfit.

They were in a saloon, wetting their pipes for the last time before they headed north, when they heard a loud-talking man boasting of how tough he was and how many men he had to have for breakfast.

The cowhand with Billy was a tough young Texan—not mean, mind you, but with a daredevil toughness that was some-times unbelievable. Those boys seemed to have wire cables for nerves and bodies of pig iron. When this braggart had worked his way down the bar to where they stood, he suddenly began to laugh when he heard them mention Dodge City.

"That's where me and my friend nicked an old bastard," he said. "Nicked him like this," and he made a motion as if holding a knife.

"Why?" said Billy.

"He wouldn't turn over his money to us when we asked him," the braggart said. "So I nicked him once, then again. He squealed like a stuck pig. Lord, how he squealed!"

Billy and the cowhand looked at each other. The cowhand turned around and slapped the man's face.

The braggart went for his gun, but the Texan was faster. He shot him in the stomach and he died a few hours later. The next day they were on the trail, heading north to Dodge.

Maybe he was lying about nicking Dave's ears. But it was a hard country.

One of the kindest men I ever knew in Dodge was C. M. Beeson, "Chalk" to all who knew him. He never killed a famous outlaw or broke an original trail or brought law and order to a lawless community like the Earps, but he was a builder. He wanted roots to push themselves into the plains of the West, he wanted homes and schools and a better way of life. There are two versions of how Chalk got his nickname. The first and probably correct one is that it was a short version of his first name, Chalkley. The second and more colorful, if not more truthful, is that he received his nickname when he was sheriff. He'd taken some cowhands into custody for hurrahing the town. Like most of the hands who made the drives, they were young, tough and full of derring-do. These boys had a code, unbreakable as the law of hospitality on the plains, and this was a cowboy's loyalty to his fellow-rider. So when the boys at the camp heard their friends were in jail, they saddled up and sent word to Chalk that they were going to take him and his jail apart.

Chalk summoned his four deputies. This outfit coming in had many guns on their side and Chalk knew he had to use what today would be called psychology.

Bob Wright gave him some lime and Chalk made a line in front of the jail.

"What are you doing?" Bob asked.

"Making a chalk line for those damn cowboys," Beeson replied. "If they cross it they'll get a load of buckshot."

Late that afternoon the hands—about seven of them—rode into town and headed straight for the jail. At various points behind the semicircle stood Beeson and his four deputies, each with a shotgun. When the hands rode up, Beeson stepped across the line. "I just want to warn you boys," he said. "I'm the sheriff and I don't want any trouble, but the first man who steps across this line gets a load of buckshot."

The seven hands just stared at him. Then one who seemed to be the leader wheeled about and rode down the street, the others following. For the next half-hour they drank and made threats at the Long Branch. Finally, they got themselves so worked up and full of liquor they forgot about the shotguns.

"Come on," said their leader, and, whooping and waving their guns, they mounted and rode down the street.

Sheriff Beeson and his deputies were waiting. Beeson stepped across the line and held up his hand.

"Boys, you had better go back to camp," he called out, "before someone gets hurt."

The hand who was doing all the talking started to move his horse toward Beeson. He had been saying all the time he thought the old man was bluffing and wouldn't dare to fire.

Chalk slowly lifted his shotgun as the horse came closer; the rest of the cowhands watching, the deputies ready, their fingers on their triggers.

Beeson backed across the line and the cowboy, now bolder, followed. The moment he was over the line, Chalk fired a blast over the head of the horse. The animal nearly leaped over the jail. The cowboy almost slipped out of the saddle, he was so surprised. About five hundred pellets whistling over one's head can make any man's guts knot up.

The cowboy knew his bluff had been called. He backed off and, after shouting a lot of nonsense, they all turned around and left. The cowhands were later fined and warned to stay in Texas.

I got to know Chalk during my stay in Dodge and when I became county surveyor of Gray County. After Bob Wright donated the land for a city park in Dodge, Chalk founded a Western museum, which he willed to Dodge at his death.

Many years later I happened to be traveling through Dodge. In the late eighties the town had been practically wiped out in a big fire and the clean model town I found simply set me aback. I had to shut my eyes and travel back down through the years in my memory to picture the old Dodge. Later I took my family to Chalk Beeson's museum, and there I caught some of the flavor of the town I once knew. But I bet Chalk, wherever he was, was probably chuckling to see "Cimarron" George Bolds walking through his museum like a damned tourist, gawking like I'd never been west of Washington, D. C.

The Biggest Little Men in the "Biggest Little Town"

T HE DODGE CITY *Times* used to boast in its columns that Dodge City was "the biggest little town in the West." Two of the men who gave it law and order with their guns and their courage, were the biggest little men in the biggest little town: Neal Brown and Fred Singer.

Neal, when I knew him, was called "Skinny" Brown. He was about five foot seven and weighed less than one hundred and thirty-five pounds when he was not carrying his hardware, which wasn't often. Back home, folks would call a slender man "slimmer than a rail," but Neal was more slender than a splinter of a rail. He could not carry his six-shooter in a belt around his waist as it would slip down, so he wore heavy suspenders to keep his pants up. Neal had a scabbard made to hold his gun on the inside of his pants on the left side, with the butt pointing to the right. He always wore a vest with the lower part buttoned and the upper part open. He'd surprise a would-be gunfighter by flipping open that vest and drawing before he could go for his gun.

I have tintypes in my old scrapbook of some of the marshals of Dodge, and Neal is among them—unsmiling, grave. He looked like an indignant deacon even when he was wading into a band of drunken cowhands who refused to surrender their guns.

Neal and Bill Tilghman were partners shooting buffalo and later in a ranch in southwestern Kansas. Neal was with Bill in the Oklahoma Run, and when Bill became a U. S. Marshal, Neal was his deputy and later his jailer. They were together the time Bill walked into the Doolin gang's hideout. Neal was waiting outside in a wagon. With a number of guns trained on his back, Bill struck up a conversation with one member of the gang. The others were lying in their bunks.

When Bill realized he could be a prime target, he said good-bye and walked out, every nerve tingling with the expectation that the gang would open up. He swung up on the driver's seat. "Get the hell out of here, Neal," he whispered, "the place is full of outlaws." Not to make the gang suspicious, Neal casually swung the team about and drove off, one hand on the butt of his six-shooter, the other holding the reins.

The second little man was Fred Singer, a slender Englishman with a good education and a wonderful, wry sense of humor. Fred came to Kansas about 1872 to settle on a tract of land near Caldwell. His small cattle ranch prospered and he hired two hands. The Atchison, Topeka and Santa Fe came through at Newton, furnishing them with a ready railhead for their markets.

Once in the 1870's Fred made a killing in Newton and after paying off his two hands, told them they could remain in town and see the sights and return to the ranch in a day or two. About a mile from his ranch he met two fellows who said they were looking for Caldwell. Fred, a genial soul, was giving them elaborate directions when a noose hissed around his neck. He was jerked out of his saddle and fell to the ground, stunned.

The two road agents went through his pockets and took the four hundred dollars Fred had earned. Fred's horse had gone on to the ranch, leaving him to walk home, a chore any cowboy detests.

"The more I walked, the madder I got," he told me. "By the time I reached the ranch I was so mad I couldn't talk. The only one at home was the Chink cook, so after he cooked up something, I saddled up and rode to Caldwell."

A livery stable owner gave him a description of two men who had ridden into town several hours earlier, but although he walked around Caldwell Fred couldn't find them. He checked in at the hotel and slept late. After breakfast he rode to Newton, told his cowhands what had happened, and then, on a hunch, returned to Caldwell that night.

There were three saloons in town and in the third one he found the two men. He ordered them to raise their hands, but one started for his gun. Fred killed him. The other one was firing wildly. Fred carefully aimed and killed him also. On searching the bodies, they found all but fifty dollars of the stolen money. Fred arranged for their burial, then returned to the ranch with the outlaws' horses. Inasmuch as he had been the victim of the holdup, the sheriff had turned the horses over to him after he paid the feed bill.

Fred, later a jailer under Bat Masterson, was known as the best cribbage player in the West. His usual question to a prisoner when he was brought in was, "Do you play cribbage?"

If the outlaw, killer or road agent played the game, Fred was delighted. He'd lock the front door, release the fellow from his cell and begin playing. But one night cribbage gave Fred quite a headache.

A young Texan was captured in Dodge and was held on a murder charge, waiting for the Texas authorities to come and get him. He turned out to be a good cribbage player. About the third day he complained of being ill. Doc McCarthy examined him and diagnosed his case as smallpox. McCarthy quarantined the jail, but since Fred had already had smallpox, he allowed him to stay on. When the Texan improved, they continued the cribbage games, the prisoner winning about a hundred dollars of Fred's money.

One night he clubbed Fred unconscious when Fred bent down to pick up a card. He took Fred's last five dollars, selected a six-shooter and rifle from the rack, locked the front door, threw the key away and left Fred lying on the floor.

Doc McCarthy found the door locked and the boys had to batter it in. They found Fred on the floor, nursing a lump the size of a hen's egg. When Fred cleaned himself up he was furious; but Doc McCarthy refused to let him go after the Texan. He was so dizzy from the beating he could barely walk, let alone ride.

A cowhand's horse was reported stolen, and all signs pointed to the Texan. Neal Brown set out after the prisoner. The trail led through Kansas and into No Man's Land to the Beaver, or north branch, of the Canadian River, then west for several miles to a small dugout, which was used as a hideout for outlaws who frequented the Strip. The fellow was taken after only a few shots and Neal put him in irons and started for Dodge. About a mile from the dugout they had run into an ambush of the Texan's friends. The gunfire was furious, but Neal killed one man and one of the bullets killed the Texan. The two dead men were strapped on the horses and Neal returned to Dodge.

Fred was miffed when he saw the dead prisoner. He complained to Neal that he should have brought him back alive.

Not long afterward the jail had another wily occupant. Fred, like all cowboys, would never walk when a horse could be had. He had a favorite one named "Rowdy." One day, when it came time to feed his prisoner, Fred rode up to jail on Rowdy, carrying the prison food in a large pan. He ground-tied his horse and entered the jail. He unlocked the cell, ordering the man to stand back.

Holding the pan with both hands, Fred entered the cell. Suddenly this fellow lashed out with his boot and the food flew up into Fred's face. Before he knew it Fred was inside the jail looking out, as the fellow ran out of the jail, swung up on Rowdy and galloped out of town.

A few hours later a deputy found Fred locked up and in a dangerous mood. A light snow had fallen and the prisoner's tracks were easy to follow. Fred took off alone and later a posse started after him. They found his trail crossing the Cimarron, and after riding about five miles, they heard the sound of rifle fire.

They came up to find Fred in a buffalo wallow, firing with his saddle rifle at a sod house. Before the posse dismounted, Fred rushed up to the door. The sheriff shouted at him to get clear, but Fred kicked in the door and went inside. We expected to hear the crash of shots but there weren't any. When the possemen arrived at the soddy Fred came out and said the man was dead.

They brought the fellow back in a slicker. Neal reminded Fred of his boast that *he* always brought his man back alive.

"But that fellow wasn't a cribbage player," Fred said.

Kate O'Leary, the Belle of Dodge

I'VE ALWAYS wondered why those who wrote about Dodge and the early West did not include the story of Kate O'Leary.

She wasn't a striking beauty, but she had a freshness that smelled of soap and water and sunshine, and her strong body was topped off by a pair of broad shoulders. Her biggest asset was her rich red-gold hair. When she walked into a saloon or dance-hall she stood out like a flame. She had no singing voice, like Dora Hand's, but she had a deep, pleasant voice. She knew all the old border songs, some going back before the Civil War. Despite her "moonlight" profession, she still looked young and not yet hardened by the viciousness of her trade. Life was still a merry game of many admiring eyes, whiskey, fine clothes and the utter abandonment which her young animal spirits demanded.

Kate was really a daughter of the border. She was raised on a small ranch by her grandmother and father. Her grandmother had been a schoolteacher and she ruled Kate with a firm hand.

By the time she was fifteen she had a fair education. Some Comanches lived not far from their ranch and the only play-mates Kate had were Indians. She rode bareback as they did and spent most of her time on the plains. As she grew older, she had the usual tasks that all ranch children had, among them taking charge of the few head of cattle her father owned.

As the influx of homesteaders incensed the Indians, they often tried to steal a steer or two or scattered the small herds. When they became drunk on trader's whiskey they usually butchered a cow for a boisterous meal and dance. There was a big spread near Kate's place and when the Comanches used to ride down on the cattle, Kate would fire off her Winchester three times. Usually some of the hands working the range would hear the echo and come a-riding. The Comanches—who were never in earnest and had no heart to tangle with any of those hot-blooded young punchers who were just looking for an excuse to shoot up an Indian—would take off.

Once, as Kate told me, a party of young bucks, all liquored up and mean as rattlesnakes, came riding past her place. They passed, but one of them said something to the others and they started to screech and fire their rifles. When they caught sight of Kate coming up with some of her cattle, they started toward her. When they reached her, they wheeled their horses and began to surround her.

But Kate wasn't one to fool with. She slid over the side of the pony as the bucks began shooting—probably over her head at the cattle, who were milling and bellowing. When they dropped one or two head, she got boiling mad. There was one wild young buck who seemed to be the leader. Kate dropped *him* with one shot. Now the firing was directed at Kate. They got her pony, but she jumped clear and started to fire from behind her saddle, which she used as a shield.

Some cowhands riding fence heard the firing and came up at a gallop. This sobered the Indians and they started to ride off. But one of them turned and killed a steer. Kate killed him with a bullet right through the head. That took the fight out of the Indians and they disappeared.

By this time the boys had arrived. "What's the matter, Kate?" they asked.

All she said was, "Killin', thievin' Injuns."

But you can't kill two Indians and not hear the end of it from their relatives. A few days later a band of them swooped down on the small herd and killed every one of them, cutting out their tongues. Roast tongue is a favorite morsel among the Nations. When Kate went out to bring them in, the buzzards were already at work.

This settled it for Kate's folks. They decided homesteading was not for them, so they sold out their holdings and moved to Kansas City. Kate was as wild as an Indian kid and had picked up more than her share of cuss words from the punchers. Kate's grandmother could probably see the way the twig was bending, so she decided to pull up the roots and plant it in better soil.

They put Kate in a school in Kansas City and she proved to be a good student. When I knew her she still had a smattering of French and once, on a bet, translated a Latin verb. But no school could hogtie *her*. She was a pretty young girl and restless.

Typhoid took both her grandmother and her father and Kate was left an orphan. Her mother had kinfolk in the East, but Kate decided to stay in Kansas City. She got a job as a waitress in a hotel that was patronized by cattlemen, and her personality and good looks made her a favorite.

One night three cattlemen came in and took over a table that was set for four. One fellow Kate knew slightly as Bill Rowdy. He was a slender, dark fellow with curly black hair. He didn't talk much, didn't blow off like most of the Texans who came in there.

Kate started to serve the meal—in those days it was all side dishes—when a young drunken cattleman came in and occupied the fourth chair. When Kate started to serve the mashed potatoes he grabbed her leg and said, "How about a date, redhead?"

Kate hit him with three plates of mashed potatoes. The puncher fell off the chair and came up roaring like a bull, his face covered with white blobs. He made a grab for Kate, but she ducked.

Then Bill Rowdy went into action. He leaned over the table and knocked the fellow down. When he came up, he knocked him down again. The man went for his gun, but one of the other cattlemen kicked it out of his hand. Then Bill dragged him out through the door and kicked him into the street.

"I'll get you and that red-headed bitch," the man shouted, but ran when Bill went after him.

The excitement died down and new dishes were brought up. Kate made a joke of the whole thing and soon had everyone in good spirits.

After the meal the other two men left, but Bill stayed on. "Where do you live, Kate?" he asked.

She smiled and said she reckoned he was trying for what that other fellow had in mind, but Bill very seriously said all he wanted to do was escort her home.

Kate thought that was reasonable and told him the address of her boarding-house. The next night he escorted her home again. And the next. Of course they fell in love. Bill asked Kate to marry him and she consented. It was exactly a month after their first meeting.

Bill had to leave town—he was always "leaving" mysteriously and returning a day or two later—and he went to the old lady who ran the boarding-house. He told her he and Kate were to be married, and after she had offered her congratulations Bill pulled out a roll of bills and peeled off a hundred dollars.

"Get Kate some pretty clothes downtown," he said, "and have her ready for the preacher in about a week."

"Are you going out West?" asked the old lady.

"I have to see about some cattle," Rowdy said. In a week he came back and they were married. The old lady gave them a wedding breakfast and all of the guests of the boarding-house were there, along with the two men whom Kate had seen with Bill when they first met. She thought it strange that none of the other cattlemen in town were there but placed it to Bill's reticence.

They took the cars to a certain town in Kansas where Bill said he wanted to settle. He built a house, hiring all the carpenters he could find. He seemed to have plenty of money, but when she asked about his business and where his ranch was located he gave her some vague explanation.

During the time he was away, Kate met some of the ladies in town, and as far as they were concerned Kate was a pretty young bride, fresh as a rose with dew on its petals. When they invited her to their homes for tea or coffee with cakes, Kate was as ladylike as any of them. Gradually she became a member of the local society.

Bill came and went. He would be in town for a few weeks, then would disappear to his "ranch." Kate begged to go along, but Bill kept saying it was no place for a lady. As she told me, "I sure was a fool. Hell, I had been born on a ranch and could ride as good as he could. But I guess any woman in love is as blind as a bat."

To satisfy her, Bill bought a riding horse and gave it to Kate. That kept her quiet for a while. But she still kept prodding Bill as to where his ranch was. Finally, one day when things came to a head Bill, to quiet her, gave her the deed to the house. It was signed over to Kate O'Leary. "Well," he shrugged when she pointed it out to him, "that was your name before we were married, wasn't it?"

During one of the periods when he was gone, a couple of cowhands were in town from Miles City. They were walking down the street when one spotted Kate. "My God, it's the red-head from Kansas City," he said. "Hey, Red," he called out, "when can I see you?"

Kate just stuck her nose up in the air and kept on walking. But the cowhand followed her and took her arm. He started to say something when Kate slammed him one.

The puncher just held his jaw and stared after her. "What the hell's she mad at?" he said. But he called out after her, "I'll see you tonight, Red."

She ignored him. The cowpuncher went to the nearest bar and began drinking. The more whiskey he drank the uglier he got. He couldn't take the idea of the red-headed gal he had known in Kansas City refusing to see him. About midnight he had made up his mind: he was going to see Kate and no one was going to stop him. From someone in the saloon he found out where she lived and went down to her house. He banged on the door and awakened Kate.

"Who's there?" she called out.

"The fellow you met on the street today. Let me in, Red."

Kate pleaded with him to go away, but the cowpuncher began kicking at the door. Finally, he started to break down the door. Kate got a six-shooter and shouted to the man that she would kill him if he took one step in the house. The puncher went right ahead and broke down the door. The moment he started for her, Kate shot him.

The wife of a deputy sheriff who lived across the street heard the shot and ran out to help Kate. When she saw the dead man on the floor and Kate standing over him with a lighted lamp and a gun, she ran for her husband, who was playing cards in a saloon. By this time the whole neighborhood was up and when the deputy came Kate had collected herself.

Some of the ladies gave her coffee and stayed with her, but Kate was as cool and collected as if she had just come back from a ride in the country. As she told me, it wasn't until after the people had gone home and the crazy fool cowpuncher was taken away that she wept like a frightened child. If she ever needed Bill, it was then.

It was generally conceded that the puncher had it coming to him and folks said it was a good thing to show the cowpunchers that the women in this town could handle themselves.

But as the weeks went by and there was no sign of Bill, Kate went to the sheriff in town and asked him if he knew where she could find the Rowdy ranch. The sheriff said he had never heard of it and he knew just about every ranch and dirt farmer in the territory. Kate told him she feared something had happened to Bill and the officer told her to return home and not to worry. "Usually two, if not four, cattlemen come in during a day," he said, "and someone must know where your husband's ranch is located." But none of the ranchers or even the drifters knew of the ranch.

One rainy night Kate had been visiting and had come home about ten o'clock, which was rather late for her. She was asleep only a few minutes when she was aroused by a loud banging on the door.

She put on a robe and went downstairs with a lamp. When she opened the door she saw four or five men on horseback. One of them said, "Are you Mrs. Rowdy, ma'am?"

"Yes, I am Mrs. Rowdy," she said. "What's wrong?"

One man got down and lifted something wrapped in a raincoat that had been lashed across a saddle. He carried the bundle over to the porch and took the lamp from Kate.

"I'm sorry, ma'am," he said, "but your husband made us promise we'd bring him home." He knelt down and tucked in a fold of the raincoat. The lamplight fell on Bill Rowdy's cheek. The man stood up. "Don't go any nearer, ma'am," he said. "It ain't right."

Kate pushed him aside, knelt down and pulled the raincoat away from her husband's face. It was a terrible sight. The rope had stretched his neck and his face was blotched and blue.

There was iron in the women of those days. Kate didn't scream and wring her hands. She stood up and faced those men.

"Why was he hanged?" she asked.

The man who had dismounted, and who seemed to be the leader, said, "He's the worst horse- and cattle-thief in the territory, ma'am." He added, "We've been trying to catch up with him for a long time. Last night we caught him and two of his gang in the act. They admitted their guilt. We couldn't do anything else. . . ."

Another man on horseback said, "He asked us to bring him back here and to give you this." He held out a pouch. It contained about four hundred dollars.

"Who are you people who hang persons without a trial?" Kate asked. "My husband was entitled to that."

"The Anti-Horse-Thief Association, ma'am," the leader said.

"Sometimes horses mean the difference between living and starving out here for people that have only a little." He got up on his horse. "And as for the trial, ma'am, we didn't need any." He touched his hat and wheeled away, the others following him down the street.

Kate was left with the stiffening body of her husband. But, as I said, she was made of stern stuff. She walked across the street and aroused the deputy and his wife.

"My husband is dead," she said impassively. "He was hanged for stealing horses last night. Please help me bury him."

Women of the frontier were a curious lot. They were snobs—they could be the wives of sod busters, with scarcely a burlap bag to cover them—but they were as proud of their purity as God of his Commandments. They'd be struck down dead before they would be seen talking to a gay lady, or a soiled dove, as the preachers called them in those days. But let one of their own kind get hurt or be in trouble and they would flock about that wounded member like a fluttering band, chattering and cooing and raising the dust with their comments to their husbands. And did they get things done!

That's the way it was the night Bill Rowdy was brought in. The fact that Kate's husband was hanged as a horse-thief was trifling. To the ladies, one of their own had been injured. The word was spread by the deputy's wife and they came from all over town, in their night-clothes, with their hair still braided and sleep in their eyes. But they came and that night—not in Boot Hill but in the town cemetery—they buried Bill Rowdy. From the folks who followed the coffin, one would have thought that a church vestryman had cashed in his chips. Prayers were said and the ladies dabbed their eyes, while Kate stood by the grave like a stone statue. When it was over, they led her back to the house that Bill had deeded over to her to help her pick up the loose threads of her life.

Well, sooner or later Kate decided to pull up stakes in that town and come to Dodge. One of the local saloons had a dance-hall which had gone to the bad. The girls were only cheap whores that the cowpunchers paid ten dollars after a drive or when they came down from Miles City and wanted a woman or for a trip to Topeka. But even the punchers didn't come in after a while.

The dance-hall place was shut down tight as a drum when Kate showed up in Dodge. She saw its possibilities and contracted to open the place again. She had the place painted and put blinds on the windows. Then she went down to Kansas City and brought back six girls. They weren't the most beautiful in the world, but they were a devil of a lot better than any cowhand had seen for the last five years in Dodge.

The girls got a percentage of the drinks, and the rule was a man danced for about three minutes with a girl, then took her to the bar. Some of the patrons tried to get rough, but Kate put an end to rowdiness. One wild kid tried to ride his cow-pony into the dance-hall one night, but Kate pegged a shot over his head and the horse almost bucked him off. Then, to show there were no hard feelings, she bought the kid a drink and danced with him herself.

I got to know Kate quite well. As time went on, she used to sit down and talk about Kansas City and the old days. She wasn't a bad-looking woman—about thirty-five—with just the hint of time and her business beginning to make their demands on her robust health. Her hair was still flamelike and her eyes were still a deep blue. Her laugh was a clear, merry one.

She took a liking to me, I guess, because I was just a fresh young kid. Every night before closing time she would bring a bottle over to the table and yarn about the places she had been and the people she had known.

One of the things about Kate's place which always intrigued me was how the girls could drink so much and never get drunk. One day I found out why. I had come in from a long ride in the country and had just picked up a letter from home at the Dodge House. My mother wasn't well and I thought I'd better think about making a trip back to Indiana. I was as low as a skunk's belly and I thought a trip over to Kate's might cheer me up.

I took my place at the bar. Although I took a drink, I wasn't what you would call an experienced drinker. It was put on more than anything else. After two drinks I usually made an excuse to get out of the place whenever I saw someone with some loose change coming up to wet the bar.

I had just leaned on the bar when a girl came up and threw her arms around me.

"Come on, kid," she said, "let's dance."

"I'm sorry, ma'am," I said, "I don't dance."

"Well, come on, I'll teach you," she said and started to drag me to the back.

"Hold on there," Kate said, coming up. To the girl she said, "You're new here, so I'll let it go. But don't do that again."

Then to me and a few others she said, "Come on, let's have a drink."

Kate was in one of her moods and I guess mine matched hers. I told her about the bad news from home and she gave me a long lecture about respecting one's parents and the beauty of having a home. I had more drinks and began to feel them. I stumbled out of Kate's place and back to the Dodge House.

"George," the clerk said, *"you're* drunk."

I tried to tell him that it didn't take the brains of a coyote to figure that out and I went up to bed. I slept all that afternoon, even missing dinner.

The next day I came down with a banging headache. Of course I went to Kate's place. There was only one girl there and when I came up she said, "You owe me a drink."

"I don't owe anybody a drink but myself," I said. And I ordered one.

The girl said she had just come in from Kansas City the night before and that this was her first day in Dodge. So to celebrate it, I ordered her a drink. We sat in the back and she tossed off half of hers without batting an eye. I just shuddered.

She excused herself when another girl came in and I switched glasses. Half a drink was all I wanted.

When she came back she said, "Mud in your eye," or something like that, and tossed off her drink.

To my surprise she gagged, spat, grabbed her throat and tears came to her eyes. "Damn you!" she said.

I just sat there, astounded. "What the hell did I do?" I said.

"Damn near strangled me," she gasped. She pointed to her glass—or the glass I had switched. I tasted it and I'll be damned if it wasn't cold tea!

"If you tell Kate I'll come after you, kid," she warned me.

"So help me, I'll never tell," I said, but I decided I'd never buy another girl a drink. Hell, I had bought those girls enough cold tea to float all of dry Kansas.

Kate stayed on in Dodge until about 1888. Carrie Nation's hatchet helped her to make up her mind. After seeing a few of her girls married off to local merchants and cowhands she closed down her place. The rest of the girls she shipped back to Kansas City to continue their after-dark life. Kate herself went to Cali-

fornia, where she married. But she returned to Kansas about
the turn of the century.

About forty years ago I visited an old-timer and asked him
about Kate. "Saw her about five years ago," he said. "Still as
nice as ever, but there ain't much red left in her hair. Mostly
white now. She asked about you, George. Said you were the
greenest kid ever to hit the West."

Then he told me about that cold tea. That fool girl had told
Kate. But Kate knew if it ever got out the boys would guy me
forever. So she never said anything.

Come In and Be Killed

THE spring made the prairie an enchanted place, but summer transformed it into a miserable hell by a burning sun and hot winds that seemed to drain every bit of moisture from a man's skin. In the heat Dodge City was just a dirty old frontier town. I was soon tired of riding, the thrill of exploring was gone, so I hung around the Long Branch and Peacock's place, drinking more than I should have and gambling far over my head.

The only excitement occurred when Bat Masterson returned to Dodge to get "justice," as he called it, for Jim Masterson, who was in partnership with J. A. Peacock in a saloon and dance-hall.

I wasn't in town when it happened, but the talk was that Bat had come in on the afternoon train, with fire in his eye, and talking of fixing Peacock, whom he accused of cheating his brother. Bat and Peacock gunned each other in the street, but no one was hurt. The mayor asked Bat to give up his guns and settle it in court and Bat agreed. The next day they fined Bat a few dollars and he left.

When I asked the clerk at the Dodge House where Jim was,

he said both brothers had gone. I was at Peacock's that night and saw Peacock wearing his guns and holding a shotgun. He just sat on a high stool and refused to talk. All he did was watch that front door.

I met Ben Daniels later at the Long Branch. He was with two ranchers from Texas who spent most of the evening talking about horses, cattle, women and Mobeetie. One of the ranchers was an old fellow with a face that had been burned by the sun into the color of old leather. When I asked where the town was located, the old rancher used the wet table to draw me a map.

He said, "It's a tough town, kid."

"Thinking of going down there, kid?" the other man asked.

"Well, it's a place I haven't seen," I said. "Maybe."

"Hell, George," said Ben. "It's a lot of talk."

That set the old rancher to telling some tall tales of this town. I think I heard more stories of badmen that night than you can find in a score of books on the frontier. Clay Allison's name was brought up and they rehashed the old story of whether or not Clay made Bat Masterson back down one day in Dodge.

It was late when we left the saloon. The streets were quiet and the cool air, after the blazing hot day, felt good. We walked down the street in silence.

When we reached the Dodge House Ben said quietly, "Look, kid, forget what those old crows said about Mobeetie . . . I know it's in your mind to go down there."

I protested. "I *would* like to see all of this country before I leave, Ben."

"Hell, that's one part you won't miss. Forget about it. Goodnight."

I said goodnight and went up to my room. I tried to get to sleep, but the more I thought of Mobeetie the more I wanted to go there. I guess it's the same old story: give a restless kid another hill and he'll climb it just to see what's on the other side. And in those days I was the damnedest kid for climbing hills.

The next day I saw Ben and told him I was going to take a ride south.

"If you wait a couple of days I'll go along, George," he said. "Any place in mind?"

"Maybe Mobeetie," I said. "I've never seen the town and I would like to tell the folks back home about it."

"Better talk to Bob Wright, George," Ben said. "He knows that country and Colonel Goodnight down there."

From the standpoint of seniority in the territory, Bob Wright had about as much as anyone in Kansas, so I paid him a visit. Bob filled me in and by noon I felt I had as much knowledge of Mobeetie as any man in Dodge.

Mobeetie, which in Indian language means Sweetwater, had been made the county seat of Wheeler County in Texas about a year or two before I arrived in Dodge. It was settled back in the fifties and its one combination hardware-dry goods store-saloon was the first commercial store in that section of the country. At one time Dodge was the nearest settlement. Colonel Goodnight's famous JA Ranch in the Panhandle had contracted with Wright's store to freight supplies to the ranch. Later, when the Texas & Pacific Railroad went into Colorado City, the JA got its supplies that way. When I got to talking about going to Mobeetie, Bob insisted I use his name and call on Charley Goodnight there. He kept telling me I should wait until I could go with his freighters. To save time and cut out stragglers the teamsters hitched about fifteen yoke of oxen to several freight wagons and chained them all together. If the heavy wagons were bogged down in the soft creek or river bottoms, they would be unchained and then brought across, one at a time.

Plenty happened to me in Mobeetie. I'm still sorry that I

didn't take the trip on the freighters. If I went along with the wagons, there would be at least five guns to hold off any outlaw gang swooping down from Robbers' Roost on the Canadian River. Anyone who traveled in the Panhandle in those days knew of the Robbers' Roost boys. They had the usual outlaw setup; a ranch, a hideaway back in the hills and plenty of informers to keep them posted on small parties and big herds. They stole horses, rustled cattle and robbed and killed stray travelers. Most of the band were Mexicans, but I recall hearing a story years later that a white man, supposedly an Englishman of good breeding, a black sheep, had been the leader of the band and was lynched later by some men whose relatives he had killed.

"I wish you'd wait until Ben Daniels would ride along with you, or else go along with the wagons," Bob Wright said.

"I think I'll ride down there myself," I said.

Bob was a slow man to anger, but my mulelike disposition rubbed him the wrong way.

"Well, go then," he said. "Get the hell out of Dodge. But you'd better leave ten dollars with me."

I stopped at the doorway. "Ten dollars? What for?"

"To send your body back to Indiana, you damn fool!" he said.

Mobeetie was a *real* tough town, I told myself. I hadn't made a name for myself in Dodge yet—in fact, that business of losing my gun twice still irked me—and in a way I thought that somehow I would recapture my lost glory by visiting a sink of iniquity. Then I could say, "Mobeetie? Oh, *I've* been there . . . a real hell-hole with plenty of outlaws. . . ."

By noon the following day I was off to Mobeetie. It was a leisurely trip and in due time I rode into the most terrible town in Western history. It was a typical frontier town, with a dirty, muddy street, some clapboard buildings and the usual saloons. There was a rotten-looking hotel, if you could call it that, so I hitched up and went in. The clerk at the Dodge House was a nice, clean-looking businessman; this clerk—unshaven and wearing a filthy shirt—was literally a bum. He certainly had a hangover.

The room was seventy-five cents a night and a dollar and a half with the livery service. I paid that and brought my horse to the stable, where I bedded him down myself. In fact, I paid the kid who took care of the horses an extra two bits to make sure he was fed.

It was twilight when I started to walk down the street. My stay in Dodge had not removed entirely the stamp of the Indiana farmboy. One or two fellows gave me a hard look, but I ignored them. I was uncomfortable and the six-shooter at my belt didn't help. It made me feel conspicuous.

I did a quick tour of the place and decided my trip had been a waste of time. I went back to the hotel, had a dinner of some beef I would not have given my hogs back home and decided to see what the town had to offer in the evening.

As I was going out the clerk said, "Going to look over the town, sonny?"

That irked me. I nodded and started out.

"Watch your step, boy," he said. "This is a tough town."

"I can take care of myself," I said.

At night Mobeetie was something to see. It was filled with noise. From every saloon there was shouting and coarse laughter, mixed with the shrill voices of women and the tinny sounds of off-key pianos.

Midway on the main street was what appeared to be part-store and part-saloon. I hesitated, and then went in—just to look around. The moment I pushed through the doors I was greeted by a wave of shrieks and laughter. The biggest man I had ever seen was dancing around the sawdust floor with a woman. Stomping would be a better description. He was taller than I and built like a beer keg. He had a thick black beard and a red face and was wearing a dirty blue or black coat, dust-stained pants and what looked like miners' boots. I watched, fascinated. They really made the dust fly.

At last when they were finished, I went to the bar and ordered a drink. The big man, who was evidently named Harry or Dutch Harry, ordered drinks all around. The bartender gave me a drink and I took it.

There was no doubt that the big man—Harry—was the boss of the place. I kept looking into the mirror while I was talking to the bartender about a drive north he'd made in the early seventies. He seemed mighty scared. By the time I came to Dodge the peak of the big drives was past. I kept questioning him about the fellows who had been in Dodge in those days when suddenly someone slapped me hard on the back.

I just caved in and the air seemed to be pushed out of me. When I got my breath I turned around. The big fellow was staring at me. I knew I was in for a bad time.

"Dodge?" he shouted. "Who's talking about that place?"

"This fellow just came in," the bartender said.

The big man just looked me up from toe to head. "So you're from Dodge," he said.

"Just came in," I said.

"Fellow whipped me up there once," he said.

"It wasn't me," I said.

He roared with laughter.

"Maybe you did, sonny," he said.

He kept laughing and walked away. There had been a moment of silence, but when he walked away everything broke out again. He started to stomp around with the woman again and I went back to my drink.

"Look out for him, kid," the bartender said. "He's mean to-night."

"I can take care of myself," I said, but this time I wasn't so sure. I wished I were back in Dodge.

But I lingered a bit and finally downed the last of the rotgut. I was just about to leave when I caved in again from another blow.

"So you're a fellow from Dodge," Dutch shouted behind me. "Let's see how you can fight."

I turned around to be hit with a fist the size of a mountain. It spun me around and across the saloon. I hit a table and saw stars. Someone helped me up and I just stood there shaking the blood from my nose. I saw him coming and tried to duck. The next blow caught me on the shoulder. I went down again. By this time I was numb. Again someone helped me up.

I don't recall what happened next—just that some kind soul kept lifting me and I kept spinning across the room and falling. When I couldn't get up he kicked me with his heavy boot. I think at that moment I was nearly crying. I just lay there. As the fog slowly lifted I realized my face was in the sawdust. I raised myself to my knees. All I could see were the heavy boots. I think it was the bartender who kept saying to Dutch, "Leave the kid alone. He's hurt bad."

They put me in a chair, where, half-stunned, I just sat, trying to wipe the blood off my face. One eye was closed and the other wasn't much good.

I could barely see Dutch standing there with a drink in his hand. When I peered up at him I got the whiskey right in the face.

"Go back to Dodge, you —— and tell them I —— over them."

I decided to retreat and think things over. The bartender helped me up, put my hat on my head and walked me to the door. I can remember as vividly as though it were today that I looked back and with my one good eye, I could see a lot of men grinning at me, while big Dutch waved a drink and shouted at me.

"Get out, kid, before he kills you," the bartender said, and pushed me through the doors.

I staggered a few feet and leaned against the building, then slowly slid down and just sat. I lay there a long time. People passing stumbled over my feet, and one or two turned to give me a good kick and a curse. I guess they were so used to drunks they figured I was one.

Finally I managed to get to my feet and find my way back to the hotel. The grimy-looking clerk was reading a newspaper and he looked up when I came in.

"Looks like you saw the town, sonny," he said. Then he got a bowl of water and helped me clean up. I told him what happened and he just made a noise like a scratching chicken.

"Dutch hates Dodge," he said. "Someone up there took his gun away once and kicked him in jail. He never forgot it. You're lucky he didn't kill you, you bein' from Dodge," he said.

"Where's the sheriff of this town?" I said. "Doesn't he do anything around here?"

He made a noise with his lips and got some more rags. "Go home, sonny," he said.

He helped me to the livery stable. The kid there just looked at me and saddled my horse real fast. I guess he had seen the same thing before.

I rode out of town very slowly. Every step that horse took

was like a kick in the stomach. But it wasn't the physical hurt that was troubling me, it was the mental. I had been kicked and stomped on by a bushy-bearded bastard for no good reason. It was the first time in my life that a man had struck me—besides my father—and I had not struck back.

That thought gnawed and gnawed at my insides. The more it gnawed the more strength came back. About a mile or two outside of town I was so mad that I swung out of my saddle and stood there in the night, cursing and fuming and swearing all sorts of revenge against that big man. I led my horse until I came to a creek and camped there to size up the situation.

There on that lonely plain I took my measure. I had been beaten and kicked and the sensible thing to do was to go back home and forget it, maybe take a few of the boys from Dodge and see if I could square accounts. Or I could do the foolish thing and go back and get myself killed.

My father was a peaceful man in his lifetime and certainly never looked for trouble, but he was dead set on the rights of a man. "This is a free country, boys," he would always say when he got talking politics, "and nobody can tell you what to do, even if he has a gun at your head."

Dan would usually say in a sly way, "Father, did you always turn your other cheek?"

Father would pitch another forkload of hay before replying. Then he would say, "Well, boys, the way I see it is, if he didn't knock me out with the blow to the right cheek, I would always give him a chance to try the left one. . . ."

I decided that would be the best course; give Dutch a chance at the left cheek. Actually, he had tried both cheeks and even my ribs.

I checked my six-shooter and rode back into town. I gave my

horse to the livery boy and told him I was staying a while. He just looked at me as if I were crazy and nodded.

The saloon was still noisy when I entered. It quieted down when I pushed through the doors. I was plenty scared, and if Dutch, who was standing at the bar, had drawn his gun at that moment, I would have been killed. I don't think I had enough strength to draw. I was shaking.

But the minute I took a step inside the saloon, I knew I was on the winning side. He looked surprised, and a surprised man is a man off guard. I didn't say anything for a moment, just looked at him. Then I walked to the bar, keeping my hand near my gun. By the time I was up to him I knew that if my bluff worked I would never again be kicked by any man.

One thing which gave me some confidence was the way Dutch carried his gun. It was hanging any which way. He carried his gun like a farmer or a homesteader, like a man who carries his weapon as part of his dress, like a hat. Killers carried their guns the way they rode a horse: it was part of them.

I was only a foot from Dutch when I made up my mind. I didn't say anything because I think I might have stuttered. My fist had been knotted like a piece of cordwood for hours, so I hit him.

He just blinked his eyes. Now, I was a six-footer, at my prime, and behind my fist were years of farm work, of splitting thousands of rails, of tramping countless miles, but Dutch just shook his head slowly. It was as though I had hit a stone wall.

"What in the hell did you do that for, boy?" he asked.

"Because you kicked me," I said. I backed up a few feet. "Now if you feel lucky—draw!"

For a long moment he didn't say anything. Then, to my great relief, he roared with laughter. He turned to the bar and banged down hard with a massive fist. I thought he was having convulsions. He pounded and pounded that bar, laughing as if I had told him the greatest joke in the world. The other fools joined in. Soon the saloon was echoing with laughter.

Finally he stopped, wiped his eyes and swung me to the bar. I groaned when my ribs hit the edge.

"Have a drink, kid," he said. "Have a drink." Then he started to laugh again. "The kid came in to kill me—"

I didn't get the joke, but I took the drink. I was tempted to press my luck and throw it into his face, but I decided not to.

We stayed at the bar for some time. Dutch stomped around with his women and he seemed to have forgotten me. The men along the bar ignored me. My wonderful feeling of self-respect regained dwindled. At last Dutch fell into a chair and slipped into a sound, snoring sleep. Everybody watched him. Finally, when they decided he was asleep and harmless, they turned to the bar, and the saloon quieted down.

"I guess I'll go," I said.

"Give the boys my regards," the bartender said.

"Sure," I said. I didn't even know his name.

I walked across the saloon. In those few seconds it took me to reach the door I had come to realize what a damn fool I had been. I felt as though I had been a man in a duel—the dead man, that is.

I rode back to Dodge City that night, wiser and older than my years.

A Black Elk's Tooth

I COULD stay put only for a short time. Dodge, for all its excitement and violence, still had its dull moments and dullness was a thing that my restless young heart could never stand.

After one period of inactivity—I think it was in 1882—I decided to travel West. I was packing my gear in the Dodge House when Billy Ainsworth walked in.

"George," he said, "I heard you were moving West on a trip."

"Yes, Billy," I said. "I'm going to do some big game hunting and look out for a nice small ranch."

"Where do you figure on looking?" he asked.

That was the damnedest thing about men with restless feet. They always want to see what's on the other side of the mountain but they never know exactly where they want to go. They have no particular place in mind—just any place over the horizon.

"Well," I said, "I've never been to Wyoming."

"Good cattle country, George," Billy said. "I hear the cattle people are having trouble with nesters."

A Black Elk's Tooth

"We may find some excitement," I said.

"I'm with you," he said. "We'll go out in the cars and hire some horses in Casper."

We both packed and after a boisterous farewell party, we left for Wyoming. From Cheyenne we went to Casper, where we inquired of the livery stable owner where we could do some big game hunting.

"Well, about thirty miles north of here," he said. "You'll find some good hunting on Alder Creek. There are some Shoshones camping there but don't pay them any heed. They're peaceable. Just mind your own business and they won't bother you."

We hired some horses, got grub and ammunition for our Winchesters and started north. We selected a fine campsite near the river, where for two days we had the time of our lives. We didn't get anything big, only small game, but it was spring and we were full of youth and zest for living. What more could any two young hellions ask?

As I recall, it was the morning of the third or fourth day when I told Billy of a small path leading toward the river. The evening before I had followed it to the peak of a grassy knoll and wondered where it led. After breakfast I proposed to Billy that we follow the path, and he agreed. We had followed it for about a mile when we heard the sound of rapids in the distance. Billy wanted to return to our camp, but something led me to urge him on. He agreed but he said he'd beat the tar out of me if any thieving squaws made off with our provisions.

A small grove of trees hid the river from us, but as we drew near I thought I heard a faint cry. When we stopped we could hear it over the sound of rushing water. I dropped my rifle and pushed through the trees. About ten feet from the bank, a small Indian boy, about six years old, was bouncing along the rocks and the water. The river at this point was only about three or four feet deep, but its force was terrific. Ordinarily it was a slow-moving stream, but the melting snows had made it a raging freshet, a racing mill-stream.

I plunged in and made my way to the boy, who was screaming and clinging to a rock. I had a devil of a time keeping my balance and fell once or twice, bruising and scratching my legs and knees. That was nothing compared to what I suffered when I grabbed hold of the child. He gave me one look, then became a wildcat. He kicked, screamed, clawed and scratched. I had a hell of a time bringing him into shore. When I did, I dropped him down on the bank.

"Any more kids fall in that river, *you'll* have to rescue them," I told Billy.

Billy looked behind me. "We have company, George."

I turned. There were four or five Indian squaws coming through the willows, gabbling like a flock of pigeons. They pushed me aside, picked up the boy, who was now just sniffling, and kissed and hugged him.

"They might at least have said thanks," I said to Billy, but he wasn't listening. I followed his glance. About ten young bucks and old men had come through the bushes. One or two were armed with what looked to be old army muskets. The others were unarmed.

They came toward us slowly. One old man, who seemed to be the chief, wore a battered old black soft hat, greasy, fringed buckskins and moccasins. The young bucks were bare-chested. They were fine-looking young men, but not the type of men I wanted to meet in a hand-to-hand battle.

When they arrived the women gabbled in their own tongue, pointing to me.

"Your six-shooter is wet, George," Billy said casually. "I'll get your rifle."

He pushed through the circle of Indians to pick up my rifle. He threw it to me and I caught it. I was relieved when the Indians didn't seem to mind. At least they weren't *looking* for trouble.

Finally the old man pointed to us, then to the trail.

"Guess he wants us to go with him," Billy said.

"Why not?" I said. "They certainly don't want to hurt us."

"Anyway, there are too many for us to handle if they did," the practical Billy pointed out.

We started up the river, the women first, Billy and me, then the men. I emptied my boots and dried my six-shooter while we walked. About a mile up the river we turned left, following a path for about another half-mile. Then we came to a small Indian encampment, cunningly concealed in a small grove.

The men ushered us to a log cabin. It was dim and cool, with two stools and a rickety split-log table. They kept the door open and the whole Indian population of the village kept passing and looking in and pointing at me. About noon an old woman with two gourds, one filled with cornpone and cold meat and the other with whiskey, came in. She placed them on the table and motioned for us to eat.

The meat was good but the whiskey was trader's swill, so raw it brought tears to my eyes. Still, it was whiskey and we split the gourd between us.

Billy was a great one for drawing the long bow and pulling my leg in those days and he said, "You know why they're feeding us, George?"

"Guess they're just naturally hospitable," I said.

He shook his head. "Nope. They're Shoshones and Shoshones eat humans. Yes, sir, they're just fattening us up."

Billy had been out in this country more years than I had so I half-believed him. I broke open my six-shooter, examined my shells and told Billy that before anyone put a fork in my hide they would have to outshoot and outrun me. Billy kept laughing and slapping his leg.

About three o'clock the old man who Billy said must be the chief came in, grunted and sat at the table. He pulled a poke out of the folds of his coat, spreading the contents on the table. Elk's teeth, about a quart of them. He motioned to us to take them, but we pushed them back. He shook his head and pushed them toward us. We in turn pushed them back across the table. Finally Billy said, "For God's sake, George, let's take one of his damned teeth or we'll be here all month."

I selected a black elk's tooth and made a great show of holding it up and exclaiming about its beauty. Billy did the same and the old man seemed satisfied.

"George," Billy said to me, "you've just selected the black one. That means you're first for the pot."

The old man was saying something in his own tongue when we heard cries outside the log cabin. "Johnny Heap Talk . . . Johnny Heap Talk. . . ."

A few minutes later a young man about twenty-five came into the cabin. He was slim as an arrow shaft, with the black eyes and copper coloring of the full blood.

"I'm Johnny Heap Talk," he said. "This is my grandfather. The people came for me to tell you how thankful they are that you saved my brother's son."

"How come you talk English so good?" Billy asked.

"About five years ago," he said, "a Chicago meat-packer came up here to hunt grizzly. He hired me and my brother as guides and the following year he sent me a shotgun. The next year we went out alone and he caught a grizzly but only wounded him. The grizzly swiped him about twenty feet and was ready to mount him when I killed him. He was so grateful he sent me to Carlisle."

"What are these teeth for?" Billy asked.

"They are my grandfather's prize possessions and we consider them valuable," Johnny said. "He was only trying to show his gratitude."

"Well, we'd better be getting along," I said. "We left our outfit down the river."

"Stay with me tonight," Johnny said. "If you're up here for hunting I'll guide you."

This sounded interesting. Johnny sent a buck back for our horses and outfits. His house was a fine log lodge—as good as any white man's. His wife was a slim young Shoshone girl who had some white blood in her. There were more books in this house than in most white men's houses and Johnny, who was the local schoolteacher for his tribe, appointed by the Indian agent, was a fine host.

We had venison, cornpone, wonderful coffee and later real whiskey. Johnny brought in the old chief and we sat before the fire listening to yarns about the early days of the West when the Shoshones were powerful and the white men few.

It was a sight I'll never forget: the old man, whose face was like the one on our nickel, sitting by the fire, shadows dancing on his dark, wooden face, framed by long black hair, as he spoke in the soft slurring tongue of the Shoshone. Occasionally he made a point by a swift, graceful sign with his hand and Johnny, sitting across from his grandfather, held up his hand to stop the flow of the words so he could interpret for us. And behind us, holding her chubby little son, whose eyes gleamed like dark stars in his round little face, was Johnny's wife, sitting cross-legged like a slim Buddha.

In the middle of one tale the door swung open and a young

buck came in. He spoke swiftly to Johnny, who then turned to us.

"Your horses are gone," he said. "The boy said he followed the tracks until it got too dark. Three men with horses took them and your food."

"Dammit," Billy said. "We never should have left them. Come on, George, we'd better go after them. We'll have to pay that livery stable man two hundred dollars—or answer to the sheriff."

"It's too dark now to track them," Johnny said. "In the morning I will take some of the men and we'll go after them."

It seemed like good sense, so after some palavering with Billy I finally got him to agree to stay the night.

There was only a small bedroom for Johnny, his wife and little son, so we slept on the floor, wrapped in sheepskins, while the old man curled up in his blanket before the fire.

I fell asleep, wondering what the folks back home in Adams County would think if they could see me now: sleeping between Billy Ainsworth, as dangerous a young man as Dodge City ever produced, and an old Indian chief who had burned wagon-trains and fought many battles on horseback against the United States cavalry.

I was beginning to find something, after all, over the hill.

We were up before dawn. Mary prepared our breakfast. When we went outside we found six young Indians wrapped in blankets and sitting on horses. Their faces appeared to have been carved from the same block of copper.

As the sun rose I could see them strung out on the trail behind me. I had the eerie feeling that I was stepping back in time and was a hunter, a mountain man, riding across land no white men had ever seen.

We traveled across some rough territory, with Johnny Heap Talk in the front doing the tracking. The horse-thieves knew the terrain and there were times when even Johnny lost their tracks on the rocks. But by late afternoon, judging by the warmth of the horse droppings, we weren't far behind them.

At twilight we called a halt. One of the bucks shot a deer with a bow and arrow—using a bow so a shot wouldn't alarm our quarry—and we boiled the meat over a small fire which Johnny started in a hole he had dug.

Meanwhile Johnny sent out one of his scouts, who came back in about an hour, to report that the gang had holed up in a small valley where they had a corral and a shack. He said there were four of them and that they were heavily armed. In the coral were about forty or fifty horses.

Johnny sent back one of his young Indians to Casper with a description of the thieves in case we didn't get them—or they got us. If we did get them, he said in the message, we would come in with them.

At dawn, just as the sun pinked the sky, Johnny spread his men on the rim of the valley and told me and Billy to take our spots. I took mine behind a tree halfway down the slope of the hill. Billy went even closer, using a large rock as a fort.

Before the fight started, Johnny told his men to weave large fireballs of grass and weeds, which they rolled down on the roof of the rickety house. The timbers began to smoke, then burst into a blaze. From behind our places of concealment we watched the flames, fanned by the fresh morning breeze. Suddenly there was a muffled yell inside the shack and a man came running out. A Winchester cracked and he spun around.

I stood up and fired my rifle. Glass tinkled and then I heard Johnny yell, "Get behind that rock . . . get back. . . ."

Just as I dived for the cover of the rock a rifle barked and the bark flew from the tree at the exact spot where I was standing. It seemed one of the men had come from the back of the house and was trying to outflank me.

He was behind a rock slightly below me. I kept splintering that rock with rifle fire, keeping him pinned down until Billy got in a better position.

He made a run for it, but Billy caught him in the head. I crawled over to where he lay. The back of his head was a gaping hole. He wore a typical cowpuncher's outfit and was unshaven. Despite his beard, I would have judged him to be no more than twenty.

We kept up a steady fire and at last the two men remaining in the house came out with their hands up. At the last minute one tried to make a break, but Johnny and Billy kept firing at his feet. After the dirt danced in front of him he decided it wasn't worth it and came back.

We drove the herd of horses and the two prisoners back to Casper, where the sheriff was ready to take off after us. Most of the horses were stolen ones. We returned our two to the livery stable owner, who thanked us warmly and, to show his gratitude, gave us each twenty dollars.

I was ready to say goodbye to Wyoming and head back for Kansas, but the sheriff said we had to stay as witnesses. There wasn't much we could do about it, so we decided to make good use of our time. Johnny lent us two horses and we rode back north with him.

But after two weeks both Billy and I were ready to claw each other to pieces from cabin fever, so we both agreed we had enough of Indians, boasting, venison and Wyoming. We saddled up, told Johnny we'd leave the ponies at the stable in Casper and headed back to town.

When we told the sheriff we were leaving he just gave us a quizzical look.

"You have to stay until the case comes to court," he said.

"Dammit, we've been here more than ten days and you haven't called us," I said. "Take our sworn testimony and let us get out of here."

"Now hold on, young fellow," the sheriff said. "How do I know you and your friend here didn't have something to do with those horse-thieves?"

"Why, that's the damnedest thing I ever heard of," Billy roared. "We brought them in, didn't we?"

"I know, but this changes things some," the sheriff said and pulled out a telegram. He read it aloud slowly: "George Bolds and Billy Ainsworth are two bad characters. Know both in Dodge as killers. Watch them carefully."

"Killers!" Billy yelled. "That's a damn lie. George here comes from Indiana and I spent a long time in Dodge as a deputy."

The sheriff shrugged. "All I know is what the telegram says."

"Who sent that?" I demanded.

He read the name. "Bat Masterson of Tombstone."

This sheriff kept saying that we had to stay in Casper or get tossed in jail. Well, it went on like that for about an hour, with Billy and me arguing so loud you could have heard us in California.

Sheriff Bat Masterson was probably on his way out to Wyoming, he said, to pick us up and bring us back to Kansas justice.

"Masterson is not marshal of Dodge," I protested. "He never was. He was sheriff of Ford County."

Billy and I were both getting worried when all of a sudden the sheriff leaned back and howled. He laughed until tears ran down his cheeks and he was gasping for breath.

We just watched him. Then we began to grin, finally joining in the laughter, although we didn't know what the hell we were laughing at.

When the sheriff recovered, he told us it had been worth all the trouble just to see how we looked when he read that telegram from Bat.

"Now that I've had my joke," he said, "I'm going hunting with you and I'll show you some real hunting."

He did take us hunting for ten days. It was the finest ten days of hunting I ever spent and the first time I ever killed a grizzly bear.

My old friend Senator Joe Randall told me about what finally happened to Johnny Heap Talk and his people.

Johnny's grandfather wasn't satisfied with what the government was giving him in the way of livestock and clothing, so he kept sending demands to Washington, denouncing the Indian agent as a thief of the worst sort. Finally he badgered the Indian Bureau so much that they notified him a commission would be sent out to investigate his needs.

When Johnny's grandfather heard this he cut the strong steers from his herd and sent them off into a valley in the far end of the reservation. The only animals he kept on the reservation were old goats, chickens, a few weak steers. The women were told to make their garments look threadbare.

Johnny argued with his grandfather, telling him it wasn't right that he should cheat the white people, but the old man would just wave his hand over the vast stretches of land which once belonged to his people and simply say, "Who has been cheated, my son?"

Joe Randall—as I recall, he was the senior senator from

Louisiana—headed the commission which had been sent out to look into the complaints of the Shoshones.

"Those poor people," he told me later, "looked like a dying tribe. The children didn't appear to have even a crust of bread. I was all for giving them more stock and improvements, but the Congressman with me was a young freshman, ambitious as hell and ready to save the government a pretty penny.

" 'The hell with them,' he told me. 'Let them exist on what the government gives them. They're a lot of trouble-makers anyway.' "

"He said this to me in a rather low tone when we were returning, but I think a young Indian heard him. I warned the Congressman, but he just laughed and said they probably couldn't understand English anyway.

"That Indian was Johnny Heap Talk. He went to his grandfather and told him he was right; if they could get something out of the white men they should.

"His grandfather was pleased and listened to what Johnny had up his sleeve. The plan was so good he called in the elders of the tribe and they listened. There's a lot of nonsense about Indians not laughing. Just don't believe that. That's true when they are with white people, but among themselves they are a happy, merry race. And that night they just howled when they heard what Johnny had planned."

The next day Joe Randall and the young Congressman were invited to a private barbecue to be held in a shed. The young Congressman had a hearty appetite and just couldn't seem to get enough to eat. The Indians just watched him. When he stopped long enough to ask what it was he was eating, the chief just grunted and said, "Goat," and the Congressman said, "It's the best I've ever eaten."

Now Joe said that, as a Southerner, he knew this was no goat he was eating, but he kept his mouth shut and just nibbled at it.

Finally the meal was over. The Congressman got up and made a silly speech, saying the government was poor and couldn't afford anything and the red men had better be good and try and live on what they had.

The chief then stood up and faced the Congressman, who was still gnawing on a sliver of meat. He was a handsome old man with a lone feather stuck in his hair and a brilliant blanket wrapped about his tall form.

He answered slowly and Johnny interpreted. He reeled off the usual long-winded Indian speech, about how the white man had cast his shadow across the land and had gobbled up the land and the mighty buffalo was gone, so now the Indians were like poor relations and must depend on the Great White Father. He said he was sorry the commission could not give him what his people needed, so perhaps he would go instead to see the Great White Father.

The Congressman, expansive with all the food he had eaten, nudged Joe Randall, and said maybe it would be a good thing for him to bring back the old chief and get some attention in Congress by showing them how much money he was saving the government.

Joe didn't say anything. He felt he was skirting thin ice. He waved the old chief to continue.

The chief then said he was very happy to see the white brothers enjoying the Indian meal, and when he got to Washington he would be sure to tell the White Father in Washington how the young Congressman had enjoyed the meal.

"Only it wasn't goat," Johnny said quietly in English.

The Congressman looked up. "Oh, no, Johnny? What was it, then?"

"Dog," Johnny said briefly.

The Congressman actually looked green.

"And boiled rattlesnake," Johnny added.

The Congressman got up, muttered his apologies and left the banquet.

The chief, of course, got all he wanted. Joe Randall explained it slowly to his young colleague—they would be the laughing-stock of Congress if the story of their eating dog and rattlesnake ever came out.

Years later I met the young man in Washington with Joe Randall. I whispered "Dog," and told him I knew Johnny Heap Talk.

"Mr. Bolds," he said, "if you ever tell that story—"

"Mayor" Bolds, Landowner

BY 1883 it was obvious that Dodge City had passed her most glorious days. The town that had won the name of "Hell City" because of the evil it had spawned was slowly dying on its feet. The drives north were becoming a thing of the past. Those which still took place bypassed Dodge for livelier towns like Miles City, where the liquor flowed freely and the girls were fresher. The men who had brought law and order to Dodge were gone. The Earps were in Tombstone, as were Bat and Jim Masterson. Killers no longer swaggered down Front Street. Dodge was now only a dirty frontier town.

I had stayed in Dodge intermittently from 1879 to the spring of '83, when I decided to pack up and seek new hills to climb. I had traveled a lot about the West and had the dust of a thousand trails on my heels. In 1881 I had worked on a couple of cow outfits in southwestern Kansas, but punching cows was not my line. When I made a quick fifty dollars surveying some town nearby I knew I was a fool if I didn't continue surveying as a way of making my living.

I was no longer as green as a gourd. I was a tall, tough kid, who could sling a gun with the best of them. I now had a mustache and had gained at least ten pounds. From exposure to all kinds of weather I was as dark as a Mex. I had been in a couple of barroom brawls and once I had knocked a man out cold with a single blow. When he threatened to kill me, I waited for him and knocked him out a second time.

I had been home to Indiana on several occasions, each time horrifying my mother. I suppose I looked like a cold-blooded killer. Although I swaggered about on my visits home for Dan's benefit, after the first time I never again walked into our house wearing a gun. I could stand up to the toughest of them, but Father was the law on high.

Portland, of course, was always a stop on my visits. I was head over heels in love with Adda Weldon, but she would have none of me—yet.

"When you come back home, George," she said, "we'll talk about it."

I blew up. "Dammit," I cried, "why can't we talk about it now?"

She stamped her foot and slapped me. "Don't you dare curse in my presence, George Bolds. You're not in some Dodge City saloon."

She was pretty as a picture when she was angry. I leaned over to kiss her and saw stars again. She weighed only about ninety pounds, but she made my cheek numb.

"Kissing a woman is a privilege due gentlemen," she stormed, "and not ruffians."

"Yes, ma'am," I apologized and then kissed her again.

But back I was drawn to the West. In the spring of '83 I finally said goodbye to Dodge City. For three years I had occupied Number Three in the Dodge House and, as the clerk said, it wouldn't be the same without me.

"God, it's a long time ago, George," he said. "Remember Mee-rage?"

"Well," I said, "I'd just as soon forget that one."

Bob Wright and Chalk Beeson had me belly up to the bar for a last one and Bob asked me where I was headed.

"Cimarron," I said.

Chalk gave me a surprised look. "That's a tough place, they say."

"That's a lot of talk," Bob said. "I know Jake Shoup up there and he's a fine man. George, tell Jake hello for me and use my name."

"I know Jake Shoup," I said. "In fact he's going to sell me some land." They both looked puzzled and I explained. I had ridden into Cimarron in '81 when I was exploring the country and had met Jake on the trail. He brought me to Cimarron, and I had visited it on and off for two years. Cimarron was in Gray County, about twenty-five miles from Dodge. As Chalk said, it was a rough town, but not violent, like Dodge in '78 or Tombstone. It had been a cowtown in the old days and the principal stopover for outfits crossing the Arkansas River.

I rode out of Dodge that afternoon, glad to go. I felt I was too young to rot. Lately I had felt restless and worried, worried at not-yet-twenty-one because I had no security. For all the hardware I sported, I was still a farmer's son, with the love of the land in my blood and a farmer's desire to own some. I wanted a home, a small ranch, even a farm, as long as it was land.

And, outside of a few hundred dollars, I was broke. On my last trip home I had bought an expensive surveyor's outfit. Now I was ready to take my rods anywhere. Gray County was the logical place, because the settlers were starting to come in there.

Jake Shoup had urged me countless times to open an office in Cimarron. "George," he'd say, "you'll make five times what a cowhand will in a month, and I'll give you a good buy on some land."

"I'll ride up in April, Jake," I had told him. "Find me an office and get ready to sell me that land."

So I set up shop as a surveyor. My first stop was the Land Office in Garden City, to convince them I was the best surveyor in the whole West. They hired me as county surveyor and as a troubleshooter for the land office. My job was to investigate claims by homesteaders and send my findings to the land office. The job bore out Jake's prediction: I got twenty-five dollars a survey and there was more work than I could handle.

I had rooms in Cimarron and became quite friendly with the boys in town—Bob McCanse, Will English, Lawyer Bryant, A. T. Riley, Charlie Dixon, Frank Luther and all the rest. In time our friendship would turn to white-hot hatred, fanned by gunfire. But in those early days we were close friends. I had a certain prestige; I was from Dodge and a few stories had preceded my arrival.

Charlie Dixon was the only one who didn't take me very seriously. From time to time he would try to rub my fur the wrong way, until finally one day I told him, "Charlie, someday you and I are a-going to tangle."

He just smiled. "It will be mighty interesting, George. Just let me know. . . ."

That day was just over the horizon.

That winter I purchased three hundred and fifty acres from Jake Shoup. Part of my land is now the Santa Fe highway. In those days, when the railroad went through the company was given ten miles on each side of the track. Promoters like Jake

Shoup worked for the railroad on a percentage agreement. I paid one-eleventh of the price down and agreed, as was customary, to pay an equal amount every year until it was paid. On the day of the final payment you were given the final deed. After I had signed the contract I had some money left, so Jake, as a good promoter, figured he might as well get that, too, before I lost it bucking the tiger or buying drinks for the girls back in Dodge.

"I have three hundred and twenty fine acres, George, three miles north of the section you bought. It's got a town on it if you're interested."

"A town?" I asked.

"Yes, a town," he said. "I'll take you up to see it tomorrow."

I was wondering how in the hell a town got out there, because outside of Cimarron there wasn't any settlement of any account and what few there were, I thought I knew about.

"Well, shall we ride out in the morning, George?"

"What's the price?" I asked.

"Why, the same price as you paid for the other section," Jake said, looking as innocent as a lamb.

Well, he had me, and I said I'd meet him in the morning and ride out.

Next morning we set out, riding quite a piece before Jake pulled up. He waved his hand. "George, this is the south section of the three hundred and twenty acres I'm going to sell you."

It was absolutely bare and desolate. Flat and hard as a Dodge House pancake.

"Where in the hell is that town, Jake?" I asked.

Jake just tipped his hat forward to hide his eyes. "Just a short piece, George, and you'll see your town," he said nonchalantly.

"How many citizens has it got?" I asked, as we continued riding.

Jake said musingly, "Oh, I reckon it must have two or three hundred inhabitants."

I almost pulled the horse to a dead stop. "Two or three *hundred* inhabitants?" I said. If he was joshing me, I was going to dunk him in the horse trough back in Cimarron, I said, but Jake insisted he wasn't.

We kept riding. At last we came to a section of the prairie, about three city blocks in length, studded here and there with little mounds from which small brown creatures darted in and out.

I just sat on my horse and stared. "Welcome, Mayor," said Jake, roaring with laughter. I knew I had been taken. I was Mayor Bolds of a prairie dog town.

The story was too good to keep, and when we got back in Cimarron Jake had a big audience down at the saloon. It wasn't until months afterward that they finally got tired of addressing me as "Mayor Bolds" with a wink.

Although Jake had his laugh on me, I had the last laugh. The next day I contracted for the land. I now had six hundred and forty acres, and the whole thing only cost me about nine hundred dollars. Of course I had given him only a small down payment and I did not have the deed, which was owned by the railroad, but I had an idea how to get the entire amount and still have the last laugh on Jake.

I knew my brother was interested in coming out and settling in Kansas, so I telegraphed him that day, telling him I had a chance to buy a large tract of three hundred and twenty acres *with a town on it* for only fifteen hundred dollars. I asked him if he wanted me to get it for him and he replied immediately that he did. He sent the fifteen hundred dollars and I transferred the contract for the prairie dog section to my brother, meanwhile paying Jake for the section which is now the town of Ingalls. All in all, I had made a neat profit and now owned a piece of land which was increasing almost daily in value.

After the deal had been made I sat down and wrote my brother a letter, enclosing the deed and explaining that I had cleared almost six hundred dollars on the deal. Five hundred dollars was clear profit and the other hundred was in payment for that moon-blind nag he had sold me a few years before when I was a horse-trader back in Indiana.

Since I was now established in Cimarron I thought Dodge City was a thing of the past. But she was unpredictable.

DODGE CITY'S GALA DAY

DODGE CITY, KAN., July 5, 1884.—Probably the most unique celebration in America took place here yesterday and today. The chief feature of the first day was the Spanish bullfight, the first ever held on American soil. Hundreds of visitors came from the East to witness the fight, and the town was crowded with sightseers from all over the West. The scene at the fairgrounds was a strange one for the United States. Men and women were crowded about the stands and amphitheatre drinking and smoking together and enjoying the sports. The events were most sensational and will long be remembered in this country. Dodge City has excelled all her past notorieties.

—New York *Herald,* July 6, 1884

The Fourth of July Bullfight

THE WEST was a violent land and an unpredictable place, peopled by an unpredictable people. It was beautiful—with savage sunsets that dyed the air saffron and gold and gave you a feeling of awe at God's handiwork. And life in the cowtowns could be as colorful as the fireworks in the sky.

I remember the time they celebrated Independence Day with a gala bullfight in Dodge City. I heard about the plans for a mammoth bullfight when one of Doc Barton's Mex hands rode through Cimarron. Doc Barton, a big cattle-owner of Gray County, whose land was at the old Cimarron crossing of the Arkansas River, was an old friend. I waved as the Mex pulled up. With my miserable Spanish I had a devil of a time understanding his mixture of Spanish and English. But at last I was able to make out that Doc was to bring in the toughest bulls in southwest Kansas. Several real matadors were coming up from New Mexico and it would be a bang-up fiesta.

I was so curious I couldn't sit still. I saddled up that afternoon and rode over to Barton's place. Doc was away, but his partners told me that A. B. Webster, the mayor of Dodge, had decided to stage a real bullfight on July fourth and fifth. Doc was now out rounding up a dozen bulls. The only requisite, the boys told me, was that the bulls had to be the meanest and orneriest in all of Kansas.

I went back to Cimarron, swearing to myself that nothing but a tornado would keep me from riding to Dodge to celebrate Independence Day.

On July 2, 1884, I rode into Dodge with Jake Shoup and some of the boys from Cimarron. As soon as we entered the town, we knew something was different. The streets were still dusty with deep ruts, the clapboard houses still unpainted and grimy. Bob Wright still stood outside his place, but the Congress Hall, the Long Branch, Peacock's Place, the Lone Star and the rest of the saloons were doing a booming business.

It was as if someone had pushed the clock back to the seventies and Dodge was again the rough, brawling town of crazy buffalo hunters and gun-slinging cowhands in from drives headed North. The clerk in the Dodge House laughed when we asked for rooms.

"I can let you have space in the livery stable," he said, "but only because George, here, is an old customer."

I thought Jake would bust a blood vessel, but I knew that the clerk was telling the truth and I persuaded the boys to take the livery space while the taking was good. We brought the horses to the stable, had them cared for, then selected places in the loft where we would bed down.

I saw Ham Bell later and he told me the bullfight would take place at the fairgrounds between Dodge and the Arkansas River. "Sure raisin' hell around the country," Ham told me. "Look here."

He showed me copies of the Ford County *Times,* which reported that protests against the bullfight had been sent to Governor Glick.

The Fourth of July Bullfight

"Somebody in Kansas City sent Mayor Webster a wire telling us the fight was against the laws of the United States, but Webster said, 'Well, that's all right, Dodge City ain't *in* the United States,'" Ham said, laughing.

Some Scottish lawyer in Paso del Norte was arranging the whole thing and it was up to him to hire the best matadors in New Mexico. "We told him we wanted the greasers in the fanciest costumes they could find," Ham said.

There were seats for thousands and an arena made of planks in which there were openings, covered with heavy mesh wire, through which the bullfighter could escape if the bull became too ornery.

We went to inspect the bulls Doc Barton had delivered. There were, as I recall, about a dozen, with the damnedest names. One, I remember, had been named after Eat-'Em-Up Jake, a desperate character who had seen service in Dodge, and whom I met in Arkansas City years later, just before the Run for the Unassigned Lands in Oklahoma. The meanest of the lot was a huge, vicious brute, weighing a couple of tons. I asked Ham what his name was.

"Doc Barton," he said.

Dodge that night was the wildest, roughest place in the West and that included Tombstone. Bat Masterson and Jim came into the Long Branch and we had a whooping time. It seemed as if every cowhand in the West had come to Dodge: they were from as far south as the border and as far west as Wyoming. Nearly all of them had money and guns and a lot were eager for a fight. We stayed clear of the tough ones. That first night there must have been ten bloody fights in the Long Branch alone.

Whiskey and beer flowed like water. The Long Branch had about five bartenders, as I can recall, and they were filling up glasses left and right every minute. There were gamblers, whores of every description, Easterners and newspaper correspondents. I remember having a drink with one from the New York *Herald*. Some of the dudes were worked over by the tough customers and some very rough jokes were pulled. Cowboys kept coming and going; you could hear them ride in, whistling and whooping like Indians on the warpath.

It went on like this for the next three days. The town was so packed with visitors and cowpunchers that a man couldn't buy a place at the hitching rail for a gold piece. We had to stand in line to get a chair at the table for meals and fight our way to the bar in the saloons.

The day before the bullfight, the Scottish lawyer from the border arrived, with his entourage of bullfighters. The chief matador was a slender, dark man, with a pencil-thin mustache. His name was Gregorio Gallardo, and he claimed that his grandfather had been one of the great matadors in Spain. He was from Chihuahua and so were his six or seven assistants, all professional matadors, like Avaristo Rivas, Rodrigo, Marco Maya and Juan Herreira.

I'll never forget the day they paraded down the street. It was a blistering hot day and Chalk Beeson's cowboy band blared and thumped like mad. The whole town lined the sidewalks. After Chalk's band came the Mexicans, riding gracefully on their horses. Gallardo was in the lead. He was dressed in fancy velvet, embroidered with gold. He wore white slippers and he carried more swords than the armorer for a cavalry troop.

The cowhands whooped and cheered and the whores called out invitations. The dark-faced men nodded and waved. There was no doubt about it now—Dodge was going to have a real live bullfight with all the trimmings.

In the early morning of the Fourth, the town started to drift toward the fairgrounds. By noon there must have been four thousand men, women and children packed in those wooden stands. I had a seat with Bat and Jim Masterson and Jake Shoup right near a spot where one of the chutes opened.

Across the arena we could see a sea of plumed hats. Mayor Webster made sure the gay ladies had their own section so they wouldn't contaminate the church-going ladies who were honoring the event with their presence. It seemed as if every cowhand had one of the girls and a bottle in tow. Kansas was far from dry that day.

About one o'clock Doc Barton's hands rounded up the bulls in the corral and brought them to the chute at the fairgrounds. I understand they cut off and filed down the sharp tips of the animal's horns.

Then the Mex matadors rode in, Gallardo in the lead on a beautiful black bay. He was dressed in scarlet and looked like a slender flame. The edges of his cloak were tasseled in gold and they shivered and shook when he rode. He had a funny tri-cornered black hat, encrusted with gold, and he waved it right and left as he bowed. Around his waist was a long wicked-looking sword, which he said was his grandfather's.

Behind him came his men, dressed in sky blue and gold and black and white. Following them came Chalk Beeson's band, all dressed in imitation velvet vests. A roar went up from the crowd. It was deafening. The cowhands, a large percentage of them drunk, pounded their boots, fired their guns and did just about everything to raise the dead in Boot Hill.

The Mexicans rode around the arena, smiling and bowing. Then they rode out and the stage was set for the first bullfight in the United States.

A hush fell over the arena. Then suddenly there was a wild bellow, a crashing of hoofs and the big black bull named Doc

Barton burst out of the chute into the arena. It just stood there, pawing the ground, whistling through his nose, his small, beady eyes studying the strange surroundings. On his back were several tiny barbs to which were attached long colored streamers.

Out from behind a screen slipped Gallardo. The bull pawed the ground. Gallardo flicked his scarlet cloak and the bull charged. As one man, we all jumped up. It looked as if the slender man would surely be crushed. It seemed that the horns missed the Mex only by inches as they plunged through the cloak.

Gallardo casually flicked the cloak like a housewife shaking crumbs from a tablecloth on her back porch. The bull pawed the ground. Again he charged harmlessly against the cloak. For almost thirty minutes that Mex whirled and sidestepped the charging horns like a dancer. The bull was wild with fury. Every time he charged, instead of hitting something solid, he bumped air and that shaking scarlet cloak. By the time Gallardo was finished, that bull had a lot of fight taken out of him.

With one voice the crowd began chanting, "Throw him . . . throw him. . . ."

The slender Mex must have weighed only about a hundred and forty pounds, the bull a couple of tons. But he had sand. He dropped his cloak, grabbed the bull by the horns and started bulldozing him. He twisted the bull's neck and, with all his strength, tried to throw the animal. But the bull just stood there, his neck twisted. He just couldn't budge the brute. At last, with a typical shrug, he turned and faced the crowd with hands outstretched, palms up. The gesture said plainly: "I'm a matador, not a cowhand."

The crowd nudged the heavens with their cheers. Two horsemen rode in and forced the bull into a chute at the end of the arena. There was a fifteen-minute interval of music by Beeson's band and all over the park you could see bottles being lifted.

For the rest of the afternoon the other matadors tried their hands with the bulls, but they weren't as good as their captain. The bulls were to blame. They raced around the arena, frightened as sheep, shredding Doc Barton's reputation as a collector of mean bulls.

The only funny thing that happened was when a cowhand got out his lasso and turned the bullfight into an impromptu rodeo. He lassoed one bull, threw him and tied him in record time. While the matadors cursed in Spanish, the cowhand imitated Gallardo by bowing and throwing kisses to the gay ladies. It was one of the funniest sights I ever saw.

Mayor Webster, realizing that the crowd was getting restless, sent Gallardo back in with the bull named Doc Barton. By now he was real ornery. I swear he was almost breathing fire. He charged the matador and had he speared him with those horns, there wouldn't have been enough left for Doc McCarthy to concern himself with. Each time the bull charged, a hush fell over the arena; it seemed as if everyone, although they were on the side of the little Mex, wanted blood.

They nearly got it. The Mex dodged—but too slowly. One side of the bull's head spun him against the plank wall and he was down. The bull started to gore him, but the horns kept striking this plank wall. Somehow, I don't know how, the Mex made it to an escape chute. The bull, now in a raging fury, charged that fence. Each time that beef on the hoof, as big as a locomotive, hit that wall, it shook and a sigh went up from the crowd. Finally the horsemen rode in and corraled him at one side while the Mex got his breath.

We all stood up and roared our approval when he returned. He was limping, but he had his grandfather's sword in one hand. This was the moment, Bat said, when they killed the bull. The trick was to hit a vital spot in his hide. We all held our breath.

The matador advanced slowly. He held his sword curved down from shoulder height. The bull charged. The sword plunged down, the dying sun flashing on the blade. It disappeared into the black hide. The bull stopped in his tracks and died slowly, its massive head bowed, as if in meditation. Slowly, ever so slowly, the animal sank to its knees. It knelt there a moment, then, as if in total submission, rolled over on one side.

It's strange, but there wasn't any cheering for a moment. Suddenly the little Mex threw his cloak around his shoulders, bowed and walked slowly across the arena. Then pandemonium broke out. All of us stood and cheered that man. He had demonstrated that he possessed what the people in those stands admired most—courage.

That night the excitement of the afternoon seemed to infect the mobs which packed the saloons. There were more fights and more gunplay than in many a year. The marshal and his deputies were up all night. I don't think a saloon closed its doors until dawn, and then only for long enough to clean up and start all over again.

The second day crowds again packed the stands, but somehow the zest was gone. The bulls were not as mean as the big one. Nothing could quite match the moment when the slender Mexican matador had plunged his sword into the heart of the meanest bull in the West.

I stayed in Dodge for the rest of the week. In three days the crowds dwindled. The painted women went back to Lord knows where. The cowhands, their money spent, their throats raw from the whiskey they had drunk, dragged themselves onto their horses and rode away. The dust settled, Dodge, once again the faded queen of the cowtowns, settled back on her weather-beaten front porch.

Incident in Santa Fe

ONE DAY in either 1884 or '85 Ben Daniels paid me a visit in Cimarron with the news that Pat Sughrue was no longer sheriff; Bill Tilghman now wore the silver star. I suddenly felt homesick for Dodge and after pumping Ben of all the gossip he knew, I suddenly decided to ride back to Dodge with Ben. I thought I deserved a holiday; I had been working hard and riding all over the country for weeks and I was just plain sick of land and homesteaders. I wanted to raise some hell.

Ben and I rode out of Cimarron early the following morning. I was full of spirit. I threw back my head and whooped like a Comanche. Ben tried to outdo me and we went on like this, whooping and howling. Then Ben bet me five dollars he could beat me into Dodge. I took him up on it and we rode into Dodge like the wind.

I spent a week there, renewing old acquaintances. It was a glorious week of seeing familiar faces, going hunting with Ben and Billy, sitting around with Bill Tilghman and—to make the week complete—Bat and Jim Masterson came in for a short visit. Now that the job in Tombstone was finished Bat was wandering about the West and for the next few years was in and out of Dodge.

I think it was on a Saturday—I was scheduled to go back to Ingalls on Monday—when Bill Tilghman rode up to the Dodge House to see me. A rancher had been killed in the southern part of Ford County and Bill was going after the slayer. He had information that the murderer was headed for Santa Fe.

"Want to come along, George?" he said. "Ben, Billy and Neal Brown are riding with me. . . ."

I hesitated. Ingalls and the surveys were waiting for me. But— Santa Fe? Maybe a couple of more days. . . .

"I'll meet you in front of Wright's, Bill," I said.

It was a wonderful journey. Despite the laughs there was a grim job to be done and Bill followed that man's trail as sure as if he'd left calling cards along the way. He seemed to be able to outguess what was in the mind of the man he was following. And he was always right.

When we arrived in Santa Fe, Bill took us to a boarding-house run by a man named Al Clark. He seemed to know what was going on in town, and after a talk with him Bill took us on a round of bars. Bill, Neal and Billy were the seniors in this expedition, while I was just a junior trailing along as an impromptu deputy. Bill told me to be sure and mind my own business and not look for trouble.

We stayed in Santa Fe for two days but didn't dig up any information on our man. But on the evening of the second day Bill came back to our lodgings with some information supplied by a man he had known in Dodge, that the murderer was holed up in a valley north of the city, where a number of fugitives had made a sort of hideout. They had a few cabins, some liquor and women; the local authorities wouldn't go there on a bet unless they had reinforcements.

Incident in Santa Fe

It seemed like reliable information, so Bill, Neal and Ben decided that they would hit this place and see if they could find any trace of the man we were searching for. It might seem that these men were fools to venture into a hell-hole when the local peace officers refused to raid the place unless they had guns at their back. Perhaps it *was* foolhardy, but thieves and gunmen as such, even though they might number many, never frightened Bill Tilghman. I have seen him walk directly up to a man who had threatened to shoot him, twist the gun out of his hand and slap him until his eyes were glassy, then turn him about and boot him out of town. It's not easy to walk up to a man with a gun who has just said he is going to kill you, but it was commonplace to these men. It seemed they *knew* they were better men. And they were.

Before they took off Tilghman told me, "Before we leave, George, let me warn you about one thing. Don't fool around with those Mex girls. They usually have a boyfriend who has a pig-sticker and they can use them."

"That's right, George, keep away from those Mex girls," Neal added.

Both told me also to keep a watch out in the saloons for our man. I had his description, and a few of the bartenders whom Bill knew promised to watch out for me. "Don't try to arrest him," Bill warned. "Just keep your eye on him and wait until we return."

I promised and they left.

I spent the better part of the next day looking over the better section of Santa Fe; it was quiet and calm and, frankly, a little boring. Across the tracks the tawdry Mex bars and honky-tonks beckoned and gradually I moved close to the tracks.

Finally I crossed them and began to make my way down the streets.

There were drunks in the shade, whores of all kinds whistling from the cribs and doorways and plenty of shifty-eyed breeds who gave me side glances. But the Colt I was wearing made me feel as if I was the toughest gunfighter in the West. I always wondered why someone didn't take a shot at me the way I elbowed my way through the crowd and winked at the good-looking gals who passed.

I bought a couple of drinks in some saloons and by the time I was deep into the section I was feeling fine. Here I was—young, cocky and armed. I was more dangerous than any of the outlaws whose elbows I had probably rubbed. They weren't looking for trouble. I was. And I soon found it.

I had about seven drinks under my belt when I reached a large combination dance-hall and gambling palace. I paused for a moment outside the swinging doors and watched a drunken cowboy come flying through the door. He landed on his back, crawled to the side of the building and slumped to sleep in the shade.

The man who had thrown him out was a stocky, red-faced white man who wore a dirty apron. He had ragged mustaches and a pot belly. Behind him was the cutest dark-eyed girl I had ever seen. She gave me a curious look, smiled and then the man—her father, as I learned later—growled at her and she went back into the dance-hall.

Bill Tilghman's warning vanished like smoke in a breeze. I pulled up my gunbelt and swaggered up to the swinging doors.

"Well, what the hell do you want?" the man at the bar growled.

"A drink," I said. "Any objections?"

He measured me with cold blue eyes and said, "All right, you can buy a drink, but keep away from my daughter and don't start any trouble."

"I'm here on law business, Mister," I said. "I'm here with Bill Tilghman."

He seemed to relax a bit. "I heard they were in town. You're kind of young to be riding with them. . . ."

"Know Mueriles?" I asked, using the name of the killer we were after.

He nodded. "He hasn't been here for months," he said. "Come on in and have a drink, kid."

I followed him inside. It was cool and dim after the bright glare of the sunlight. After my eyes got accustomed to the dimness I could see the beautiful young girl seated at the bar near the door.

"My name's McCarthy," the man said. "This is my daughter."

I took off my hat and mumbled something about being pleased to meet her. I noticed her father didn't give out her name.

"Dolores," she whispered, as her father turned around to pick up a bottle.

"George," I said.

Her father poured me a drink and started to complain about how hard it was for a man to make some money. He told me his place was only for Mexicans and breeds, and as I looked around I was sure he was right. We were the only white men in the place.

"It's the only way I can make any money," he said. "And those damn cowboys come in here looking for trouble and wanting to shoot up the place. But I stop them."

"How?" I asked.

He picked up a sawed-off shotgun from under the bar. "With this," he said. "You don't argue with a shotgun, kid."

Then he started to ask me about the man we were looking for and promised to notify us if he came in. When he left to serve a customer I started a polite conversation with Dolores, keeping one eye on her and one eye on her old man.

I can still see her in my mind's eye—slight, with dark eyes and long eyelashes and a warm olive-tinted skin. Her hair was long and glossy, and she had plenty of curves under the silk blouse she wore. She was about sixteen and the prettiest girl in the Southwest.

She told me her mother was Mexican and her father Irish. He had been a wagon-master for the Union Pacific after the war, when they were laying track in Kansas. With the small pile he'd saved he bought a small saloon in the Mex quarter. Then, after he'd married the Mex woman, he'd managed to get enough together to buy another saloon. He was now quite a power in the Mex quarter and knew all the outlaws and breeds who were on the dodge.

The way she told me about his prominence made me feel uneasy. Maybe, I told myself, I had made myself an easy mark, putting on the brag the way I did. But after looking into those deep black eyes and feeling the whiskey crawling up my veins, I pushed the foreboding behind me and concentrated on the whiskey and the girl.

The next day I was on the edge of the tough quarter of town and I went into a small cigar store and bought a couple of cigars. It was just a little hole in the wall with a counter facing the street. As I was given the cigars I noticed two young Mexicans, about eighteen or twenty, standing on each side of me. One said, "Cigar." I didn't think anything of it and handed them each a cigar.

Then I turned around to get the change of my five-dollar bill and I'll be damned if one of them didn't reach out and take my money. I came down on his wrist with the edge of my hand and he dropped it quickly and set up a howl. The other fellow started to move in on me when the little man behind the counter reached down and came up with a sawed-off shotgun. He told them to vamoose and they backed off, rattling something in Spanish.

"What did they say?" I asked the storekeeper.

"They said they were going to get that change from you later, kid. You had better keep your eye out for them; they're a couple of bad customers. They'd cut your heart out for a peso."

I had supper early that night after another session down at McCarthy's and I returned to the rooming-house. I talked for a while with Clark, the owner, before I went to bed. I had always made a habit of taking precautions against robbers when I stayed in strange hotels. What I usually did was to raise the window a bit and stick my knife in the sash so that it balanced. If anyone tried to push the window up higher, the knife would clatter to the floor and wake me up. I followed this procedure, hung my gunbelt around the bed post, kicked off my shoes and started to doze off.

It was early morning when I woke with a start. The knife had clattered to the floor. I turned on my side and in the moonlight saw a man's sombrero. Then a hand reached in and carefully raised the window. Then another hand appeared, holding a stiletto. When a man's head appeared I reached over, slipped my six-shooter out of its holster and took a quick snap shot. The head and sombrero vanished without a sound. I lay there with the gun in my hand, in case my visitor appeared firing. But there wasn't a sound. I heard steps on the stairs and Clark began banging on the door. "Open up, George. What's wrong?"

I opened the door and explained what had happened. We went over to the window and looked out. Just below the window was the roof of a small shed. On it lay a sombrero and a knife, and there was some blood. Against the side of the shed was a ladder. Clark went out on the shed, picked up the sombrero and the knife and kicked the ladder back into the alley. "You can sleep anywhere tonight," he told me. "You won't have any more trouble from them."

He was right, but it certainly took me a long time to get to sleep. Every time there was a noise out in the street or a creak on the stairs I leaned over to feel the cool assurance of the butt of my gun.

In the morning I came down for breakfast and saw a policeman talking with Clark. Once in a while he'd look over at me. Finally, he came over with Clark and said, "Mr. Bolds, you'll have to come down to police headquarters. The chief wants to talk to you."

I said, "What for?"

"Something that happened that the chief wants to talk to you about."

"Am I considered under arrest?" I asked.

"No, not at all. You just come down and listen to what the chief has to say."

Clark said, "You go along with him, George. It's going to be all right."

Down at headquarters, the police chief, a roly-poly man, said, "Let me congratulate you, Mr. Bolds, for helping us get rid of one of the most vicious young outlaws we've had in this town in a long while."

"I didn't get rid of anybody," I said. "I don't know what you mean."

"You killed that young thief who tried to get in your room last night. Clark told me all about it."

"I didn't mean to kill anybody," I said. "I just wanted to scare him off."

"One of my men found his body just beyond the alleyway by Clark's place with a crease in his head."

The other policeman spoke up, "We followed the trail of blood back into the alley and found the ladder Clark told us he'd kicked back away from the shed."

"I'm sorry," I said. "I don't like to kill anybody."

"Well, you did," he said, "and good riddance. We've been waiting for some time now to try to get something on him to hang him. You just saved us a job."

That night I went back to McCarthy's. As always I met Dolores and we sat around and talked, sometimes with her father. I had been noticing the last few times I'd come there that one of the five poker tables was reserved for a richly dressed Mex of about forty, who seemed to be some sort of a boss. "Who's that?" I asked Dolores.

"Black Jack Gonzales," she told me. "He's the leader of all the Mexicans down here."

"He has his hand in everything," her father later told me. "Some people say he's on the dodge and has been running with an outlaw gang. He's not a man to tangle with. He's killed a few in his time with a knife."

As I watched Black Jack I noticed that every time there was a large pot on the table, something would happen just before the showdown. One of the dance-hall girls would scream or a waiter would fall down with a loaded tray or someone would threaten to draw a gun and McCarthy would have to come running with his shotgun to preserve order. This would distract the attention of the other players momentarily and I would notice Black Jack's hand dropping below the table and—in the wink of an eye—come back up with a new hand.

I'd been watching Black Jack about three nights when about nine o'clock that evening Bill Tilghman walked into McCarthy's. "I've been looking all over town for you, George," he said. "We've got the fellow we were after, along with two others. Ben and Neal have him in custody now."

I noticed there were two Army officers with him and I asked Bill what they were doing. He said they had come in at the request of some of the local citizens who felt that there was a lot of ill-feeling between the Mexicans and whites in the town and that there had been some talk of the Mexicans going out to kill all the whites they could find.

"Well, George," he said. "You coming along?"

"No, I think I'll sit in on that game over there," I said, indicating the Mex. Then I told him about the suckers that had been taken in and the little tricks the Mex had played to get the pots.

"Look," he said. "Come along with me and forget about that. You'll only get yourself killed and then there'll be hell to pay." He walked to the door and added, "I'll see you at Clark's."

By now I was feeling my oats. I had swaggered around in this tough section long enough and I had made a brag to Dolores about what a gun I was, so I figured I could stand up to the Mex and maybe come out on top.

I gave Dolores a wink, waved to her and walked across the room. I took the vacant chair directly across the Mex. He didn't say anything for a moment. He had just raked in another pot and was carefully stacking his chips in neat little piles. The other fellows at the table nodded and I nodded back.

Black Jack looked up, gave me a long, hard stare and then

grunted to himself as if dismissing me as a fresh-faced kid who was still wet behind the ears. "Stranger in town?"

"Yup."

"Ante's fifty dollars."

I pulled out some bills and bought some chips.

"We play table limit."

"That's fine with me," I said, "but where's your money? I don't see any."

Black Jack gave the other two men a smile as though he understood my naïveté, then reached down and put a small wooden box on the table. It held easily a thousand dollars.

"Let's play," I said, and we began.

We must have played for a couple of hours. As I remember, I kept my head above water, losing and winning about evenly. The pots that I won were usually very high.

Gonzales kept giving me quick glances. Finally, the opportunity I had been waiting for arrived. The pot was more than three hundred and fifty dollars. I put in another fifty and Gonzales studied a while, then said, "I'll raise you fifty."

He motioned toward the bar, as though he were looking for someone or had suddenly remembered to say hello to somebody. Then he added, "I'm raising you fifty dollars."

Suddenly a waiter came hurrying past, balancing a tray filled with beers and glasses of whiskey. His feet seemed to fly out from under him and he let out a whoop, spun around and the glasses flew up in the air and crashed down on him and some girls who were sitting at a table with a couple of Mex cowhands.

They, of course, let out some healthy screams. Everyone at our table automatically turned around to laugh. I made believe I did, but out of the corner of my eye, I watched Gonzales. Just as I expected, his hand went under the table. When everyone turned around and things quieted down I said, "I'm calling you—but not *that* hand. The hand that's under the table."

At the same time I yanked my six-shooter out of the holster and just put the tip of the barrel over the edge of the table, aimed directly at Gonzales. The others started to move back in their chairs, but I said as quietly as possible, "Stay where you are. I don't want any commotion." I knew that Irishman behind the bar would blast me with his shotgun if he caught what was going on.

I thought for a moment Gonzales would go for me, but after a time, which seemed like a century, he said, "Take the pot. You win."

I didn't have to show my hand. In this case the six-shooter was my hand and he knew it. I reached over with my left hand and grabbed some of the bills and put them in my pocket. Then I carefully transferred the six-shooter to my left hand and reached over with my right to scoop up the rest of the bills.

Just as I touched the money, his hand—quick as a snake's tongue—appeared with a stiletto and curved down in one slashing blow. He missed pinning my hand to the table by a fraction of an inch but cut my hand from the knuckle of the second finger to the wrist. I bear the scar to this day.

As he struck I fired. The slug caught him full in the chest. It's strange about men who have been shot. They don't screech or moan but just stand still for a moment or just lean back in their chair as if they've been struck by some terrible blow. Perhaps it's the shock that numbs them.

The next few minutes of that night will never be erased from my mind. Gonzales seemed to blanch for a moment. His mouth opened a little and he slowly put his hand up to his chest, where a widening red stain had begun to appear on his silk shirt.

I can remember that the other two men just stared at him. The place suddenly became as quiet as a tomb and at the far end of the bar was Dolores, just looking at me, her eyes wide. Next to her was her father. I remembered the shotgun. "Keep your hands on the bar," I said, "or you'll get it, too."

McCarthy didn't say a word. He just stood there, towel in one hand and the other hand resting on the bar. He was sure I meant what I said. I knew now that I was one against all of them. I was in Mex territory. I had killed their leader. The walls seemed to be pushing in and the silence was deafening. I wanted to run out of the place, but I knew if I didn't back out I'd get a knife or a bullet in the back or a blast from the shotgun under the bar.

But I had to have my last bit of bravado. I reached out the last few inches toward the money, grabbed the crumpled bills that were now drenched in blood and put them in my pocket. Then I stood up slowly. I tried to cover every man that was staring at me. I didn't have to look at Gonzales to know that he was dead or dying rapidly. The blood was drained from his face and his chin was slumped on his chest.

I edged along the bar, wondering if someone would peg a shot at me. I could feel my stomach muscles tense, waiting for the crack of a six-shooter. But none came.

When I got up to McCarthy, I said, "I'm sorry, but it was either him or me."

He didn't say anything but just stared.

"Goodbye, Dolores," I said.

She whispered, "Goodbye, George."

When I got my back to the swinging doors I could see the trail of blood from the table. It was draining out of my hand fast. I made a motion with my six-shooter and said, "Don't follow me. I'll kill the first man that shows his face outside this door."

Then I plunged through the door and ran as fast as I could down the darkened street toward the depot. I knew if they got up a quick posse and came after me I'd be lifted higher than a goose at Thanksgiving. And I think also some of the horror that comes to a man after he has killed someone was beginning to engulf me.

As I ran I twisted my neckerchief around my hand. Finally I saw the light of the depot and it was the most welcome sight I could remember.

I stumbled into the depot. Neither Bill Tilghman nor the Army lieutenant he'd introduced me to was there. There was a sergeant sitting reading a newspaper, his feet propped up on a chair. When he saw me his feet came down with a crash and he jumped up.

"My God, what happened to you?" he said.

I identified myself and told him I was with Tilghman and then he took me outside and put me in a buckboard and drove over to his barracks. There an Army surgeon took care of the wound and stopped the flow of blood. "You're a lucky young fellow," he said to me. "If that gash were on the inside of the arm instead of the outside, the arm might have been useless."

The sergeant gave me a couple of shots of whiskey and sent a soldier out to look for the lieutenant and Tilghman. The soldier returned in a short time, running and out of breath.

"Sarge," he said, "he shot Gonzales and he's dying. There's going to be hell to pay with the greasers."

"Gonzales!" the sergeant repeated. He turned to me. "All hell will break loose if that old thief dies."

The surgeon, who was putting his things away, said quietly, "Sergeant, you'd better get this man out of town."

Just then the lieutenant came into the room. He looked as if he'd been riding hard. "My God!" he said. "Bolds, why did you have to shoot him?"

I started to explain, but he waved his hand. "Sergeant," he said, "take three men and yourself and escort this man to the siding and put him on the first train back."

"I want to see Bill Tilghman before I go," I said.

"Tilghman is taking care of his prisoner. I'll explain why you had to leave. Now get going. The train will be here in about an hour and I'll explain to the conductor that you'll be waiting at the siding and why."

As we went out the sergeant picked up a newspaper and pushed it inside his jacket. The horses were outside and we started off at a gallop. It was the most terrible ride I had ever experienced. That gash was now paining me terribly and every time a horse's hoof struck the ground it felt as if someone had slammed my hand with an iron bar. I was dizzy and thirsty and feverish.

To make matters worse, it began to drizzle. And for the five miles from the town to the siding the rain soaked all of us clean through to our skin. The night was cold, dismal and terrifying. Finally we reached the siding on the Santa Fe east of town and I slid off the horse. I was so weak I could barely stand.

One of the soldiers helped me to the side of the siding and propped me up against the wall while the sergeant went up the track a way to wait for the train. A thousand years passed before I heard the far-off click of the wheels. The pinpoint of light grew larger and larger.

Up the track a torch appeared. The sergeant had lit the twisted roll of newspaper and was waving it back and forth. My heart was in my throat. It seemed to me as if the train was gathering speed instead of slowing down. I wondered if the officer had not had a chance to notify the conductor.

Then suddenly we could hear the brakes, and the engine and cars came to a grinding stop. The first man to get off, holding a lantern, was Pat Donnelly, a conductor I had known from Dodge City. He said, "Get on here, George, quick."

I thanked the sergeant and the soldiers. Pat helped me into the car and the train moved.

"It's a lucky thing for you that you got off as easy as you did, George," Pat said. "There were more than a thousand Mexicans down at the depot just watching to see if you got aboard."

"What about Gonzales?" I asked.

"He's dead, George."

I looked at Pat, but I couldn't say anything.

"And they tell me that wasn't the only Mex you killed, George. They say you killed one the night before."

"That was in self-defense," I said. "He tried to rob me."

"You know, you're getting to be known as a young fellow fast on the gun. Back in Dodge they'll say you're a killer, even though the the tough boys don't count greasers and Indians. Is that what you want, boy?"

"No, Pat," I said. "I didn't want to kill those people. But it was a question of either me or them."

"I believe you, George," Pat said. "But the trouble is no matter how many times you tell it, when it's repeated it will never be told like that. Right now, back in Santa Fe, there's a dozen stories about how you went after that Mex. They even said you killed him over that Mex girl."

"That's a damn lie," I said, and I held up my bandaged hand. "He cut me and I fired at him. I didn't mean to kill him."

Pat just shook his head. "I believe you, George. But there are a lot of people who will only know that you killed a couple of men and have a reputation as a gunfighter. And because they want that reputation, too, they'll force you into a fight. And if you kill them your reputation gets bigger.

"And if you kill another man who comes along, it will get still bigger and finally it will be like those characters that used to come into Dodge before you got there, when the town was really tough. They'd walk in a saloon and nobody would stand near them for fear of getting a slug in the belly, because everybody knew they brought fighting and death as sure as a drought brings grasshoppers. And then the next thing you know you'd read in the Kansas City *Star* or the Denver paper that this gent what was so handy with the guns that you saw in the saloon finally met a gent who was still faster, and they buried him." He shook his head. "George, I don't know what we're going to do with you. You're a young kid, but you're always getting into trouble."

During the time he talked I didn't say a word, but it all sank in. My craving for attention and my tough-man act had made me take that chair opposite Black Jack Gonzales.

But what could I say now? It was all over.

Staying Out of Trouble

I SAT UP most of the night in the railway coach, brooding about life and death in Santa Fe and suffering a great deal of pain from my gashed hand. I was ready for a long spell of peace and quiet.

Early in the morning, just after dawn, we reached Tucumcari. There was a long wait there, and finally Pat Donnelly came into the coach. "George, there's been a wreck two or three miles up the track and we'll be held up here for a few hours. Why don't you go out and take a walk up the street? As soon as I give some orders and take care of a few things I'll join you and then we'll have breakfast."

As I started down the steps of the coach, Pat came out on the platform and called out after me, "And for God's sake, stay out of trouble."

Pat didn't have to tell me that. That morning a dove of peace was hovering over my head, although I still carried my six-shooter on my hip. Trouble was the last thing I wanted.

In those days Tucumcari was just a small community with one street running through the heart of it. There were elevated wooden sidewalks and a few stores. I walked slowly down the wooden sidewalk, occupied with my own thoughts. I noticed a lot of horses hitched up and some people hurrying back and forth across the street but paid little heed.

As I passed one small place that looked like a store, three men standing by the door were talking earnestly among themselves. One man saw me, stared at me for a minute, then nudged the others. They stared at me as I passed, and for a moment I was tempted to turn around and say, "What the hell are you looking at? There's no flies on me."

But that dove of peace just fluttered her wings a bit and I went on. I figured that a bedraggled character like myself, with one hand in a sling, would naturally attract attention in the early hours of the morning in this tiny town.

When I reached the end of the street I turned around and walked back toward the depot to join Pat. Suddenly, as I passed the little store someone behind me yanked my six-shooter out of my holster and spun me around. Two officers were on one side of me and the third, whom I recognized as the one who had nudged the others as I had passed, grabbed my left hand. He was dark, with a hooked nose and big bony hands.

One of the officers said, "Put the irons on him."

The other said, "Don't put the irons on him. Let him try to get away. I want to kill him myself."

"What's this all about?" I said.

The man with the big nose snarled, "You know damn well what we're holding you for. You killed old man Gaston last night and robbed him of his money."

"My God," I said, "I've never been in this town before. I don't know the man."

"His old lady said the man who killed her husband was a stranger just about your size and build," one of the officers said. Then he pointed to my right hand. "Mrs. Gaston said just before you killed her husband she slashed you with a bread knift in the right hand, and there's your right hand bandaged and with blood on it."

"I got this out in Santa Fe from a Mex who tried to cheat me," I said. "I've never been in Tucumcari before in my life, and I don't know Mr. Gaston *or* his wife, and I spent last night on the Santa Fe coach with Pat Donnelly, the conductor. . . ."

"*That's* a likely story," one of them said. "You'll have to tell it to the judge."

We started down the street to the marshal's office. They opened the door and pushed me in and I nearly fell down. They *knew* I was a thief just by looking at me. I was a robber and an outlaw and probably a horse thief as well. The only way *I* was going to leave Tucumcari was in a box, because before nightfall I was going to be strung up for the murder of that old man. A group of people had started to follow us, and it seemed to me that the only law in Tucumcari that morning was lynch law.

The judge was a short, fat fellow, who was also the marshal. He looked as if he controlled the town. The fellow with the big nose told him he'd caught me leaving town, running for the train. He pointed to my hand and said, "Judge, this is the bird we want. He fits the description Mrs. Gaston gave us and that right hand bandaged is a dead giveaway."

"You're a damn liar," I said. "I never was in this town before. I was in that Santa Fe coach all last night, and I just came in this morning."

"It looks bad for you, boy," the judge said.

"It certainly does," I said, "what with this man lying all over the place about me. Judging from the way you handle the people you take into custody, it certainly looks as if I don't have much of a chance. I'd like to send a few telegrams—one to Santa Fe and one to Dodge."

"You're not sending any telegrams," Big Nose said. "You'd better close those blinds, Judge," he added. "If the town ever finds out we have this killer in here, they'll mob us and we'll lose the pleasure of hanging him."

They closed the blinds and then they tied my left hand behind my back. My right hand was still in the sling.

"Did you search him?" the judge asked Big Nose. No, he hadn't. He had only taken my gun. Then the judge ordered me searched. The deputies turned my pants pockets inside out and of course they found the crumpled, blood-stained bills.

"That settles it," Big Nose shouted. "That's old man Gaston's money with his blood on it. Joe," he said to one of the other men, "get that rope."

One of the fellows went into a small back room and came out with a rope. They quickly made a noose of it, threw it over my head and tightened it around my neck.

"Now just a minute, boys," the judge interrupted. "We have to make sure he's the right man, and if he's going to be hanged he's going to be hanged legally."

"We have all the evidence we want, Judge," Big Nose said. "We have his description from Mrs. Gaston, wounded in the right hand, a stranger running for a train, the first train out of here, and he's got blood-stained money. Mrs. Gaston said the man who killed her husband took the money from his tin box and we saw blood in the box, so the bills must have been blood-stained."

The other two deputies kept nodding and agreeing with everything this fellow said. "We'll hang him after dark," one of them said. "We can use the hooks down by the butcher store." I knew what he meant. In a lot of western towns when outlaws were caught and there weren't any trees, they'd string them up by the hooks used by butchers to hang sides of beef outside their shops.

These men were going to hang me! I might be dead in a few hours, the very breath of life strangled out of me by the rope that now hung around my neck. "Dammit," I shouted. "I'm no outlaw. Let me send those telegrams to Dodge."

Big Nose grabbed my left arm and pushed it up my back until I thought it was wrenched out of the socket, and the other two jerked my head back with the noose until I thought the blood vessels would burst in my temples. Then they slammed me against the wall and into a chair. The pain of my arm hitting the wall was so great I almost passed out. The three of them just stood there, looking down at me. They wanted a hanging and, by God, they didn't care who they were going to hang.

When I had recovered my breath I said to Big Nose, "You can hang me and you'll probably kill me. But when word of this gets out, by God, you and those two friends of yours and even the judge had better get out of this part of the country . . . because I have friends in Dodge who'll come down here and wipe you and your kind and this rotten little dump of a town right off the face of the earth."

For almost an hour they kept up a line of talk about what they were going to do to me and how they were going to do it and how a man feels when he's kicking away his life at the end of a rope.

I didn't bother to answer them. I just sat there, trying not to pass out from the pain in my arm. The pushing around they had given me had opened up the wound, and I could see bright red stains appearing on the bandages.

"It doesn't make any difference," the judge said, "but who was it you'd planned on sending telegrams to?"

"Bill Tilghman in Santa Fe, and Bat Masterson and Bob Wright in Dodge," I answered.

The judge looked surprised. "Do you know those people?" he said.

"I certainly do. I was with Tilghman in Santa Fe when this Mex stabbed me in the hand in an argument over a poker hand."

The judge turned to the others. "Maybe we'd better let him send those telegrams. If he's really a friend of Tilghman and Masterson I don't want to get mixed up in this."

Big Nose just waved his hand. "He doesn't know Tilghman or Masterson any more than I do," he said. "He's just a damn robber who's trying to delay what's coming to him." He kept going over what he described as the "evidence" when suddenly we heard the sounds of a lot of boots coming toward us on the wooden sidewalk. I grew cold all over. I thought it was a mob coming to take me. Then there were some voices and someone began banging on the door.

The judge went over to the door and shouted, "Who's there?"

"Let me in," a voice outside said. "Open up this door."

"Don't open the door, Judge," one of the deputies said. "They might rush us."

However, the judge opened the door an inch and started to say, "I'll let one man come in here," but the door was flung back and Pat Donnelly burst into the room. Out in the street were some conductors, the engineer and a growing crowd of people.

"My God, George," Pat cried, "what are they trying to do to you?"

"I don't know, Pat," I said. "Looks like they want to hang me, and from the way they're talkin' it looks as if they mean it."

Pat turned to the judge and said, "You've got the wrong man."

"How do you know we've got the wrong man?"

"That's George Bolds. He came in on the train with me this morning."

"Was he with you last night?" the judge asked.

"Of course he was," Pat Donnelly replied. "He got on my train at a siding five miles outside of Santa Fe and he was in my coach every minute until this morning when we pulled in here. I told him to walk around the town and then to meet me for breakfast. I was waiting for him in the depot when I heard about the murder. Someone said they had picked up a stranger with his right hand in a sling and I knew it was George. So I came up here on the double."

"What about that wound and the blood-stained money?" Big Nose said.

"George got it in a fight with a Mex in Santa Fe. He went there with Bill Tilghman. If you men want me to send a telegram to Tilghman I'll do so immediately."

The judge said, "No, no, there's no need of that. We know we've made a mistake, Pat. We know you and we know you'd only tell the truth."

He took my six-shooter from the desk and handed it to me. "Here's your gun. I guess we made a mistake."

"Maybe we did," Big Nose admitted, and he took the rope off my neck. The other two fellows stepped back. With all the strength I had left I slapped Big Nose across the face. He fell back against the wall and rubbed his cheek.

"You made a great arrest, you hook-nosed horse-thief," I said. "Now, if you call yourself a man, go out in that street and we'll settle this." I reached over to my right side, took the six-shooter out of my holster and put it in my belt on the left side. "I haven't got the use of my right hand, but I'm sure I could gun you with no hands."

Big Nose just looked at me. It was plain to see that he didn't want any part of me.

"I'm waiting," I said. "Let's see how much sand you have."

Just then Pat Donnelly stepped in front of me. "You damn young fool," he said.

The way he said it, in a very quiet way and directly to me, just wilted me. The anger I felt just drained away. A few moments before, there I stood, a young hot-headed fool, ready to right a wrong by killing a man. What remorse I had felt the night before about killing two men in Santa Fe seemed to have been quickly forgotten. I took the gun from my belt and slipped it back into my holster.

"I'm sorry, Pat," I said.

"Let's have some breakfast, George," he said, and we walked out.

Big Nose didn't say a word, just kept rubbing his cheek. I was suddenly glad that I hadn't gunned him. Hell, I thought, he wouldn't have been worth the trouble.

On the train heading for Dodge, Pat brought up the subject of what had happened only once. "George," he said, "you're the damnedest young fool I ever did see. You go down to Santa Fe to hunt a man on the dodge, then you wind up by killing two men, being run out of Santa Fe and almost hanged by those fools in Tucumcari."

"Well, Pat, I can say one thing," I said.

"What's that, George?"

"I was run out of Santa Fe, but it took the Army to do it."

He chuckled and shook his head. "That's the straight of it, George," he said, "and no man can deny it."

And that was one of the stories they used to tell about me in the cowtowns, that I was such an "ornery cuss that the Army ran me out of Santa Fe."

The Callahan Place

IT WAS about a year after the Santa Fe incident that Jack
Callahan stepped down in Cimarron from the Santa Fe train.
He was a tall man, well over six foot, and wearing the gambler's
usual costume—polished boots, long black coat, black hat, heavy
gold watch chain and a six-shooter strapped about his waist.
A thin white scar on the left side of his face gave him a sinister
look. We didn't know much about Callahan then, but later
Buffalo Joe Reynolds, then the sheriff of Gray County, found
out he had been run out of Wichita for running a regular
hell-hole.

That first day Callahan ignored the loungers at the depot.
After a quick perusal he started to walk south toward the
Arkansas River bridge. Halfway across the bridge he stopped,
leaned on the rail and studied a small island some forty feet
west of the bridge. This narrow strip of land had been given
the name Beaver Island sometime after the Civil War by some
French Canadian trappers who had camped on this island to
count and cure more than six hundred beaver hides. God knows
where they ever got them in that country.

Callahan seemed to know exactly what he wanted. He studied the island for about ten minutes, glanced at his watch, then hurried back to the depot just in time to swing aboard the eastbound local.

A week later, five wagons loaded down with all kinds of building material passed through Cimarron on up to the bridge. I recall I was standing outside the courthouse with Jake Shoup when they passed. The sight was so unusual the whole town saddled up and rode out to the bridge.

By the time we arrived at the bridge, five or six men were unloading plans and other material. "What are you doing, boys?" Jake asked.

"Building," one said.

"Building what?" Jake persisted.

The carpenter cocked an eye at Jake. "A castle for a queen, Mister," he said.

Jake wasn't too happy with the carpenter's humor. "I asked you a civil question, Mister, and I want a civil answer," he said.

The carpenter eyed Jake and his gun for a moment, then shrugged. "Mr. Callahan told us to build a house on this island and we're doing what we're paid to do," he said and walked off.

"Who the hell is Callahan, George?" Jake asked me.

I shook my head and said I didn't know. We rode back, wondering why anyone wanted to build on a flat island when they could buy plenty of homestead tracts.

Three days later, two carloads of furniture and furnishings, brilliant red draperies, chandeliers and things of that kind arrived at Cimarron in charge of a Chinaman, who chattered excitedly. He hired four drays and wagons to haul the stuff to Beaver Island. Tarpaulins were spread over the things which the workers dragged into the shell of the big house.

All day and far into the night, when they worked with

torches, the carpenters filled the air with the rasp of saws and the slam of hammers. I walked out to the bridge with Jake one or two evenings during the week to watch the progress of the building; it was long and squat with a corrugated tin roof. But the curious feature was a wide porch and a sort of foot-bridge leading from it to the river bridge.

"Looks like he wants company," murmured Jake.

The house was finally completed and the Chinaman sent a telegram to Callahan in Kansas City. Several days later the west-bound train stopped at Cimarron and Jack Callahan stepped down. His boots were polished so brightly that a man could shave by them and he had not one, but two guns strapped about his waist. Behind him came two hard-looking hombres—hired guns. Following Jack's men were six or seven beautiful girls, shepherded by a woman with a brightly rouged face.

The mystery of Jack Callahan's place was now solved. We watched the ladies in silence as they climbed aboard a surrey which the Chinaman had brought down from the town's livery stable. As they drove away they giggled and waved their hand-kerchiefs.

"Come along tomorrow and see us," the madam called out.

"Just wait until the wives hear about this," Jake said.

Not having a wife, I could chuckle. There wouldn't be many poker games in Cimarron any more. At least the married men wouldn't be dealing a hand. News of Callahan's bagnio and gambling house spread along the frontier with the speed of a prairie fire fanned by a high wind. In those days a young fellow didn't have too much to occupy his time; there were just hunting, playing poker, racing your best horse, maybe making a trip to Dodge or even Kansas City. For the young cowhands, especially the Texans, there were usually only whiskey and women and—if they had both time and money left over—cards.

The Callahan Place

Riders out of Cimarron carried the news around Gray, Finney and the other counties. Soon Jack Callahan's place was booming. But when the gay ladies started to come into town, swishing down the street, their hems mopping the sidewalks, the women of Cimarron put their foot down.

One day Jake and Charlie Dixon stormed into my place. They were fuming. Both their wives had been on their backs day and night.

"We've got to do something about Callahan's place," Jake said.

"Not me," I said. "You and Charlie here. Not me. I've got enough trouble surveying tracts and settling arguments. I probably have more than my share of men wanting to kill me."

"I'm going to see if Reynolds can do anything," Jake said, and left.

That night, when I met him, he looked low-down. I asked him if Reynolds had been able to help, but he shook his head.

"Reynolds said he couldn't do anything until Callahan did something that would constitute breaking the law." In those days, breaking the law, so to speak, was either killing a man or stealing his horse.

Gradually Beaver Island lost its air of bawdy fun and assumed a more evil mask. There were rumors that men had mysteriously disappeared after winning a large pot. When one cowpuncher found himself on the bank of the river, badly beaten and without a cent left of a month's wages, Reynolds talked to Callahan. Still nothing came of it. The cowhand left before the sheriff completed the interview. The hotel clerk said one of Callahan's hired guns had paid the cowhand a visit. The puncher probably felt he would rather continue living than be a dead civic hero.

But matters came to a head one fall day in 1884. A rancher

who lived forty miles south of Cimarron had shipped four cars
of cattle to Kansas City and the proceeds for the head were to be
shipped to him to Cimarron by express. The rancher sent in his
foreman to receive the package. The straw boss picked it up
late in the evening and then went for a walk to see the town.
He was never seen again. One man said he had last seen him
walking toward the bridge with a woman. The sheriff and a
deputy visited Callahan's place, but they could not find any
evidence to indicate that the foreman had been there, so there
wasn't anything that could be done but send out a description
of the missing man to the other towns and search for his body.
A party of us did go up and down the river, but didn't find a
thing. I can still remember Jack and his men standing on the
porch while the girls waved at us and shouted invitations.

As the months passed, Callahan became bolder. He brought
in two more hired guns and they swaggered around town as if
they owned it. A strange thing about small towns—they will
allow themselves to be pushed so far; then there is a savage
counter-attack, a deep growl of anger and the ordinary citizen
is suddenly a fighting, clawing wildcat and God help the bullyboys.

It happened in Cimarron. The people of the town were
shocked to learn that Callahan's girls were using the Cimarron
swimming hole. The girls would sport around in their shimmies, sitting in three or four feet of water, splashing and cavort-
ing, shrieking and giggling like schoolgirls. But they weren't any
schoolgirls; they were salesladies displaying their wares. They
would occasionally shout up to the men on the bridge, "Come
on up to see us, honey, and we'll have a dance and a drink."

That did it. A group of citizens met and decided to find the
owner of the land. A man came forward and he was persuaded

to file suit in federal court in Garden City to have federal authorities oust the Callahan gang.

The suit was duly filed. I was summoned by the judge. As official county surveyor, it was my job to locate and survey homestead claims and to settle disputes. My verdict in homestead claims was always accepted by the court as the final verdict. As one judge said, "Men lie, but figures do not."

The day before the case was to be called Callahan walked into my office. He was an arrogant fellow and I disliked him from the beginning.

"I want you to make a survey for me, Bolds," he said.

"The fee is forty dollars," I said. This was higher than I usually charged for such a job, but he nodded. "Suppose we ride over to my place?" he said.

When we got to the island he said he wanted to measure the area of the island and the distance from the island to the north and south banks. That was an easy assignment and I was finished within a short time.

"Can you make a sketch of the island?" he asked.

"Certainly," I said and began to look in my box for some drawing paper.

"I have some paper inside," he said and started walking down his plank bridge.

My curiosity was stronger than my civic pride, so I followed Jack down the bridge. The main room was large and luxurious, furnished with rugs and deep sofas and crystal chandeliers overhead. I also noted that in one corner was a stack of Winchesters. Callahan, I thought to myself, would be a tough hombre to oust by force.

Off the main room were small siderooms and there was also plenty of gambling equipment. Jack disappeared into the back and the Chinaman came out with some glasses. Callahan gave me a glass and downed his. I followed suit. It was damn good whiskey, probably not the kind served to the paying customers.

I completed the sketch in short order. Callahan took it, put it in his wallet and said, "I want you to come to court tomorrow, Bolds."

"I'll be there," I said.

"Not for the government," he said. "I want you to testify that the river is navigable at this point."

"Of course it isn't," I said. "It's not more than three or four feet deep except when a spring thaw makes it overflow."

He came closer. "Bolds," he said quietly. "I want you to testify tomorrow—my way. I would suggest you not testify against me. . . ."

"Callahan," I said, "I don't like you. And, frankly, you can go to hell."

He didn't say anything but just kept looking at me. After a long time he turned away and left the room. I was collecting my equipment when I suddenly became conscious that someone was looking at me.

It was the woman I knew as Mrs. Callahan. She was about forty, with her face painted like a Sioux buck getting ready for war. "Mr. Bolds," she said, in a voice as sweet as boiled sugar, "I would like for you to meet my girls."

They came out one by one. As she introduced them, each girl came forward, gave me a smile, then stepped back. My breath was just taken away. They were dressed in almost nothing. At a signal from Mrs. Callahan they began crowding around me, smiling and not saying a word. The room was heavy with their perfume and a feminine scent. They didn't have to offer me an invitation; it was plain Callahan was offering them to me instead of money.

I was certainly no saint in those days and I guess if Callahan's two guns hadn't swaggered into the room, picking their teeth and grinning as though I were a farm boy being played for a sucker, I just might have allowed myself to be bribed and to hell with civic duty. But those two bullyboys set me on edge.

"My name is Libby," Mrs. Callahan said. "Please join us this evening."

I picked up my gear. "I'm sorry, ma'am," I said, nodding in the direction of those two tough characters, "I don't like to eat with skunks."

The following day's court session was brief. The judge was an old man, so small he looked like a child with an old face, lined and weatherbeaten like soft, wrinkled leather. His spectacles were constantly slipping to the tip of his pointed nose, and he had the impatient nature of an old bear.

Callahan had as his attorney Harry St. John, the son of a former Kansas governor. He tried to make an issue of the navigability of the stream, but the judge waved away his argument. "That's not the issue here, counsel," he squeaked. "Who owns this island?"

"A citizen of Cimarron," one of the Cimarron people said. "Here he is."

The alleged owner then made his claim, and the judge ordered me to make a survey showing the exact site of the island. The case was then adjourned for five days.

The following afternoon I collected a crew and set out for the bridge. When we reached the river bank south of the island, Callahan and two of his hired guns were leaning on the bridge. I paid them no heed and started to make the survey. Callahan and his men climbed down and walked along the bank toward us. One of my men had driven in a peg and Callahan bent down, pulled out the peg and threw it in the stream. Then he and his men began shooting at it. It jumped and splintered under the hail of bullets. "Now get out of here, Bolds," he said in that quiet way of his.

The crew I had were all unarmed. It would have been foolhardy for me to have started anything. I had no desire to join the other poor suckers who had ended up as catfish bait.

"This is a federal order you are violating, Callahan," I said.

"I don't care if the President of the United States ordered this survey," he said. "I'll kill the first man who drives another peg in this river bank."

"I'll be back tomorrow," I said.

"I'll be waiting."

"You had better be ready."

He just smiled.

I had all I could do to keep my temper from boiling over. Had it been just Callahan and me, I'm sure I would have asked him to try his luck.

I rode that night to Garden City and saw the judge. I never saw him so excited. He cursed like a trooper and said he would have troops sent to enforce the law. "Dammit," he said, "why didn't you Cimarron people throw that fellow out before this? I'll send a telegram to Fort Scott asking for troops."

"There's no need for that, Judge," I said. "I would like your permission to handle it in my own way."

"What way is that?" he asked. I told him and he said to go ahead. He even chuckled. "The law will back you to the limit."

The next day I paid a visit to Dodge to see Bill Tilghman. He wasn't around, but Jim Masterson happened to be paying a call in Dodge. Jim just sat there, nodding, as I told him the story. When I had finished he stood up. "Let's see if Neal and Billy are about, George."

We found them and they said they would like to see Callahan and his sporting house, so we rode back to Cimarron.

The next day their presence created quite a stir in town and some of the people stood outside the stores and watched us ride off.

Our plan was simple. Jim, Billy and Neal could cross the bridge as though they were just passing through, then would circle back. Meanwhile, I would come up to continue my survey.

I gave the boys about ten minutes to cross the bridge, then I rode up with my crew. Callahan was sitting on his porch, his men lined up alongside him.

"Bolds, I guess you're hard of hearing," he called out.

"My ears are just fine, thank you," I said. "If anyone is going to kill me Callahan," I added, "I guess I'll have to prevent him any way I know how."

I climbed down from my horse and gave orders to my crew to take the equipment to the bank. The water looked about five feet deep. I took off my clothes and hooked some chain together which would reach the point in question.

"Want your hardware, George?" one of my men asked.

"No," I told them, "but if they do hit me, you men get out of sight and let Masterson, Ainsworth and Brown take care of matters."

Dressed only in my long johns and holding the chain over my shoulder, I waded into the water. It was swift and cold as ice. The water was bubbling about my knees when the first shot cracked. A tiny water spout leaped up about four feet in front of me. Another foot, and two guns went off. Two more plunks. I stopped for a moment. There I was, dressed only in my underwear, with the river swirling about my waist, and me tugging at the chain as I pulled it higher on my shoulder.

"I wouldn't come any nearer, Bolds," Callahan shouted. "I don't want to hurt you, but you are trespassing on my land."

"I'm following the orders of a federal judge, Callahan," I shouted back.

"Well, it's *your* neck," he answered and picked up a shotgun.

The next minute I looked up I was staring at a shotgun. The barrel seemed as large as a cannon. One of the hired guns casually took aim and fired. Water jumped up, off to my left. I cursed Masterson, Brown and Ainsworth. Where were they? The hell with them, I thought. I'm going to plant that stake and lash up that chain and no damn pi was going to stop me.

I started to move deeper into the river, my guts cold as lead. Any moment I expected to hear the blast of that shotgun—probably the last earthly sound I would ever hear.

The crack of the .44 almost made me lose the chain and stake. Callahan lowered his shotgun and was looking across at the bridge. I looked up. The heads and shoulders of Jim, Billy and Neal appeared. "Taking a bath in your drawers?" Neal shouted.

There was another crack and the slug raised the dust on the tin room. Someone—it was Jim, I learned later—called out. "We can bring our shots down, Callahan." More shots banged that tin roof.

The shots brought out the women and the Chinaman on the run. They must have thought the citizens of Cimarron were coming to bust up their place, because they started to jump into the water and go for the bank. Some of them just had their shimmies on and stayed in the water, with only their heads sticking out, shrieking at the top of their lungs.

I started toward the spot on the island where I had to drive the stake. Callahan and his men seemed frozen; they didn't move a muscle. I emerged from the river, dripping as a dipped rat, with the seat of that damn long underwear hanging behind me like a sack, to drive my stake and fasten the chain.

I passed within about twenty feet of Callahan. "Next time you come into town, Callahan," I said, "I would be pleased if you and I would try our luck."

He didn't say anything, but I could feel his eyes follow me. Across the water, leaning on the rail, were Jim, Billy and Neal.

"You look real cute, George," Neal called out.

I went back into the river and splashed up on the bank, put on my pants, gathered up my stuff and piled it in the wagon. The girls were running back up the bank of the island to the porch of the house. When I looked back, Jim, Neal and Billy were certainly enjoying what they were seeing.

But Callahan won the suit. Ironically, my survey helped to prove that Callahan did have a right to claim the island. He rubbed salt in my wounds by nodding at me outside the courthouse. "Thank you, Bolds, for such honest testimony," he said.

"Left your gun home, Callahan?" I asked bitterly.

Now there was no holding him. His place became worse than ever. There were new robberies and assaults and more men vanished. The following spring a rancher came in from New Mexico and went to Callahan's place, wanting to know what had happened to one of his young nephews. Callahan denied any knowledge of the boy. We helped drag the river, but the lad was never found.

By this time the place was a state scandal. Several attempts were made to get him out by charging that he was a public nuisance, and once or twice we got cowhands to claim they were assaulted. But Callahan's men always got to them first and either by bribe or threat all of them were forced into riding out of town before the cases came to court.

Finally, after a man had been found almost beaten to death, we decided to do something. In my days in Cimarron there was an active vigilante group known as the Anti-Horse-Thief Organization. It had been started in 1859 in Fort Scott, Kansas, to combat the rising threat of horse-stealing and after the war had spread to many Kansas communities. In our district the leader was a Civil War veteran named John Logan, who was as tough as sun-baked rawhide.

One night we called on him and plans were made. Riders galloped across the county and men gathered in barns and on the plains. We rendezvoused outside Cimarron on a Saturday night and rode along the main street to the bridge.

The Callahan place was alive with music and laughter and lighted by many lamps.

"Give them a round, boys," Logan ordered.

Rifles and six-shooters made the roof a sieve. The music and the laughter stilled. It was a strange sight—the horsemen lined up on the bridge, moonlight glinting on the gun barrels—and across the water the now quiet, well-lighted house.

Suddenly the door opened. Callahan came out on the porch, flanked by his henchmen.

"Callahan?" Logan called out.

"I'm Callahan," he shouted. "What do you people want?"

"You have until two o'clock tomorrow afternoon to get out of town," Logan called back. "If you're not, we'll come back with a rope for you and your men."

He turned and all of us galloped after him. Within an hour a guard we had left behind reported the customers were leaving the place in droves.

It was an uneasy Sunday morning. Most of us wore our guns and watched the clock. At about noon Callahan rode down Cimarron's main street in a surrey with his wife. Behind them came other carriages filled with his gay ladies, all waving their handkerchiefs and crying out invitations to come and see them.

But it was too damn far. Who in hell wanted to go to Creede, Colorado?

In time, some homesteaders took Callahan's place apart for the lumber. Many a homestead shack on the plains was built with the best lumber that Jack Callahan could buy in Kansas City. And many a worn farm woman carefully placed ragged antimacassars over the deep plush chairs which had once held the voluptuous bottoms of Jack Callahan's beauties.

"There are now 225 men and 360 horses and mules digging Soule's ditch. The monthly payroll will be $15,000! It is said the ditch will make the valley bloom as the rose. . . ."

The Kansas *Cowboy*, 1884.

Asa Soule and the Railroad
to Montezuma

I T was in the winter of 1884-1885 when Asa Soule appeared on the Western horizon. I think of all the strange men who came out into the West, he was the strangest. I don't know much about his early background, but I believe that after the Civil War he founded a patent medicine business in Rochester, New York, which brought him huge profits. By the time the West was opening up he was looking for new lands to conquer. He was a typical Easterner: a dandy with thick sideburns, a brisk, businesslike manner, a trace of arrogance and the manners of a man born to blood royal. When he came to Kansas he came in a hired train. He didn't spend thousands, only millions. He built colleges, bridges and canals. Before he died he was one of the most powerful men in the West.

His two lieutenants were John and George Gilbert. Evidently they were hired by Soule in the early eighties to find a "Western Empire." Finally they decided on the north side of Arkansas River and bought a large tract on the river from the

Atchison, Topeka and Santa Fe. The Gilberts were plotting their section of Gray County for a town site, which they named Soule City. Soule, however, insisted they name it Ingalls after his friend Senator Ingalls. The railroad knew there were millions behind this venture, so they built sidings and a depot and hired an agent. Before long a trainload of lumber, accompanied by carpenters, arrived. I believe Soule's two nephews, Eugene and Lou Soule, arrived a few days later.

The two boys were in charge of construction and the Gilberts had the financial end. One day they rode into Cimarron and said they had discovered that my land, the north half of Section 31, cornered the townsite of Ingalls.

"That's fine," I said. "Now I'm part of a town."

"Why don't you come in with us, Bolds?" John Gilbert asked. "We can use a surveyor."

Well, why not? I asked myself.

"Going to Ingalls?" Jake asked, when he saw me loading a wagon with my equipment.

"You're right, Jake," I said.

He eyed me for a moment, then said, "George, I wish I had never sold you that land," and walked away.

When Soule himself first visited Ingalls in about 1885 it was a raw collection of clapboard buildings and not too impressive. The boys told him the place needed water and Soule said, "Build them a canal."

A few weeks later the Eureka Irrigation Canal was started. It was to start one mile above Ingalls and run through the northern part of Gray and Ford Counties and end in Pawnee County, a total of some eighty miles.

Every farmer and sod buster within miles around grabbed a shovel and began pitching dirt. The people of Cimarron, the oldest town in the county, didn't take very kindly to "Soule's ditch," as they called it, and before long, Soule's surveyors came riding into Ingalls and quit.

"What's wrong, boys?" the Gilberts asked them.

"We're surveyors, not gunmen," they said and collected their pay.

I was living in the makeshift hotel that had been built in Ingalls at the time, and when the Gilberts came to me and asked if I would finish the survey, I agreed.

The next day I went out and started my lines. A few minutes later a rifle cracked and the slug made me dive for the earth. The rifle fire kept me and my rod man pinned down for an hour. I knew when I was licked, so I called off my crew and went home.

That night I rode into Dodge. I hired Ben Daniels and a few of the boys to come along with me the next day. At dawn we rode out, but before we hit the spot where I had been fired upon, we split. I went on with my men to continue the surveying job and Ben and another fellow made a wide circle and came toward me to outflank the would-be killer. I had my rifle ready.

About fifteen minutes after we had begun work a rifle cracked and we jumped behind a mound of dirt. I tried to locate the shot and get a bead on the fellow, when a second shot rang out, dashing dirt in our faces. My crew was getting restless.

"I ain't coming out here tomorrow, Bolds, unless you get that bastard," one called out.

No sooner had he spoken than there were several shots, then silence.

"They got your man," I said. We stood up to watch Ben and Fred Singer ride across the prairie and flush the gunman from a buffalo wallow. They started toward us, the man with his hands up, the others as nonchalant as if they were going to a picnic.

When they came closer I was shocked. The assassin was a man I knew from Cimarron. He had been associated in business in Cimarron with me and had shared my table many times.

"My God, why did you want to kill me?" I asked.

"I wasn't going to kill you—I was just trying to get you out of here," he said.

"But why?" I asked. "What has this canal got to do with you?"

He pointed to the canal. "You and that damn Soule," he shouted. "You'll ruin all of us. You're no friend of mine, Bolds. And don't come to Cimarron unless you want trouble."

"What do you want us to do with this skunk, George?" Ben asked me.

I picked up the man's rifle, and emptied it of shells.

"Get out of here," I said, throwing him his rifle, "before I kill you."

He caught the gun and without a word walked back to where his horse was hidden. A few minutes later we heard the muffled sounds of hoofbeats. The last we saw of him he was riding hard for Cimarron.

"The hell with working today," I told the crew. "I'm going into town and get drunk."

"Maybe we'll join you," Ben said.

"You're welcome," I said, "and it's on me."

I just couldn't go on working. I felt sort of sick to my stomach, as though I had caught my own brother out to kill me.

This was the kind of hate which simmered in Gray County in those days, simply because men wanted *their* town named county seat.

The King of Hop Bitters, as they called Asa Soule, made good his promise to the people of southwestern Kansas; he gave them a canal. Every farmer, homesteader and jobless cowhand who could lend a hand joined the gangs slinging picks and shovels—and they dug a ditch eighty miles long across the sun-baked plains of Kansas!

It was a marvelous thing. But there was only one thing wrong with it. It never held a drop of water!

Meanwhile, the bad feeling between Ingalls and Cimarron intensified. Once when I rode into town—with my gun in plain sight and ready for use—I met Jake Shoup.

"George," he said, "I wouldn't be seen around town too often if I were you."

"Jake," I said, "you know so-and-so tried to kill me?"

"I heard about it," he said.

"Well, you can tell him and anyone else who wants to try and stop me from coming into Cimarron that I'm ready to see them."

"I guess that's the way it has to be," Jake said and walked away.

I thank God I *didn't* run into my former friend that day. I hate to think what might have happened.

It was soon plain that Soule wanted Ingalls to be the county seat of Gray County and the most important town in southwestern Kansas. Cimarron's businessmen knew that if this happened their town might die on the vine. Immigrants were pouring into the county, but they'd naturally settle near the county seat and do their trading there.

Cimarron girded herself for the wars. She won the first victory, not by gunfire, but through a political maneuver. It was very simple. The Cimarron men realized that Soule was buying all the votes he could with his million-dollar projects and that to combat him in the open polls would be disastrous. So they went to the governor, who was friendly with some of the town's leaders.

A petition was quietly prepared and Governor Martin acted at once. He named three commissioners for Gray County and they in turn immediately named a county clerk and a sheriff—all Cimarron men, of course.

When we heard the news in Ingalls there was plenty of rough talk. But a few months later tempers really mounted when Martin, acting on the recommendation of the three commissioners, named Cimarron as the temporary county seat.

The Gilberts were troubled. They sat in my office in Ingalls, with their big, thick cigars, just thinking and smoking. Finally one brother figured they had the majority of votes in the northern part of the county, though many of the homesteaders in the southern part were still friendly to Cimarron.

He telegraphed Soule and the Hop Bitters King wired back: "Come to New York at once."

When the brothers left on the next train we all wondered if this was the end of "Soule's bubble." But within two weeks the Gilberts were back. The older one had a carpetbag. Folks always said it was loaded with money.

"What's Soule going to do now?" I asked.

"Give them a railroad," the brothers chorused.

And that's what he did. The railroad was to start at Dodge City, pass through Ensign and end at Montezuma. The Gilberts promised that the road would be continued southwest. The right of way was obtained and the settlers in the southern part of the county were invited to help build the road.

I don't think there was ever a short line of railroad completed in such a short time.

The opening of the road was set for July 4, 1887. The Gilberts told Soule he should be on hand.

The brothers must have spent a small fortune making arrangements. They went to Dodge and hired Chalk Beeson's famous cowboy band, and hired a small army of housewives to cook the food they purchased. There was enough beer and whiskey to inundate the whole county.

That Fourth of July was a memorable one. Soule arrived in Dodge City about the time the town was getting real drunk. Cowboys were racing up and down outside town, firing pistols.

Soule was delighted with his reception. He made a speech, which was punctuated with shots and shouts. The Gilberts were corraling people to board the coach and four flatcars, making sure the drunks were wedged in so they wouldn't fall off. When the coach was filled, the boys climbed on the roof or clung to the windows. Those who couldn't find any room piled into wagons or drays or rode their horses alongside the train.

Soule, his face dripping with perspiration and covered with Kansas dust, sat in the locomotive cab with the "best citizens" of Dodge. Behind the locomotive came the coach, filled with the shouting, drunken fools firing their six-shooters and the flatcars, groaning under a varied load—some cowpunchers had even dragged their animals aboard. And above all rose the most dreadful clash of metal on metal and wailing horns and the thump-thump of a bass drum ever heard in the West—Chalk Beeson's band. To add to the din, loco cowhands raced alongside the tracks, whooping like Comanches attacking a wagontrain.

At Ensign more citizens fought for a seat and many fist-fights broke out. When they couldn't find room the Ensign people joined the cowpunchers riding alongside the train. More shots were fired that day than at Gettysburg.

At Montezuma the Gilberts attempted to form the unruly gang into a parade and we all marched around in the blistering heat, cheering and whooping behind Chalk's band. The ladies threw aside the cloths covering the tables of refreshments and the mob rushed toward them. I thought the ladies would surely be trampled under, but they braved the tide to form lines so the boys could be served. With all mouths occupied the din died down.

I found Soule an amazing man. He had a brain like a hair-trigger and he made his decisions that way, too.

During our conversation he suddenly asked me, "Mr. Bolds, does Ingalls have a church?"

"Not yet, Mr. Soule," I said. And before I could go on, he said, "We had better get one built at once."

He said no more about it, but went on talking about the country and its great prospects. When the feast was over there were several speeches before at last Soule was introduced. He was given a noisy ovation.

I can still see him holding those people spellbound with his dreams. He told them he was going to build a bridge across the Arkansas and a college in Dodge City for the people of the county. He said he intended to make Ingalls the largest and most prosperous town in the West.

"I've only started doing things for you people," he said. "I've paid you people for your work and I've helped you stay on your claims and I have not asked you for one cent. All I want is your good will. Common sorghum can easily be grown in this soil. My chemists are now working on a formula to make brown sugar from the juice of the cane, and if they are as successful, as I hope they will be, there will be a mill in every town in this county, where you can deliver this cane for a good price. But this is only the beginning. I have many more projects in mind for your benefit which will be started shortly. They will be for your benefit and won't cost you a cent. . . ."

The cheers and applause which greeted his words almost started a stampede among the horses. Asa Soule was undoubtedly the most powerful man in the West on that bright, hot day.

By twilight his audience was drunk not only with dreams, but with whiskey.

The day finally came to an end and the people piled back on the train. It was only then that the realization came to all of us: no one had built a turntable at Montezuma.

The engineer did the next best thing. He backed that damn train all the way to Dodge City.

A Preacher for Sunday

BEFORE he left for the East, Asa Soule made a quick inspection of Ingalls. "Should be a church here," he said.

"We haven't had time to build one," someone said.

"Should have a preacher," he said.

"We have to wait until one rides circuit, Mr. Soule," I told him. "The nearest one is in Dodge."

Soule shook his head. "A town is not a town unless it has a church and a minister," he said. "I want a church built here within sixty days and a minister hired. Select a representative to hire one, and my people will take care of the details."

By nightfall he was on his way back East and we had our orders. Asa Soule wanted a church and a preacher in Ingalls, and it just had to be done.

As always, I was the goat. The boys elected me to build a church and find a preacher. The first job wasn't too difficult—we put up a frame building on a little hill—but the latter was almost impossible in that wild country. I kept hoping *someone* would come up with an idea.

The old folks in town had taken the thing seriously and

every day one white-haired gentleman named Clark would stop by regularly to see me at my office. "Now see here, George," he would say, "you had better get after that minister. We want a fine service on Sunday."

Finally I realized there was only one thing to do and that was to start hunting. So I saddled up and rode the twenty-five miles to Dodge. I found the minister there was too busy. So I rode to Garden City. There they told me, "Sorry we can't help you, Bolds. We have only one minister and his contract with us calls for his dismissal if he preaches outside this town. And, besides, you boys are raising so much hell down there we wouldn't let him go for fear he'd be shot."

I rode all over that country, even traveling by train the three hundred and fifty miles to Kansas City, looking for a minister, but I couldn't find one. The boys in Ingalls kept saying, "George, as long as you can't get a minister, why don't you do some preaching yourself? Hell, you were baptized in the Cimaron, weren't you?"

The ladies were the worst. They would stop me on the street to pass the time of day and would inevitably end up by saying, "We trust you'll have the preacher this Sunday, George."

"Yes, ma'am," I would always reply cheerfully. "He'll be there bright and early Sunday morning, preaching God's word and full of fire and brimstone."

One evening John Wemby, the town banker, came by my office and when he asked me how I was I replied I felt lower than a snake's belly.

"Why, George?" John asked. "People are still coming out and there's plenty of land to be surveyed. What makes you feel so low?"

"I just can't find a preacher and the whole town's depending on me for a fine service Sunday."

"That's an easy problem to solve," John said. "We'll put off the meeting until we get a preacher."

"That might be two months, six months or two years," I said gloomily. "I guess the only thing I can do is leave town for a while."

"You're not going, George," he said. "I'll insist that the meeting be postponed."

I went home, but I didn't sleep a bit that night. I felt I had let the town down. Many of the people of that period were well-read despite their meager schooling and were as upstanding as shellback Baptists. In most frontier communities Sunday was a great day. The people wore their go-to-meeting clothes. The children were dressed up and on their best behavior. The carriages and surreys were polished and the horses well brushed. After receiving a liberal dose of fire and brimstone and a chance to test their vocal cords in a hymn or two, the folks would gather outside, no matter what the weather, to chat with their neighbors. Sunday and the meeting made a break for everyone in a long week of dawn-to-dusk work in a wild, new land. A great deal of this ran through my mind as I tossed and turned on my bed.

The next morning my spirits were at a pretty low ebb when I threw myself on my chair in the office, stuck my boots on my desk and stared out of the window. My mind happened to wander to the grocery store across the way and the sign above it, which read "Douglas and Turner, Groceries."

The name "Turner" suddenly struck me like a blow. I leaped to my feet, shouting, "Turner!" Why hadn't I thought of him before?

Six months before, I had been asked by the land office to straighten out the boundaries on a tract thirteen miles west of Ingalls which belonged to a man named Turner. I had completed most of my surveying by midday and was invited by the family to share their meal.

When I sat down at the table in their small sod house and saw the battered china and the pitiful furnishings, I suspected that Turner, a slight, brooding man, was having a hard time of it. When mealtime came I was sure of it. I knew that Mrs. Turner, who seemed to be a real lady, was offering me the best dinner that she could scrape up in her humble larder. There were pitifully few black beans and sow belly.

Before we set to, Turner stood up and, with his eyes closed, said grace. This was dinner. But it was damn near supper before he finished. I marveled that a man could talk so long with his Maker on an empty stomach.

When he had finished, Mrs. Turner explained, "Mr. Turner was a minister in the Ozarks, Mr. Bolds."

The family had completely disappeared from my mind, but in the quiet of the morning when I saw the same name above the grocery store the memory of her words came back to me with a rush. I ran out of my office, saddled up and rode out of town as fast as my pony could go. I don't think any pony express rider could have made better time than I did in traveling fifteen miles from Ingalls to the Turner place. When I arrived I realized that Turner should have remained a preacher. He had an old cow teamed up with a swayback mare and he was trying to plow a section of land. It was pitiful to watch him.

"Why, Mr. Bolds," he said, "you should be ashamed of yourself using a fine horse that way." My horse was dust-covered and heaving like an old bellows. "What's the matter? Is the law after you?"

"The whole town of Ingalls will be unless I fulfill my mission," I said.

"What mission?" he asked.

"Well," I said, "you know we have a church that Soule gave us and we *have* to have a meeting on Sunday."

He nodded. "Yes, I heard about it, but I wasn't sure I wanted to go down to see it. I heard there are a lot of rough characters in Ingalls."

"All the rough ones are in Cimarron, Mr. Turner," I said. "In Ingalls we have only peace-loving people."

"Well, I'll have to go down and see the new church someday," he said.

"Now look here, Turner," I said. "Your wife told me the last time I was here that you were a minister in the Ozarks. I want to hire you to come down and preach a good sermon at our Sunday meeting. How much will you charge?"

He shook his head. "Well, Bolds, I haven't done any preaching in a long time and I don't know any of the people there."

"Never mind that," I said. "Myself and a few of the others will appoint ourselves as a committee to introduce you to the folks in town and make sure no harm comes to you."

He stood there for a minute, gazing reflectively at that miserable cow-and-horse team and then said, "Let me consult with the good wife. I always talk over important decisions with her."

Then he went into his sod house. I sat on my horse, making plans to kidnap him and bring him back to Ingalls if he *didn't* agree.

"Well, we talked it over, Bolds," he said when he returned, "and I'll preach your sermon. But I don't know if you'll meet my terms."

When I asked him what they were he hesitated a minute and then asked, "Would a dollar a sermon be too much?"

I damn near fell off the horse. He came close and looked up into my face and said, "What's the matter, Bolds? You look sick. Do you think that a dollar a sermon is too much?"

"No," I said, "that's quite all right. Now I'll go back and tell the folks that you'll be down Sunday morning."

"My good wife has a little organ we'll fetch along," he said, "and we'll have a little music."

When I got back to Ingalls a couple of the boys lounging near the bank called out as I rode down the main street, "George, did you get your preacher yet?"

I replied coolly, "Yes, I did. I've had him all the while. I've just been fooling you fellows."

That took some of the wind out of them and they soon spread the word around town that Bolds really had hired a minister.

Friday night I rounded up the boys and we had a meeting in my office. I explained to them that the minister had heard a lot of things about the town and that we should try to present our best appearance on Sunday morning.

"You mean wear a clean shirt, George?" someone asked.

"Yes, a clean shirt and leave your gun home unless you're an officer of the law," I said. "I think that's what we all ought to do."

There was a lot of discussion, but Buffalo Joe Reynolds, the sheriff, agreed with me. Then Billy Ainsworth, who was stopping over with me, piped up, "But suppose you're an officer of the law, George?"

"A peace officer is welcome with his guns in any church," I said. They left me that night, promising they'd leave their hardware at home.

The next day, Saturday, I seemed to notice that a number of the boys were carrying tin cans home. They didn't say anything, but just waved their hands, gave me a grin and passed by.

It turned out to be a beautiful Sunday morning, as beautiful as only Kansas can produce. The word that we had a Sunday meeting had sped around Gray County. Folks from all over came into town by wagon, surrey and on horseback. I can still close my eyes and see the farmers in their Sunday best, with their wives in starched dimity and their children freshly scrubbed, walking slowly up the hill to where the church had been built.

I was on hand to greet Turner and to introduce him to most of the families. Before long I discovered why so many tin cans had been taken home the night before. Every male inhabitant had cut himself out a tin star which he pinned on his shirt. And on every hip, of course, was a gun.

"All right, you coyotes," I told them. "I just dare you to put twenty-five cents in the collection plate." They all thought it was a good joke and promised nothing but green stuff.

Soon the church was filled and people were forced to stand outside. The meeting opened with Mrs. Turner at the organ, and I think one of the most beautiful sounds I ever heard was the sweet notes of the hymn coming through the open windows and finding their way through the quiet Sunday morning. As I recall, the first song was "That Old-Time Religion." When Turner asked everyone to join in, the voices lifted in song that morning almost took the roof off Soule's new church.

Then Turner started his sermon. It went on for more than an hour and I began to get a little restless. I got up and began to pass the hat around. I remembered I had to pay the preacher. The boys were as good as their word and soon the hat was three-quarters full of silver and bills. I brought it down to the small table by the preacher and carefully laid it out.

Preacher Turner ended his sermon, closed his Bible with a final prayer, then carefully counted eight bits from the pile of money.

"I believe we agreed to one dollar a sermon, Mr. Bolds," he said. "Good day and God bless you all."

He stood outside with Mrs. Turner for a spell, greeting the folks—which wasn't included in the bargain—and everyone told him it was a fine meeting.

"See you next Sunday, Preacher Turner," I called out as he was leaving with his wife. He nodded and tipped his hat. Behind that old cow and swayback horse at his place he had seemed like a tired old man. Now he looked ten feet tall and his eyes were shining.

The Great Ingalls Mail Robbery

I HAVE had some terrifying experiences in my life, but I think the worst was the time I was accused of robbing the United States mail.

It was about the time Ingalls was booming and I was just getting established that the Santa Fe cannonballs passed through Ingalls. The westbound train always took the siding, but the eastbound never stopped, only taking a mail-sack from the hanger. The mailman was Billy Turner, who was the one helped me to decide to make my home in Ingalls. He was to spend many a night with me in my office, which was located a half a block from the station. He was a great cigar-smoker and I always bought him Williams stogies, then two for a nickel. Billy always knew he would have a smoke on me.

One Saturday evening in early spring I came to Ingalls from Cimarron and hitched up outside a saloon. I met Billy Turner carrying his mail-sack.

"Hello, George," he said. "Just a-visiting?"

"Just a-visiting, Uncle Billy," I said. "I'm thinking of settling in Ingalls."

The Great Ingalls Mail Robbery

"Walk up a ways to the depot with me and I'll tell you what's good about us," he said, and I accompanied him to the depot, watched him hang that mail-sack on the hanger and then walked back with him. We had a smoke and then I stayed overnight. That Sunday I had about decided to settle in Ingalls and started to look around for an office.

Monday there was a flock of detectives, postal men and the local sheriff in town. It seemed that the mail-sack containing about two thousand dollars in bonds and cash had disappeared. The trainmen swore they never took it from the hanger at Ingalls.

The detectives questioned Billy and me. We both told the same story and the detectives checked my background and reputation in Dodge and Cimarron. Although some of the boys swore I was a no-good horse-thief and a gunfighter who'd kill his own brother, the bankers and business people like Bob Wright convinced the detectives I was fairly well fixed, with no reason to steal. As for Uncle Billy, the whole county swore by him. Still the detectives persisted in questioning me. I nearly gunned one of them who had the gall to say to me, "Bolds, *did* you take that money?" I had the notion that people were looking at me queerly as though they were not sure that they wanted anything to do with me. I got jumpy and was sure glad when the great mail robbery simmered down a bit.

Then about a month later a stranger appeared in town. He said he was a cattleman just passing through, but I knew damn well he was no cattleman. But in those days you never questioned a stranger's name or inquired into his background. That was his business, and to question it was asking for a dose of lead poisoning. He was a nice enough fellow and a great hand at poker. We had quite a game going in Ingalls and he always sat in.

It was a few days before I began to realize he was striking pretty close to me. A couple of times he even shared my quarters. Once when I had ridden out I noticed on my return that the papers I had left in my temporary office had been tampered with. I now came to the conclusion he was a railroad detective.

I decided to fix him and make sure at the same time whether I was right or wrong. One day I had to ride to Garden City.

"That's fine, George," he said. "I'll ride with you."

"It's twenty-five miles," I said.

"That's a nice ride," he said.

He hired a horse from the livery stable and we rode off. First, though, I had made up a mysterious package and held it close, as if I didn't want to lose it. Inside were some buffalo chips.

When we arrived in Garden City I told the detective I had to see my old friend Buffalo Jones and he should wait around town for me. I told Jones the story and asked him to get his boy to take the package and put it in the trash-can they had outside for burning garbage. Jones chuckled at the idea and we both schooled the boy, who thought it was a funny idea.

Then Jones looked out the window. "Dammit, there he is outside the hotel. Let's make him wait."

We made the poor fellow wait for about two hours. Then the boy went out the front door and made a great show of looking up and down the street, then threw the package into the can. He ran inside and we all watched through the curtains.

The fellow was off like a shot. He first sneaked around the corner of a nearby house, then headed for the trash-can. In the meantime I left by the front door and hurried down to the depot just in time to catch the train. Jones promised to send my horse back by his boy and to give me an account of what happened after I left. I got in the last car and waved goodbye.

The train was clicking down the track when the detective

came around the depot at a dead run. I went out on the rear platform and waved my handkerchief. And I'll be damned if Jones didn't wave his in return! There was no other train out until the next day and the detective must have spent a sleepless night in the Buffalo Hotel.

When he returned to Ingalls, I made a great show of telling him how absent-minded I was and how I didn't think of my horse until I was on the train. But he wasn't satisfied, and kept even closer than ever on my tail. A few days later I noticed my gun and cartridges had been tampered with. I suspected what he was up to and told Billy Ainsworth to examine the shells while I took the fellow out hunting. When we came back, Billy told me my suspicions were correct; he had removed the powder from my shells and put back the lead. It is obvious he intended to arrest me soon and wanted to make sure I didn't have a chance to kill him.

"Let me have your Smith and Wesson .38 short, Billy," I said. "I don't trust this fellow."

Now John Glynn, the cashier of the Ingalls bank, and I sent our laundry together to Cimarron by a dray which went from Ingalls to Cimarron every morning. About eight o'clock I went over and saw John and got his telescope, which had our laundry in it, and brought the bag over to my office.

There was my faithful old watch-dog, waiting for me to open up.

"Hello, there," he said. His eyes fell on the telescope. "Going on a trip?"

"Yes," I said, "a long one."

"Hmmmm," he said, "you just came from the bank, didn't you?"

"Yes," I said. "I just robbed it, killed the cashier and five lady depositors."

He just grinned and walked out. He didn't waste any time getting to the bank. Later John said he came in and asked him if I had a lot of money banked there. John told him to get the hell out, it wasn't his business or anybody else's for that matter, how much I had there. Then the fellow showed his badge, but that didn't faze John.

"Mister, this is a federal case, and you had better have a United States warrant from Garden City," John told him.

The detective left the bank and walked into my office. "Bolds," he said, "I'm arresting you for the robbery of the Ingalls mail. Are you going peaceful or do I have to take you?"

He was watching to see if I'd go for the gun in my desk drawer. Instead, I took out the .38 from my pants pocket and leveled it across the desk at him. A more surprised man I never saw.

"You have to take me, Mister," I said. "Now if you think you're lucky, go for that gun you've been toting around all these days."

"I'm a detective," he said. "I demand that you turn yourself over to me."

"You're just a lot of hogwash," I said. "You're a no-good tin-horn detective who wants to try for that six-hundred-dollar reward and you'd hang your own mother to collect it!"

John came in just at this moment and said, "Is the laundry ready for the dray, George? The driver is outside."

I nodded and John bent down to pick up the telescope. The detective lunged at it. "Don't you pick up that bag," he shouted. "That's evidence."

Roy Draper, the deputy sheriff, was passing, and seeing the commotion, came in.

"What's up, George?" he asked, looking from the detective to me and John.

"This damn fool wants to arrest me for the mail robbery," I said.

"I have the evidence right here," the detective said, and started to pull it away from John. Glynn, a well-built young fellow with a quick temper, just lifted the detective off his feet, opened the door and threw him out into the street. The detective got up and came for us with his gun out. A shot at his feet drew him up short.

I pushed aside Draper, who had fired the shot, and told him this was my affair and not his. But he said very quietly to the detective, "Put that gun up."

The fellow saw so many guns aimed at him he was glad to put his up. Then Draper knelt down and opened my telescope. All he saw were long johns, socks and shirts.

"Is this your mail-robbery gold, Mister?" he said.

The detective was silent, but Draper said, "I'll walk you to the depot."

They walked down the street. That was the last I ever saw of him.

That was in July. In the late fall, John Denham, an old friend, stopped me on the street one day and said, "George, isn't it about time you went for some plover?"

I promised him he'd have some that week. The next day I locked the office and went on the prairie with my dog, who in some respects, had more brains than I did. We followed the river and got a good bag by the afternoon. I fired my last shot in the late afternoon and one of the birds, wounded, got away. The dog followed it to the railroad track and there he pointed. I sent him under the tracks and he came out with the wounded bird.

I was turning away when I saw in the frozen woods something which had a familiar look. I knelt down and parted the grass. It was the mail-sack, frozen and dirty and rain-soaked. I didn't touch it, of course, but highballed down to the depot. Si Burns, the section-hand, rounded up Draper, the county attorney and Uncle Billy. We all trooped down the tracks, where they retrieved the sack. Back in the depot, they opened it and, intact inside, were the bonds and letters and the money.

That was the finale of the great Ingalls train robbery. They sent me the six-hundred-dollar reward from Garden City, but I returned it. Then a man came over with it again and they said I was entitled to it. But I insisted that Billy Turner, who had a large family, should be given the money.

We never discovered just how the mail-sack ever got forty rods south of the depot. The train's hook probably slipped in some fashion, missing the sack and knocking it off the hanger but onto the car. There was a bend in the track where the sack must have slipped off the train and into the weeds.

Old Si Burns was the only disgruntled one. He swore he had scoured that section of track every day but was done out of six hundred dollars' easy money by a bird dog and a wounded bird.

Doc Barton and the "OS" Brand

I GOT to know Doc Barton of Gray County well after I settled in Ingalls and in time we became good friends. His cattle were famous and he was now making a fortune in grain.

"Know how I came West, George?" he said to me one day when we were trading yarns in my office.

"No," I said, "how did you?"

It took the best part of the afternoon to tell me the story. He wasn't pulling the long bow, for his brothers told me the same yarn.

Doc and his brother Al caught the Western fever in 1866, and after they pooled their money together, they persuaded their friends Ben Eubank and Tom Connell to join them on a trip from eastern Tennessee to south Texas to corral some wild cattle and start a ranch. They were all only about eighteen years old, and as Doc said, "rarin' to go." The other two boys joined them and pooled their savings, which amounted to a few hundred dollars.

They purchased an old prairie-schooner, repaired it and loaded it with barrels of salt and corn meal. They purchased five horses and four mules, partially on credit. Most of their folks had been killed in the war, so their goodbyes were few.

Game was plentiful and some they could shoot from the wagon. In southern Arkansas they followed an old wagon trail until they arrived at a cabin that had a fence around an adjoining half-acre. In the lot were about ten hogs.

They noticed the hogs all had great long snouts. If you'd cut their heads off, you'd be cutting them in the middle. On the end of each of their tails was a large ball of mud as big as the cannonballs you could pick up back home after the Civil War.

When an old fellow came out of the cabin, Doc asked, "Will you sell a shoat, Mister?"

The old fellow said, "Yes, I have one here that has lost the knot off his tail. He's no good nor ever will be."

Doc then asked, "Why all the mud balls on their tails?"

The old man rubbed his chin.

"It's this way, Mister. If those balls were not on their tails, they could not root. Every time one of them would stick his snout in the ground he'd fall over if it wasn't for the ball of mud holding him down. That's the way he makes his living, rooting around stumps for worms."

"Will you take a dollar for the hog without the tail ball?" Doc asked.

The old fellow said a dollar was enough for the shoat, so they tied his feet together and threw him in the wagon.

A few miles further on they spied another cabin. A woman came dashing out, ran past them and dived in the brush at the side of the road like the devil was after her. Then a fellow waving a basket ran out of the cabin. He was a big, lanky fellow, more than six foot tall. When he was near the wagon he stopped and asked Doc, "Mister, did you see a woman running this way to hide?"

"Sure did," said Doc.

"Well, that's my mother," the fellow said. "She's trying to wean me. I always suck before I go out to pole hogs."

"Ain't you weaned *yet?*" Doc asked.

"No, sir," the fellow replied. "Mom never weans her boys until they are eighteen, as it makes them tall and stout, so as to get good wages poling hogs."

"How old are you, boy?" Doc asked.

"Sixteen, but more than six foot, and if Mom don't wean me until I'm eighteen I'll be six foot four and earn lots of money," the fellow said.

"Poling hogs? What's that?" Doc asked.

"You see this basket," the fellow said. "I fill it full of these little pigs. Then I shove their tails with the balls of mud on the end through the holes there, and they can't jump out of the basket. Then I put the basket on top of my head and walk around under the best acorn trees and hold them up to eat the acorns before they fall. That gives them a darn good start to be ahead of the rest. The taller you are the better wages you get. So that's why I'm after Mom. She's sure a good dodger, runner and hider."

"Well, son, what's your dad's politics?" Doc asked.

"He's a moonshiner, sir," was the reply.

"Where is your dad?" Doc asked.

"I ain't going to tell you, sir. If I did tell you and you went up there you'd not come back," the boy said.

"Why don't you get married, son? You're old enough," Doc asked.

"Oh, hell, not me. I had a friend that was with me poling hogs. He got married and his wife hitches him to a jumper plow and drives him like a mule. Get married? Not me. I'd rather pole hogs," he replied.

"Do you have many good neighbors?" Doc asked.

The fellow pointed, "You see that cabin down by the creek? A fellow and his family live there and they're just damn mean."

"How?" Doc asked.

"Well, it's this way. He claims all that land near the creek where the best acorns are. If our hogs get near the creek he dogs them back and raises hell and is liable to start a feud."

"Have any trouble with him?" Doc asked.

"A while back a big storm came up and this fellow was not at home," the fellow said. "When a big rain comes the creek gets full of water. You see that island there in the bend? We took our dogs and drove most of his hogs on the island just as the creek began to rise. We held them there until only a speck of the land was out of the water. We hurried home and got ready for a feud, but it never came."

"Why?" asked Doc.

"Well, it's this way, Mister. He was wanting to butcher his hogs, but couldn't catch them. He came home and found his hogs all dead on the island after the water went down. The balls of mud on their tails kept them from floating away."

The fellow started to walk away, but Doc called to him to tell what happened next. The fellow returned.

"Well, he took his family to the island and dressed all those dead hogs. In a couple of days we saw him coming up the road with two wagons. One of them was piled full of hogs like cordwood and the other wagon had three barrels of chitlings. We got our guns and was ready for him. When in front of our house, he stopped and said, 'You're good neighbors and I want to thank you. When you drove those hogs on the island the mud balls on the end of their tails held them there. I'm on my way to town to sell the hogs and chitlings. So anytime I can help you out, just call on me.' "

Doc's friend Eubank asked, "How long was it since you drove the hogs on the island?"

"At least a week, Mister."

"Those hogs was spoiled," said Eubank.

The boy nodded, "They couldn't tell if they was spoiled or not, as they are snuff-eaters and couldn't tell if they was rotten, as their mouths are always full of snuff."

Eubank climbed into the wagon, cut the strings that held the shoat and threw him out. "I'll never eat pork again," he said. "I'll like squirrel much better from now on."

The four young fellows continued on to the Southwest. South of Austin, they saw the country was full of cattle and good grass, so they camped for the night by a small stream.

In the morning they heard a funny noise near their camp and investigated. They found an old Texas steer down in a bog hole, nothing showing but his head and horns. They pulled him free and tied him to a tree. He seemed tame or was too weak to object and became very docile.

Doc said, "Here is where we stop and begin gathering cattle for our herd." Then they branded the captured longhorn with "OS" on the right side and marked it with a crop out of the right ear. This was the start of a great herd.

Doc and the other three found the brush full of cattle and they soon had as many in the OS brand as they could handle. The steer they rescued never left camp. They put out salt and this helped to attract others, so all they had to do was throw and brand them. Doc rode to Austin, only to find that cattle were bringing only about what the hide and tallow were worth. The country was overrun with cattle, but there was no real market.

Doc was the oldest of the bunch and they looked to him for advice. After he returned from Austin, they held a council. Doc said, "We're not making our wages here. I'm going on a trip up in Kansas, as I hear the Santa Fe is building west. If I can find a good location we'll be near a market. I'll go by way of Austin and register the OS brand."

The next morning he saddled up and gave the other three last instructions.

"You fellows hold the camp and only brand the she stuff. Don't bother with those old moss horns, as they never can be tamed."

Doc was gone three months. When he returned he had a Mex with him and said, "Some fellows was going to hang this Mex up near the Territory. They claimed he stole ten dollars from their camp. He pleaded so bad for my help I paid the ten and he claims he'll be my slave for life. We can use him."

"Are we going to head north, Doc?" his brother asked.

Doc nodded. "I've found the right place west of Fort Dodge along the Arkansas River with plenty of grass and water. We will need more help for the drive."

The Mex said, "In three days I can go and get my cousins, who know cattle and will be glad for the work."

The Mex, whose name was Felipe, returned in two days with three of his cousins. They began collecting cattle of the OS brand and saw they had more than 3,000 head, all they could handle. The Mex help seemed to be in their glory and knew how to handle wild cattle. They left Texas in 1872 and headed for Kansas. They were forced to abandon their original plan of crossing the Indian Territory for fear of outlaws and hostile Indians.

Instead they headed west for the Pecos. One morning when they broke camp, Eubank discovered a dead Mex near where the herd was bedded that night. Doc called in all the Mexicans to learn why a dead Mex was near the herd. Felipe said, "He came to me in the night and wanted us to help steal the cattle and murder you white folks. I refused, and he got mad. I just had to kill him."

"Well, let's plant him," Doc ordered. "We've got to get going."

After the Mex was buried, they started the herd west, with old Tex in the lead. They crossed the plains without much trouble and landed on the banks of the Pecos. It was a tiresome trip and Doc ordered a two-day layover.

Felipe said, "I know this country. Some of my cousins live in a little hamlet downstream. I'll go visit them and be back tomorrow." Eubank remarked after Felipe left, "That's the last we will see of that damn Mex. I don't trust them."

"I'll bet you ten dollars he comes back," Doc said.

"How about fifty to make it interesting?" Eubank said. They shook hands on the deal.

Felipe returned to camp the next day, accompanied by a Mex woman. He looked as if he'd been fighting mountain lions. His face was bruised and cut and one arm was in a sling. Through his bruised lips he introduced the woman to Doc.

"This is Carlotta, my wife. We were married by the padre."

"How did you get beat up?" Doc asked.

"I had one bad fight to get her," the Mex said, "as we need a cook. Carlotta is one fine cook and she make me good wife and good cook for the camp, so there won't be any more fights who's to cook."

As Doc said, he collected his bet and Carlotta took charge of the camp like a veteran. Then she learned she was a distant cousin of one of the other Mexicans and all was happy.

They started the herd north and Old Tex was in the lead. He seemed to smell the rich buffalo grass up in Kansas. The second day out they met two Texas Rangers. When Doc told them the route they'd taken and their destination, they were surprised to learn he'd had no trouble with outlaws. They cautioned him to be careful when his spread crossed the west end of No Man's Land, as it was full of rustlers and outlaws.

They met with no trouble and days later reached the Arkansas River, crossing over to the north side. They continued east along the north bank and their first stop was where Garden City now stands. Later they established camp at Pierceville along the river.

The OS brand was the first herd to come in western Kansas between Fort Dodge and the Colorado line. The Santa Fe was just building west from Dodge City and Doc knew he was near a good shipping point. For the next ten years their OS brand numbered in the thousands. Felipe and Carlotta sent for more cousins and they soon had a Mex settlement. The OS brand had sixteen Mex cowboys on their payroll and all of them knew how to handle cattle.

Doc decided he wanted to be a permanent resident of Kansas and selected land at the old "Cimarron Crossing" at the point where the Santa Fe Trail crossed the Arkansas River. He filed on a homestead and tree claim where the old ruts of the Santa Fe Trail showed on the south side of the Arkansas River near what is now Ingalls, Kansas. His partners also filed on claims that gave them over two square miles of acreage.

In the spring of 1885, Doc said to his partners, "The sod busters are here and more are coming. It's the end of the open range. I suggest we gather and ship all we can during the summer and fall. We must reduce our herd."

They all agreed and during the summer and fall you could see many trainloads of OS-brand cattle rolling east to Kansas City.

By the late fall of '85 they had reduced their herd to about two thousand. Some were full-blooded Herefords and short-horns. The terrible blizzard of '86 pushed all the OS cattle south, where nearly all of them perished. The summer roundup showed there was not enough of the OS cattle to pay expenses.

That marked the end of the OS brand in Kansas. Doc and his brother Al bought out Eubank and Collins before they left for California and the Mex cowboys went home to south Texas.

The settlers had shown that wheat could be grown in western Kansas without irrigation, so Doc and Al went into wheat. They were as successful with wheat as they had been with cattle. The Bartons built a fine place and their combines were the talk of the countryside. I did some of their early surveys and my office was usually Doc's first stop in Ingalls.

In 1888 I was one of the delegates asking Doc if he would run for sheriff of Gray County. There was always trouble in the air over where county seats should be located, so many a sheriff's job went begging.

Doc shook his head. "George," he said, "I've had enough hell in my time and now I want to live in peace, unless I can get one job. . . ."

"What's that, Doc?" I asked.

"Poling hogs in eastern Tennessee," he chuckled.

The White Killer

IT WAS a raw day for April one dark afternoon in 1886, and the clouds hung low, gray and swollen with the snow that was soon to fall. I had been unusually busy all that week and I was ready to bed down early when Jake Shoup walked into my place.

"What's up, Jake?" I asked. "How are the boys acting in Cimarron?"

"Fine," he said. "There are some strangers in town. Came in yesterday."

I sensed something was up. Jake didn't ride five miles to tell me about some strangers.

"What's the straight of it, Jake?" I asked.

"Claim-jumpers," he said. "They got one last night." He drew on his cigar. "Do you know that this is the last night you have to spend on your claim?"

I suddenly realized, after consulting the calendar, that I had completely forgotten about my land. I thanked Jake and saddled up in a big heavy mackinaw. Within five minutes I was galloping out of town. Jake agreed to stay overnight in my place in Ingalls, which had two cots. It was a raw, dull day and the wind was in my face, blowing the low, heavy clouds across the sky like billowing, dirty cotton.

Before long it began to freeze and the sleet came whistling down like sprays of solid shot. The high buffalo grass, stiff with ice, sounded like crackling matchwood under my horse's hooves. Soon his mane and tail were encrusted with ice. By the time I reached my tiny cabin I was in the midst of a howling storm. The wind screeching in the sky sounded as if all the dead Indians had gathered together for a war dance.

A small lean-to served me for a barn, but to my dismay I found that the wind had blown it away. For a moment I was dumbfounded, but after gathering my wits I did the only sensible thing: I tied the reins to my saddle horn and gave my horse a slap on the rump and shouted for him to go home. He gave a neigh, kicked up his heels and in a moment disappeared in the sleet, now mixed with snow, that hid the rest of the world as if by a solid curtain of ice. I hated to send a fine saddle horse out into the storm, but I knew his chances of getting home were good. Without at least a lean-to to break the wind, he would have frozen to death.

I knew I was in a tough spot, alone on the prairie, horseless and with just so much firewood. I had been in many a wild storm in the West, but I knew, as I fought my way to the cabin door, that this was the worst I had ever experienced. As was the custom in that part of the country in those days, there was no lock on the cabin door. There was fuel, coal and food for anyone to use. The only unwritten law was "Replenish if you can what you have used."

I had a small iron pot-bellied stove, a bin of coal, some wood, a bucket of water and some dried antelope meat hanging from the wall near the one tiny window. There was no glass in the window—glass was a luxury—but nailed across the window, and reinforced by strips of wood, was greased antelope skin, scraped of meat until it was like a piece of membrane. It let a thin lemonish light through on a bright day and that was about all. But it kept out the rain and snow and the draughts.

Physically, at this time, I was in perfect shape. I weighed about one hundred and ninety pounds and was six foot two. I had never been sick a day in my life, and I was as hard as a spike and as straight as an arrow shaft. I had thick, coal black hair that I used to keep rather long.

By the time I had fought my way to the cabin I was as battered and breathless as if I had run a mile while struggling with some huge buck who kept banging me on the chest with his war club. The ends of my hair were as stiff and sharp as splinters from the sleet.

The wind was like a living thing. It plucked the air from my lungs, then battered me to my knees. The hail was like buckshot fired at close range, and the cold, in spite of my heavy, sheep-lined coat, seeped through my flannel shirt, then my skin, then my veins, to rest in the marrow of my bones.

I virtually crawled to the door, and throwing all my weight on it, threw it open and fell inside. To get it closed was comparable to shutting it against the weight of several angry men.

When I finally got my wits together and rubbed some of the blood back in my hands and feet, and my blue fingers were able to hold a match, I took off my wet and frozen clothes, lit the lantern and started a fire. Gradually, the heat began to penetrate and my blood began to pump again through my veins. Outside, the wind increased and there were gusts which also grew in intensity.

I fed the fire carefully, hoarding my coal and wood. Every once in a while I would open the door just an inch and peer out. Whenever I did, however, it seemed as if someone was waiting outside and, at the first streak of light, would slam their shoulders against the door and begin pushing against it. The rush of the wind would fling hail and snow inside, and it was so murky outside it was like peering into a black sombrero in a darkened barn.

As the wind increased the house began to shake. The gusts shook every timber. As the lantern swayed I swear I could see the side of the cabin, taking the full force of the northern blast, begin to bend in. Suddenly there was a terrible wrenching noise—like a giant tearing a fresh pine plank in half and having a hell of a time with the last few splinters—and I felt the house begin to move off the blocks it was on. I held on, for I knew what was coming. And it did. Another blast lifted that small house and it began to slide down the slope toward the Arkansas River.

The stove gave a lurch and the door opened and a shower of hot coals flew out. The barrel of water began to tip and I made a lurch for that. There I was—hot, smoldering coals on the dry plank floor, the lantern swaying like a mad thing, and I clinging for dear life to the barrel of water—while the house was slipping down the slope as if it were on a greased spillway.

Suddenly, it slammed against something. I suspected it might be the well curbing. This gave me time to stamp out the coals and stop the swinging of the lantern. I knew this wasn't the end of my journey in this madhouse, so I sat on the floor, my back propped against the water-barrel and waited.

Another wild gust lifted the house off the well curbing. Again the house began sliding down the ice-coated buffalo grass. Again it stopped, started, stopped. This time I knew I had to get out of that house before it slid into the river.

I knew from the size of the window I would have to remove some of my clothes. I took off my mackinaw and extra shirt and lowered them out of the window with a length of rope. Then I stood on a chair and started to crawl out the window.

Halfway out, my gunbelt caught on the sash and I was stuck, half in the shack and half out, in a raging blizzard. The hail and snow were driving across the prairie on the wings of a seventy-mile wind that slammed me in the face. I couldn't see, and all I could do was struggle as hard as I could and twist in such a way as to unbuckle the gunbelt. As the belt and guns fell inside, I fell out. I landed on my shoulder and almost jarred my teeth loose.

For a moment the wind pasted me against the wall of the shack and then, on hands and knees, I groped like a blind man for my mackinaw and hat. By a miracle I found my mackinaw, but my hat was gone. I started to stumble through the snow— to keep moving was my only hope of staying alive. The wind was at my back, propelling me forward as if by an invisible hand. It was impossible to fight the wind; all I could do was rush forward with it. I could only pray that I was going in the right direction. If I wasn't, I was moving away from town onto the blizzard-locked prairie. If that happened I couldn't hope to last very long.

The thought of death occupied me in those first few steps I took away from the shack. I knew how men died in the snow; the terrible numbness, the strange fading away of strength, the lassitude and then the final moments of slipping into an eternal slumber.

I resolved to fight to the last minute to live. I thought to myself, it would be horrible to end it all now, and I wondered what my mother and father would say. I could see them grieving, my father dry-eyed and grim-faced, telling himself he should never have let me go West in the first place, and my mother, never a crying woman, stony-faced like my father, and weighed down by the grief that clung like a millstone about their hearts.

I can still relive the moments when I stood in the storm, with the breath almost sucked out from my lungs by the howling winds, and swore I would fight it out. I would lick it. Maybe I was out of my head with fear, but I tried shouting my defiance. The words were snatched away before they left my lips.

That I must keep going drummed in my mind. I stumbled through the snow. It was like trying to move in a strange vortex. On all sides unseen forces tripped me, buffeted me, shrieked in my ears with a devilish glee, while high in the sky was a weird, keening noise. There was a wet blackness all about me.

Gradually, the feeling went out of my body. It started in my toes and began spreading upward. After some time—I never knew just how long I was out in the storm—my feet felt like stumps of lead. I tried to warm my hands under my armpits, but it didn't do any good. It seemed as if the only thing alive in my body was my beating heart.

Once I fell and it took all the strength I had to raise myself to my knees. I rose to one knee and said a silent prayer. I knew I was going to die, but I prayed for that one last burst of reserve strength. It came slowly, and somehow I got to my feet again. . . .

The rest is a blank. I dimly recall falling against a wall of a house, hitting it with my fist and crying violently. I was sure I had made a complete circle and had come back to my own shack.

Then suddenly the darkness was speared by a shaft of yellow light. People seemed to be shouting in my ears. Then I slipped into unconsciousness.

I awoke in an old-fashioned tin tub filled with ice and snow and coal oil. Doc Clark was slapping me in the face as hard as he could and shouting orders to the people in the room. I think the only thing that bothered me was that I was naked in a tub and old widow Tubbs was present.

I can recall being rubbed, slapped and battered by Doc and later lying on a bed while the Tubbs woman rubbed me down with towels.

When I tried to rise she shoved me back.

"Land sakes, George," she shouted, "do you think you're different?"

They poured enough whiskey down my throat to float the whole town of Ingalls and finally I could feel the blood beginning to warm my body. It was dawn before Doc said he guessed I would pull through. By that time I was so damn drunk from the whiskey and fatigue I gave a whoop and a holler and tried to get up out of bed.

Of course I collapsed and the widow Tubbs pushed me back. I fell asleep hearing her growling, "Do you think you're different, George Bolds?"

A Swig of White Missouri Mule

IN 1887-88 I made about four trips back home to Indiana, because of Mother, who seemed to be failing. When I came home for Christmas, 1887, a cold hand clutched at my heart when I saw her. As always she was smiling, but her heartiness had been replaced by a frailty I had never seen before. The vivid beauty of the wild rose had been replaced by the fragile beauty of the lily.

Father was grave. When I walked out to the barn in the winter twilight, he slowly shook his head.

"Mother's failing, George," he said quietly.

"Yes, Father, I know," I said. "I wouldn't have known if Dan hadn't written," I reproached him.

"Once a year you come home—last time you left two days after Christmas," he said.

I had no answer. There was no bitterness in him, only an unsaid hurt. To try to make up for my thoughtlessness, I threw myself into the work on the farm. I didn't realize how my muscles had softened until I tried rail-splitting. Dan swung his axe with effortless ease for hours; in half an hour I was puffing, my hands raw.

"Why don't you shoot 'em, gunfighter?" Dan said slyly.

"The hell with you," I told him, and swung that blade until the palms of my hands were skinned. But I didn't give up.

Twice I took a ride over to Portland to see Adda. I had always considered her one of the prettiest girls in Indiana, and now she was at the prime of her beauty. Her father still owned the Merchants' Hotel and they still lived there.

Adda and I went for several rides and once went to an opera, which put me to sleep. I would stay over Saturday and Sunday at the hotel and leave Monday for the farm. On my second visit I was disturbed. I couldn't put my finger on it, but Adda, although as pleasant as always, seemed thoughtful, distant.

"Adda, what's on your mind?" I asked.

She only shook her head and began talking about something else. I had found, too, there were long periods of silence between us now. It seemed as if I had come from a different world; we had little in common to talk about. As always, in the first half-hour of my visit she would chatter away excitedly about this and that—all of which had happened in Portland.

I had only Ingalls to talk about: Ingalls, Dodge and Cimarron. Could I tell her how Jake Shoup had burned the coattails of the town drunk in a Cimarron saloon? Or of Bat Masterson, who was now operating a saloon and gambling place in Denver? Or how the Bartons' OS brand was vanishing from the plains and I was thinking of buying Charlie Eubank's quarter horse when the Eubanks sold their share of the OS spread and went to California . . . ?

We were drifting apart . . . I loved her as much as life itself, but I knew I must come soon to a decision. Adda was not going out West. If I married her, it had to be Indiana. And on her terms. What to do . . . ?

The question whirled around and around my brain on the

ride back to the farm. After I had returned home, Dan saw I was disturbed and asked why. I told him.

"George," he said, looking uneasy, "I heard Tom Devers is courting Adda...."

I could feel my temper rising. Dan always said my eyes narrowed and my face sort of tightened up. I guess it did this time, because he grabbed my arm and said he wanted me to help him with the stock. The more I worked that afternoon, the hotter I became under the collar. It was just getting dark when I threw down my pitchfork. Without saying anything I saddled up Dan's mare.

"It's a long ride to Portland, George," he said calmly. "Don't ride her too hard."

"Tell Father and Mother I'll be back tomorrow," I told him.

When I reached Portland I walked up to the desk of the Merchants' Hotel and asked the amazed clerk to send a boy up to the Weldon suite and ask if Miss Adda could see me. The boy came down and said it was all right for me to go up.

Adda, looking both sleepy and frightened, opened the door. "George! What's wrong?" she asked.

"Adda, are you seeing Tom Devers?" I burst out.

Adda looked at me a moment, then opened the door. "Please come in, George."

I came in and sat down. Adda sat across the room from me. She looked mad. And, as usual, when she was angry she looked her prettiest.

"Do you mean to say, George Bolds, that you rode all the way from Adams County to Portland to wake me up and ask me that?"

"And I'm riding back immediately," I said, "after I find out what's going on."

"There is nothing going on," she said, in a voice as cold as ice.

"We are not engaged, and no man is going to dictate to me."

"Are you seeing Tom Devers?" I asked.

"I am not only seeing Mr. Devers but any gentleman who chooses to call on me," she said. "Does that answer your question, Mr. Bolds?"

We stormed at each other for about an hour, her voice snapping like a lash. She was as distant and cold as a fifth cousin from Alaska. I remember we went over the whole thing about me going out to Kansas and sending her only a few letters and seeing her once, perhaps twice a year.

Suddenly she stopped. After a moment's pause, she said, "George, what is it that keeps you out there? What is it that's stronger than your mother, your father, your home . . . ?"

"And you," I added.

"And me," she said.

Answer her, I told myself. But how to answer her? What was out there? Adventure? Even that had paled by now. The towns were only dirty, dusty streets and clapboard houses; the fame of men whom I had pictured as great heroes rested only on their ability to draw a six-shooter faster than another man.

What was it then? Perhaps the sense of participation in history in the making; the sense of being part of that which will never be again; the sense of walking with the last . . . ?

I tried to put all this into words. Adda sat and studied me as I talked. When I had finished, she said in a soft voice, "Go back there, George."

"I want us *both* to go back, Adda," I said.

"The choice is yours to make," she said. "I will not live on the frontier. I've seen some of the women from out there." She shook her head. "I don't have to, George."

"Your mother and my mother came out here," I said.

She stood up. "I'm sorry, George."

"I'll be back, Adda," I said. At the door I leaned down and kissed her. I felt her arms around my neck and I knew that she loved me as much as I loved her. But I also knew Adda Weldon; wild horses couldn't drag her to Kansas. If she were to come, she would come only because she wanted to. I knew there was no asking her about Tom Devers.

She slammed the door so hard the knob almost came off. I started across the lobby and if that clerk or bellboy had said one word I would have knocked their heads together.

I'm surprised Dan's horse wasn't wind-broke by the time I got him back to the stable. The poor beast just stood there, his lungs working like bellows as I rubbed him down. Half the time I wasn't even following the roads. I was getting madder and madder by the hour. I knew Tom Devers was in the banking business. He was a nice enough fellow, but it took what little common sense I still possessed not to look him up that very night and tell him to keep away from Adda or suffer the consequences. I'm glad I didn't. Adda, who was a spitfire when aroused, might have refused to see me again . . . or Tom might have beaten the tar out of me.

I wasn't much good the next week. Father probably guessed at the reason and didn't say much. The only thing that took my mind off the subject was Mother's improved health. It made us all happier. Along about February or March of 1888 I began thinking about making tracks for Kansas. After all, I did have a business and some land and they had to be seen to. But Mother and Adda were closest to my thoughts and I put Kansas behind me.

It was Uncle John Pine who decided for me. Since I had left Indiana, Cousin Joe, who had developed into a handsome young hellion, had drifted across the West—logging in the Northwest, working a claim in the Dakotas, trading with the Indians and just drifting. He hadn't been home in three years, Father told me.

That night we were eating supper when a rider came up. It was Joe's father, Uncle John, and he got to the straight of it as soon as he sat down.

"Joe's been arrested as a horse thief in Cassville, Missouri, and they'll probably hang him," his father said. "Here's a letter from the sheriff."

I read the scrawl, which said that Joe had stolen a horse in Cassville and was being held for trial. The sheriff urged that someone come at once from his family. Horse-thievery may be a joke today, but on the frontier it was a monstrous crime. You didn't steal just a horse, you stole a man's form of livelihood, his only means of transportation and probably the most expensive thing he owned. The horse-thief was lucky to reach jail; usually a posse stretched his neck as soon as he was caught.

Uncle John pulled another letter from his pocket. It was from Joe, explaining he had borrowed the horse to visit a girl in the neighborhood and while he was a-visiting the horse was stolen. A logical excuse, but the owner of the horse wanted his horse and not excuses.

"What can we do?" Dan asked. No one said anything, but they all looked at me.

"Send a telegram to the sheriff offering to pay for the horse," I said.

"The man wants his horse or the money, George," Father said, "not a piece of paper. Who's going to take him the money?"

"George will," Mother said, sweet as her own warm apple pie. "He's leaving for Kansas and that can be on his way." She turned to me. "You were leaving in the morning, weren't you, George?"

I just stared at her, open-mouthed. "Yes, ma'am," I said at last.

Uncle John looked relieved as he counted out two hundred dollars.

"I guess that should take care of it, George," he said. "Lord, what a relief, Leah."

"When that boy of yours comes home you'd better keep him under better control," Mother said firmly.

"Yes, ma'am," Uncle John said grimly. I wondered whether it wouldn't be better for Joe to stay in jail.

After Uncle John had gone, I started to talk, but Mother just hushed me.

"You've been like a disturbed hen on an egg, son," she said. "I don't blame you. I'd like to get away myself."

"Will you come out, Mother?" I asked.

She smiled at me. "Perhaps next summer," she said. "Perhaps Father and I will come and see your Wild West."

Father was a little more practical. When we were saying goodnight he added, "You can think things out better away from here, George."

"Adda wants me to come back, Father," I said.

He held up his hand. "It's up to you to decide, son. You and Adda. Will you be leaving in the morning?"

I nodded. He looked me in the eye. "Don't make it too long next time, George."

"I won't, sir."

At St. Louis I learned that Cassville was the county seat of Barry County in the southwestern part of the state. I had to buy a ticket on the 'Frisco to a small place called Exeter, then go by stage to Cassville.

It was a long and boring journey. I reached Exeter at five

o'clock in the morning. I had to wait at the deserted depot for two hours until the station man came along and opened it. I was almost frozen stiff by the time he rode up in his buckboard. He said something about it being cold and then unlocked the door. Inside the station, it was as damp and chilly as a tomb. When I told him where I wanted to go, he said he had to send someone to the house of the man who drove the stage to Cassville. I gave him a fifty-cent piece for a boy, but he went himself while I stood behind his counter to tell people he would be back soon.

I didn't sell any tickets and he returned in about fifteen minutes with a lanky, bearded fellow who looked as if he should be in jail instead of driving a stage. He said he would pick up the mail and drive me over for ten dollars.

"Ten dollars!" I said. "That's the price of a ticket to Kansas City."

"Five dollars," he said.

"Two dollars, you old outlaw," I said.

We settled on two dollars and fifty cents. The old driver went out to hitch up the stage while I had breakfast.

On the way out of Exeter the driver asked me if I had a gun. When I said I had one in my carpetbag, he asked me to take it out. Road agents, it seemed, had robbed the mail stage two weeks before. I took out my gun, put on my gunbelt and rode to Cassville on the box, while he took generous swigs from his jug of white Missouri mule.

When we entered the village, he asked, "Where do you want to stop, Mister?"

"The jail," I said.

He pointed with his whip to a ramshackle old building with slats across the windows.

I told him to pull up and I swung off with my bag.

"When are you riding back?" I asked.

"Anytime you say, Mister," he said. "For five dollars."

"But you only charged me two-and-a-half dollars from Exeter," I pointed out.

"You had a gun and the mail needed protection," he said. "I ain't got nothing going back 'cept you."

After telling him to pick me up at the one hotel in the place, I entered the jail yard. It was littered with trash. I knocked on the front door, but there wasn't any answer so I walked inside. I found myself at the entrance of a narrow corridor about fifteen feet long and about four feet wide, with four small cells facing each other.

As soon as I entered, two rats, nibbling on some stale bread, looked up, but didn't stop eating. I walked down the hall and looked into the cells. All were empty and incredibly dirty.

There was an old chair near the door, so I sat down and watched the rats gnaw away at the crust. After about an hour I heard footsteps and stood up. A man with a rusty mustache and a beard so stained with tobacco juice that it looked dyed brown on one side, swayed in. He looked as if he had slept in his clothes.

"How did you get in here?" he demanded.

"Walked in," I said.

"What do you want, young fellow?" he asked.

"My business is with the sheriff," I said.

He pulled himself up to his full height. "I'm the boss here, sonny, and you tell me your business or get out."

Suddenly a rat leaped right between us and I almost jumped out of my shoes.

"How much do they pay you?" I asked.

"Fifteen a month with board when I have prisoners. When we haven't any, I only get the board," he said.

"Why don't you take care of those rats as long as you don't have any prisoners?" I asked.

"Too damn many," he said.

Then I told him I had heard that if you shoot around where rats are, they'll leave. I pointed to a big rat sitting there washing its face, its whiskers twitching, and suggested to the jailer that he peg a shot at him. He unbuckled the top of the holster that held his gun, and after sighting, fired. A hole appeared in the wall about three inches over the rat's head. The rat jumped a bit but went back to licking his paws. The black powder fogged up the place, and the jailer began cursing like the devil.

"Where's the sheriff?" I asked.

"None of your damn business," he said.

The rat was still washing himself and I thought maybe this fellow needed his memory jogged. I slapped leather and blasted the rat. It spun around and kicked a few times. The jailer seemed impressed, although anyone who was a fair shot could have killed the rodent. All you had to be was sober, which he wasn't.

"No black powder," he said. "What do you use?"

"Fanamite," I told him. "Now where's the sheriff?"

"He'll be back at noon," he said, "and I don't think he'll like it when I tell him you were shooting up the place."

I gave the fellow a dollar and he finally told me that Joe Pine was in a barn not far away, tied up, because the jail had no windows and the prisoners were always running away. I persuaded the jailer to send a boy down to the hotel and get some food for Joe. When it arrived I gave the kid two bits to bring the stuff to Joe and to tell him I would see him when the sheriff arrived.

In about five minutes the kid came back, shouting that Jim, the Negro who had been left to guard Joe, was dead. My heart dropped like a stone in a brook. I thought Joe certainly had a noose around his neck now. We ran down to the old barn and found an old Negro, nursing a swollen eye and looking as if the sky had fallen in on him.

Joe had managed to untie his bonds and had slugged the old fellow. And to top off the morning, he had stolen the sheriff's horse. The jailer tried to put me in jail, but I pushed him aside and told him to inform the sheriff I would be at the local hotel.

The stage left without me, but the old thief said the price would be the same the next day.

The sheriff came in at noon, mad as a hornet after listening to the story told by the jailer. He rode off, ordering me to stay put until he came back, which I promised to do. I was in the hotel's saloon when I heard some of the town boys talking about the jail-break. My God, you'd think someone had broken out of the Jeff City Penitentiary, the way one fellow told it.

I couldn't get to sleep, which was not surprising when I considered the mattress, which seemed to have been stuffed with rocks, so I got up about midnight and sat by the window. There were lamps along the one main street and I thought I saw a man standing by a gate under one lamp. I watched him. After a while he moved up and down a few paces and I could see he was carrying a rifle.

There was only one reason why a man with a rifle would be watching the hotel—and the reason was me. I dressed, strapped on my gun and went downstairs. I went out the back door, up a few alleys and made a wide swing to come up in the rear of the figure with the gun. It would have been foolhardy to outline myself against the light by crossing the street.

I entered the back gate of the house across from the hotel and walked up the yard as quietly as I could. Just beyond the pool of lamplight was the man, his greatcoat buttoned up about his neck and an old knitted hat pulled down about his ears, stamping up and down in the bitter night air. He had a rifle cradled under one arm.

I crept up behind him, drew my gun and said quickly, "Drop that rifle and turn around."

I thought he'd jump over the moon. The rifle fell and his arms shot up.

"Don't shoot," he kept saying. "Don't shoot. . . ."

It was the drunken jailer. When he turned at my order, the smell of Missouri white mule was so strong it almost melted my gun buckle.

"What are you doing here?" I asked.

"Guarding you," he said.

"On whose orders?" I said.

"The sheriff's," he answered. "He came back after supper and said to guard you. I'm getting two dollars."

I suddenly had an idea. "I don't trust that man," I said.

"What man?" he asked.

"Your sheriff," I said. "He looks like an outlaw who's wanted in Dodge. A mean-looking cuss if I ever saw one."

"Boone White?" the jailer said. "He's been here for ten years."

"Just about the time that killing was done," I said. "Murdered a saloon-keeper and his whole family."

I went up to him and showed him my Gray County deputy's badge. "I'm the law, Mister," I said, "and if you're a good citizen you must obey my orders. I'll pay you three dollars."

It was the three dollars that got him. "I'm a law-abiding man," he said.

"Take your rifle and guard the sheriff's house," I said. "If he leaves, come a-running. I'll be waiting."

I gave him the money and he was off like a shot. When I went back to my room I laughed so much I wore myself out, and those rocks in the mattress felt just like balls of cotton.

The next morning it was the jailer, of course, who notified me the sheriff was coming to see me. He looked so numb with the cold that I bought him breakfast and a new pint.

A short time later the sheriff hitched up in front of the hotel. He was slightly mollified because his horse had come back during the night with a note from Joe attached to the saddle. Joe apologized in the note for having borrowed it and promised to send back fifty dollars, when he had it, to pay for the other horse.

The sheriff wasn't a bad fellow, but there was still the question of the jail break and the Negro guard Joe had hit. He was all for sending out a poster of Joe to the other counties, but I kept talking, telling him about the Pines and what good people they were.

"Where are you from, Mister?" he asked.

"Ingalls," I said. "Five miles from Cimarron—although we don't brag about it."

"Isn't that in Ford County?" he asked.

"No, Gray. Dodge is in Ford," I said.

"Know many fellows in Dodge?" he asked.

"A few," I said cautiously, "all lawmen."

"Colonel Harvester?" he asked hopefully.

"I've sat at Jane Harvester's table many times," I said. He became all smiles. "Jane's my cousin," he said. "I had a letter from her last month. Let's have a drink."

We went over to the saloon and lifted a few. Before we shook hands and said goodbye, we both agreed that Joe should have his pants lowered and his backside tanned, but that he was a good kid and fifty dollars should take care of the farmer whose horse he had borrowed. Ten dollars made the Negro guard my friend for life and two dollars and another bottle of white Missouri mule took care of my friend the jailer. The sheriff did me one last favor: he told the stagecoach driver I was to ride back to Exeter for two dollars. The old thief didn't say a word on the return trip.

When I reached Kansas City I sent the rest of the money back to Uncle John Pine by a brakeman I knew, along with a letter explaining the whole matter. I also sent a note to a certain young lady in Portland, but I didn't think it would do much good. It didn't.

Curiously, none of us ever saw Cousin Joe Pine again. We had all kinds of reports as the years went by, but I guess Joe never stopped climbing those western hills.

I reached Ingalls at the height of a snowstorm. I was the only one to get off the train and it seemed to me the conductor was so damn glad to get out of there he practically pushed me off the last step. I stood there for a moment, watching the caboose lamp wink out in the swirling snow. Then I started up the street for my office.

I didn't feel just right somehow. Perhaps it was the feeling that my mother was ill; perhaps it was a guilty conscience, perhaps it was the fear that I had lost Adda. Perhaps it was a combination. I don't know. I *do* know that if someone had come along to my office that day and given me a hundred dollars for the whole outfit, I would have taken it and highballed back to Indiana.

I wish I had, for trouble was just over the hill.

"Bleeding Kansas"

INGALLS prospered and Cimarron simmered, as Asa Soule made good his many promises. A hotel was erected in Ingalls, along with many business rooms, as we called them in those days. A large mercantile house was established to supply the needs of the settlers, and my old friend John W. Glynn was placed in charge. A newspaper was another one of Soule's donations. It was called the Ingalls *Union*, under the editorship of Bob Turner. Many new people came in with capital and soon all kinds of businesses were represented.

Meanwhile, the county seat wars were erupting across Kansas. The law was a six-shooter around a man's waist. To understand the reasons for these county seat wars, one must be aware of the conflicts which reached a final peak in the Battle of Cimarron in January, 1889. There were other episodes of violence in the state which preceded the struggle in which I was to play a major part.

I was astounded to learn that in an address made some years ago by a learned Kansas judge that we of Ingalls were "ruffians," "outlaws" and "hired gunfighters" because of what we did in

Cimarron that January day. How that judge could describe Bill Tilghman, one of the great marshals of the West, in that fashion, I'll never know. We were all deputy sheriffs fulfilling a civic duty: removing county records to the county offices. The judge is gone, along with most of those who took part in our county seat war, and I'm the last survivor. I will tell you what I saw. The slugs in my body should give testimony as to my participation in that bloody event.

But first I must go back to the few years before I settled in Ingalls. By 1885 the vast tide of immigration which streamed into Kansas had overflowed the short-grass prairie as far as the Colorado border and beyond. Perhaps this was the result of the land promoters' campaigns. Any quarter-section—one hundred and sixty acres—was supposed to be the most fertile farmland in America. They said Kansas sod held more water than any other part of the United States, that the breaking of the sod had increased the retention of moisture. I believe that's where the phrase, "Rain follows the plow," came from. This was the state of affairs I found when I first left Dodge for Cimarron and Ingalls.

In riding around the country I got to know some of the people in other counties. Everyone was a promoter for his own township. All you would have to do was to light up a cigar and say in a courteous way that you liked a town and suddenly you were the center of attention. Five people would be filling your ears with the glories of the future and pleading with you to settle right there. A campaign for a county seat was sometimes started by a speculator who raised a few pine board shacks and spent some money on promotion. If your spot was made a county seat, all you did was sell your land, which you'd bought dirt cheap, to the new immigrants at a nice profit.

I think my first experience with the county seat wars in

"Bleeding Kansas"

Kansas began about 1885, when the Grant County people held an election to decide whether Appomattox or Ulysses would be the county seat. In the election each citizen was paid ten dollars apiece for voting! Both towns also checked to make sure there were no repeaters. However, the Supreme Court of Kansas upset the vote, declaring that any balloting carried on in moonlight on the prairie without a ballot box or ballots was highly irregular and, in fact, invalid.

Blood was almost spilled a short time later when the votes were to be cast again. I rode up to Appomattox with some of the Cimarron boys to see what was going on. Evidently the bosses of both towns had made some secret agreement, which had leaked out while the voting was going on. The citizens of Appomattox had come to the conclusion that they had been sold out, and when we rode into town more than one group had their guns ready and were making nooses.

For twenty-four hours an uneasy quiet hung over the town, while the sheriff frantically tried to work out a compromise between both sides. Finally an agreement was reached and the representatives from both towns were released and rode out of town in a hurry. Tempers cooled, but this was an indication that "county seat" were fighting words in Kansas.

In 1887 in Ingalls we heard of the gun battles in Coronado City; a gunfighter named Coulter started to gun some people who were sponsoring another town. They buried him in Boot Hill, but some of his friends came up from Texas and there was hell to pay for a while.

About the same time in Stevens County the county war situation erupted into blood and gunfire. It began when Hugoton made claim to the county seat. Woodsdale, a neighboring community, insisted *it* was more centrally located and should be the seat of county government. In Woodsdale, Sam Wood, a young fire-eater, was the spokesman. I think he was an attorney. Sometime in 1887 a gang from Hugoton kidnapped Sam and took him to the Nations Strip. The leader of the gang returned to Woodsdale and said Sam had been bought out and had gone farther west. Nobody in Woodsdale believed this, so they rounded up a posse and set out to look for Sam.

They found the trail of the kidnapper in the Nations, and one of the men discovered a campsite with a scrawled piece of paper bearing Wood's name. That same day they caught the gang on the banks of a creek in what is now Beaver Creek, Oklahoma, and "arrested" them. I was in Garden City the day Sam and his men returned and I believe more whiskey was sold under the counter that day and night than at any one time in dry Kansas.

The following year Hugoton was temporarily named the county seat, but a dispute over railroad bonds brought the feud between the towns back to life. It got so bad that the marshals brought the leaders of both sides to Voorhees, a smaller town nearby and a sort of neutral ground, to effect a peace. The dispute was so violent that a gunfight broke out and the sheriff of Hugoton wounded his own deputy.

Ironically, the warrant for the arrest of the Hugoton sheriff was put into the hands of the Woodsdale sheriff, and it was at this point that the pent-up hate in the southwestern part of the state exploded. The sheriff of Woodsdale, probably chuckling with satisfaction, tried to arrest the sheriff of Hugoton. They met in the main street of Voorhees and fought it out with guns. But they were miserable shots, and all they did was smash some windows and kill a horse. The citizens of Voorhees, sorry they'd ever volunteered as peacemakers, wired Governor John A. Martin, and he sent in the militia.

"Bleeding Kansas"

That summer the most terrible episode of the whole county seat wars occurred. Sheriff Robinson of Hugoton left the county after that shooting match; Sheriff Short of Woodsdale got a posse together and rode into the Nations to search for him. He captured him after another gun battle but, fearing the reaction of Robinson's friends, sent a rider back to Woodsdale for reinforcements.

A posse of about five or six men from Woodsdale saddled up and rode into the Strip, camping at a spot called Wild Horse Lake. Robinson of Hugoton, meanwhile, had managed to escape by slipping his bonds while the others were asleep. He started for home. Meanwhile, his town's citizens had raised a posse of about fifteen guns and were searching for him when Robinson encountered the party. He ordered his men to join him in vengeance by raiding Short's camp. On Wild Horse Lake they came upon the relief party sent out from Woodsdale on Short's orders. When the gunsmoke cleared, five or six men were dead. One man, who had been left for dead, swore that the Hugoton people lined them up and shot them down in cold blood. From that day on, it was always referred to as the Haymeadow Massacre.

Sam Wood of Woodsdale was in a frenzy when he heard about the killings and swore he'd find the murderers. He saddled up and with the help of his fellow townspeople hunted relentlessly day and night until he had every man behind bars. When he had his prisoners roped together he brought them back to Woodsdale, which was under martial law. The head of the militia escorted his prisoners to the nearest federal court, which was in Texas. However, their convictions were reversed and they were set free.

I saw one of them sometime later in Ingalls; he never let his gun away from his side. He even wore his gunbelt to bed.

"If I ever meet Sam Wood," he said to me, "I know it's going to be either him or me."

By 1888 or so, six counties in southwestern Kansas had been combined to form one judicial section. We were interested to see who the governor was going to appoint as judge. The bitterness which had developed between Ingalls and Cimarron was now even more intense, and the bad feeling between Hugoton and Woodsdale had not lessened. The new judge was from Topeka: Theodosius Botkin, a well known Kansas lawyer, a slight, mild-mannered man, but a hell-raiser once he was aroused.

In the beginning Sam Wood and Botkin were very close, but they fell apart. Some years later came the Wood-Botkin feud—which lasted even after one of them was dead. Botkin was holding court at Hugoton one day when Sam Wood rode into town with his wife. He left his wife and her lady friend sitting in the carriage and went into the courthouse on an errand. In the courtroom was a man who had testified for his brother in the Haymeadow Massacre case. The moment he saw Sam he went outside and waited by the front door.

Sam came out about fifteen minutes later and walked to his carriage. The man calmly took aim and shot Sam in the back. He staggered to the side of the courthouse and reached for his gun, but the man followed him and, while Sam's wife screamed, carefully took aim and shot Sam in the back a second time. Sam was taken inside the courthouse and died an hour later in a courtroom.

The killer was taken into custody but never brought to trial. Partisanship in the county wars had taken such a hold on the citizens that out of a hundred eligible voters, the sheriff was unable to get an impartial jury. One half said Sam was a martyr;

the other half said he was a damn scoundrel who should have been hanged long ago.

I don't think I am stretching the long bow when I say a "reign of terror" was sweeping over southwestern Kansas. The fact that Sam Wood's killer was not brought to trial and was even released within a few days seemed a license to kill without retaliation. Men were bushwhacked and dead men were found on dark roads. County issues became personal issues, and there was more feuding in the counties of Kansas than in the Ozarks.

A short time after Sam's murder, Judge Botkin opened court in Springfield. Feeling ran so high that the sheriff of the county sent out deputies to gather a posse to protect Botkin on his way to court. About four o'clock in the afternoon the sheriff and his men—about ten of them—started for Judge Botkin's home. Midway, anti-Botkin people bushwhacked the party. The sheriff was shot out of his saddle and was dead before he even hit the ground. His deputy had his arm shattered and the rest of the men scattered. They soon regrouped and the twilight echoed with the crash of rifles and six-shooters. It kept up until after dark, when the bushwhackers crept away.

When word reached Judge Botkin he was furious. He changed from a mild-mannered little frontier judge into a fire-eater. Riders galloped along the lanes and back roads of the county that night, summoning his followers to his place. By morning, instead of a white clapboard house, his home resembled a Civil War outpost. Lines of men were strung out before the house and pickets were posted far up the road. You couldn't come within a mile of Botkin's place without being stopped by a man with a gun who demanded to know who you were and what business you had with the judge. Even those who were going to visit persons who were neighbors of the judge were turned back.

The people of Springfield sent a wire to the governor and he ordered the militia out. Judge Botkin was indignant. "Send me guns and ammunition," he wired back to the governor, "I have the men." But finally the militia took over and a calm settled over the countryside. But Judge Botkin refused to open his court. In the end he resigned, because he knew it was worth his life to ride into any one of those counties.

Bullets and Ballot Boxes

WHILE KANSAS was seething internally with these county wars Asa Soule was proceeding with his campaign to make Ingalls the county seat of Gray County. He was also building up Montezuma, in the southern part of the county, and Ensign, just east of Montezuma. Ingalls was booming and the people of Cimarron were getting worried. They petitioned the governor for a special election for the county seat and finally a date in November, 1888, was set for the election of the county seat and a full slate of county officers.

Violent days followed. If an Ingalls man rode into Cimarron he was a marked man. He was in for a beating or he would be cornered until he was forced to draw. When the reports of the violence reached Soule in New York, he offered to buy up the town of Cimarron and consolidate it with Ingalls. But the people of Cimarron—my friend Jake Shoup was one of the leaders—refused because, as they later explained, they thought Ingalls was only a boom town and would soon vanish from the prairie. But many new settlers seemed to be attracted by Soule's rosy propaganda and they wanted to see what Ingalls was like.

And, liking what they found there, they stayed and built their homes.

I had switched my allegiance from Cimarron to Ingalls simply because a large section of the land I owned was in Ingalls. I had built the third business house in the town and I felt that my roots were really in this mushrooming frontier community. Soon all kinds of threats reached me: I would be shot on sight as soon as I roamed down Cimarron's main street. But I sent word back to any interested party that two make a shooting match.

After numerous petitions had been circulated around the county by the Cimarron people, the governor ordered a special election. Soule, confident he controlled the votes in the northern part of the county because he had given farmers work on his various projects, thought we would win. Everyone in Ingalls was confident our town would be the county seat.

The rest of the boys from Ingalls and I were congratulating ourselves when a rider came up to my surveying office and said, "George, I think we're going to have trouble with Foote Township." Foote Township, in the northern part of the county, had seventy votes and I had heard rumors that the town's leaders were saying, the hell with Soule and the railroad, they wanted cold cash for their votes. I had heard reports of night riders holding meetings in barns, so the talk of bad news from Foote was no surprise to me or the rest of the leaders of Ingalls. The rider told us of a society called the Dark Lantern Society, which had put a price of seven thousand dollars on their seventy votes.

The leader of the Dark Lantern Society rode into Cimarron a few days after the election announcement was posted and put the proposition before several of the town's leaders. They were turned down. Then they rode into Ingalls and paid the Gilbert boys a visit. John Gilbert told them politely to go to hell. "If we can't win the county seat honestly, we don't want it," he told them.

The Dark Lantern Society men rode back to Cimarron. That afternoon they had a meeting with the town leaders and indicating, without saying as much, that the Ingalls people were ready to buy their votes. The Cimarron boys held a secret meeting and, after a long conference, told the men from Foote Township that they would pay them seven thousand dollars for their seventy votes. The Foote Township people agreed but demanded the money in advance. That led to an impasse. The Cimarron people went back into conference.

Finally they came up with a proposition: they would draw up a contract agreeing to pay the Foote Township voters seven thousand dollars for their votes, the money to be paid immediately after the election. What one of the Foote Township men said about the deal seems to sum up their feelings: "We don't have much of a hankering for Soule, his hop bitters, for your damn town of Ingalls or for Cimarron, for that matter. We don't care who wins the county seat. So as far as we are concerned, our votes are for sale and they go to the highest bidder. Let Ingalls and Cimarron fight it out. . . ."

Finally, the contract was drawn up and signed in Cimarron by both parties. When news of this became known the bitterness between the two rival towns became more intense. One day a delegation from Cimarron, all packing guns, rode to Ingalls. They stopped on the outskirts of town and a rider came in to find me to escort them in.

They rode into town, with me in the lead. I had the feeling that a thousand guns were trained on us; one wrong move from the Cimarron people and I think Ingalls would have resembled a Fourth of July in hell. We stopped at my office, where a number of Ingalls men were waiting. For a minute it was tense. Then Jake Shoup said, "We don't want any trouble. We just want to make a proposition to you people."

"Go ahead, Jake," I said, "spout your piece."

"Well, it isn't that we don't trust you people," Jake said, "but we know you people don't trust any Cimarron people. So we thought that you could appoint a man to be at our poll and we'll have one at yours. That way there won't be any chance of any shady business."

"Well, that's fair, Jake," I said.

We stood there a few minutes, talking about the crops and the folks coming into the territory. Then someone in our crowd said, "George, why don't we bring these coyotes down to the hotel and give them a feed?"

Jake just looked at me and I knew damn well he thought this was a plan to poison the whole bunch. The look on his face was so funny I couldn't help laughing. The rest of the boys began chuckling and that broke the ice for a bit.

Later we walked over to the hotel. We must have been a sight to the townspeople—a lot of tough-looking hombres ankling down the main street with enough belly hardware to shoot our way out of Gettysburg.

The hotel put up a nice feed, but the air was slightly strained. Our people sat on one side of the table, Jake and his boys on the other side. Any moment I thought sure some fool would open the ball. Luckily, everything went along peaceful.

As the Cimarron boys walked out, Jake drew me aside. "Tell me one thing, George."

"If I can, Jake."

"Where in the hell does this Soule get all the money?" he asked. "Lord, he's building bridges, canals, towns and what not. We thought in Cimarron he'd go broke long ago."

"Well, Jake," I said, trying to act as smooth and cool as he was, "Old man Soule has hundreds of barrels of money back East, and to tell the truth he hasn't even got down to the bottom of the *first* barrel...."

Jake gave me one look to tell me I was too damn smart for my own good and walked out.

I knew as they rode up the street and out of town that despite the polite words and the big feed and the glasses of redeye we'd downed together there was still trouble in the air.

Inside my office, I met one of the Ingalls men. He had broken open his six-shooter and was looking it over. I took off my gunbelt and did the same thing. We didn't exchange a word. We didn't have to. I guess trouble has a way of knocking on a man's heart before it enters.

The morning of the election dawned clear and crisp. It seemed as if the whole town was astir at sunup and most of the men were at my office at dawn. When I came in they stopped talking and looked at me. I knew what they had in mind: I was to go down to Cimarron.

"Now look here," I said, "I'm not a-going. That's the sheriff's job." But they wouldn't take no for an answer and they had a lot of logic on their side. Most of them were newcomers and I had lived with the Cimarron people and was friendly with them. As one man said, "Hell, George, they'll shoot us without an argument. At least they'll *listen* to you."

Suddenly I was the only man in the world who had even *been* to Cimarron. I was the only one to talk to Jake Shoup. You'd think, to hear them talk, George Bolds was the oracle of the West. Well, I said to myself, I'm the goat. So I told them I would go and supervise the Cimarron election as Ingalls' representative. To look at their faces you'd think I had just given them a dozen gold pieces.

I took off my gunbelt and put it in the drawer with my surveying instruments. I answered the blank look on their faces with, "There's a law in this part of the country that says you can't shoot an unarmed man. I'm going to make damned sure I'm going into Cimarron without being shot."

I saddled my horse and rode across the prairie toward Cimarron. It was a beautiful morning, but any man in my position that morning who can say he wasn't a frightened man is either a fool or a liar. I wasn't sure I would ever get out of Cimarron alive.

When I got to Cimarron I hitched up and went to the place where they were going to hold the election. One of the Cimarron men, Bob McCause, saw me and said, "What the hell are you doing here?"

"Just a-visiting," I said. Then Charlie Dixon, a great bull hog, said, "Get out of here, Bolds. We don't allow any Ingalls people in Cimarron."

Bob McCause was the lawyer who'd drawn up the contract with the Foote Township people. I handed him a letter which was signed by the sheriff and some of the other leaders of Ingalls, certifying that I was to be one of the official representatives of Ingalls at the Cimarron voting. Bob just read it quickly, grunted and tore the letter in half. "You'd better get out of here, Bolds," he said, as he threw the scraps on the floor.

"You people made an agreement with us that we were to exchange representatives at the election. I don't give a damn whether you have someone at Ingalls or not," I said. "All I know is that we're keeping our part of the bargain."

"You're going to get hurt, George," Charlie Dixon warned.

I pointed to my belt. "I'm unarmed, and if I get shot by any of you people there's a couple of hundred people in Ingalls who would raise more hell in Cimarron than you could handle." I said this with a great deal of bravado. But the truth was, I was shaking in my boots.

Meanwhile, Charlie Dixon, Bob McCause, Jake Shoup and several others, after a whispered conference among themselves, picked up the ballot boxes and hurried out. I ran after them. When they entered a small building down the block I was at their heels. "You going to vote *here,* boys?" I asked.

Bob McCause, who had the ballot boxes under his arm, said, "None of your damn business," and Charlie Dixon, looking mean as the devil, put his hand on the butt of his gun.

"Look here," I said. "If you vote here it's going to be declared illegal. I'm going to follow you to every hole in the wall you've got in this town to see that this election is carried off in the proper fashion. But it won't be according to law if it's not held in the city hall, so I suggest we all go back there and do it right."

"Let me throw this young squirt out the window," said Charlie as he started toward me.

Jake stepped between us. "Hold on, Charlie," he said. "Let's have a conference."

After they had whispered again together Bob McCause said, "Let's go back to City Hall."

On the way back to the city hall I walked in the middle. Jake called me aside. "Look, George," he said, "we've all known you for a long time, and if you don't get the hell out of here you're going to be shot."

"You wouldn't shoot me, Jake," I said. "I haven't got a gun."

"Maybe *I* wouldn't, George," he said, "but those fellows would. Look there."

I followed his finger. A couple of fellows in the windows

across the street, Winchesters laid across their knees, were watching us. "You going now, George?" Jake said.

"You don't think I'm going out in the street to get shot at?" I said.

Once back in the city hall, Bob and the others grabbed the ballot boxes and ran out again toward the building we had just left. Immediately there was a sharp crack and a metallic ping. After a moment of silence there was another crack and a window crashed, not far from where I was standing.

I looked out quickly and saw gunsmoke drifting out of one of the windows. I knew I was being gunned. I crouched under the window, heading toward the back of the room, where I hoped to find somebody's gunbelt or a rifle hung up on the wall, which wasn't unusual in those days.

I didn't find a thing except the ballots the Cimarron people were going to use. The ballots in those days were about the size of our present dollar bill. There were four small packages tied together. I put the packages in my coat pocket. Bob McCause, I thought, might have the ballot boxes, but by the good Lord in heaven, *I'd* have the votes.

The boys with the Winchesters across the street opened fire. Glass splintered and slugs shook the front door. George, I told myself, you're a fool to stay here to be shot at like a clay pigeon when you haven't even got a gun. Get out of here, George, I said. I edged up to a window and shouted, "The train will be in the depot in about ten minutes. If you let Jake Shoup walk with me to the depot I'll go back to Ingalls. If you don't, you'll have to kill me because I'm not a-going to leave."

The firing stopped. Someone called out that they would agree to my terms. Jake stepped into the doorway a few minutes later. I stepped up behind him, flipped his gun out of his holster, spun him round and pushed him ahead of me outside.

There was a large group of Cimarron people, all heavily armed, standing by the barber shop. Out of the corner of my eye I could see the men in the upstairs windows half-raise their Winchesters. We started to walk slowly past them. No one moved, but I saw Charlie Dixon's hand drop to his gun butt. When I came abreast of him I stopped.

"It's agreed I'm going to get that train back to Ingalls?" I asked.

Bob McCause and some of the others said, "That's agreed, George."

I nodded to Charlie Dixon and a few of the other men standing about. "If I'm shot in the back this cocked hammer is going to put Jake in a very bad fix. In fact, it's going to blow him to hell."

"Go ahead, George," Bob called out.

We continued along. Just as we got to the depot the train pulled in.

"Feel all right, Jake?" I asked Shoup.

"Sure, George," he said. "I knew you was a-bluffing, but I wouldn't tell those fellows. Hell, I knew you wouldn't shoot me . . . we've been friends too long for you to do that."

"Jake," I said, "you'd be surprised what friends do to friends. Now take your gun and go your way and I'll go mine."

He waved and began walking up the street. I hopped on the train. The conductor, a friend of mine named Adams, took my ticket money and remarked as he looked out the window, "Looks like there's a hangin' or a funeral in Cimarron."

I could see the men milling about in front of the barber shop. I knew if they ever got back in that city hall and found the ballots gone I'd really be in trouble. "For God's sake, Adams," I said. "There's going to be a hangin' and a funeral *both* in Cimarron if this train doesn't get out of this depot!"

He didn't ask any questions but jumped down the steps of the car and waved his hand to the engineer. To me it seemed a million years before that rickety old train creaked its way past Cimarron.

When we were out of sight of the town I took the ballots out of my pockets, tore them in half and left a trail of paper from Cimarron to Ingalls.

Back home, I reported to the committee. There were lots of hard words and more than one gun oiled, but cooler minds prevailed. The Ingalls people stayed home and waited.

The next morning Bob Turner, the *Union* editor, came riding up to my office. He grinned as he held out a press dispatch. It read: "Ingalls man steals Cimarron ballots. . . ." The rest of the story was devoted to the report that the deputy sheriff of Cimarron was coming to arrest me.

I strapped on my guns and waited. So did most of the men in Ingalls. But the Cimarron people never showed up.

After they gunned me out of town the Cimarron people had more trouble. The Foote Township Dark Lantern Society demanded their seven thousand dollars. They produced their "contract," but the town leaders pointed out that the names of the Cimarron leaders were forged. The Foote Township riders were furious. Jake told me later that more hands were on gun butts than at any other time in the history of Cimarron. But the Foote people left without any blood being spilled.

The election did take place. Cimarron won, but only because they stuffed the ballot boxes. The case was taken to the courts, which found that my ejection from Cimarron, the Foote Township "contract" and the brazen ballot-box stuffing had made the election illegal. The court designated Ingalls as the proper county seat. But A. T. Riley, the county clerk, and some of the other town leaders sent word that they and the records would remain in Cimarron as long as the city hall remained standing.

The Cimarron officials doggedly took the case to a higher court. "It is claimed by the citizens of Cimarron," wrote Chief Justice Horton in his decision, "that the friends of Ingalls bribed many voters. We have no doubt but that that charge is true." He went on to castigate the Ingalls voters because they had been bought "by Soule's railroad." He also pointed out that the "people of Montezuma had openly declared their intention of voting for Ingalls (as the county seat) in return for the railroad. In fact, Mr. Soule had posted a $70,000 bond to fulfill this promise." In declaring Ingalls the county seat he also pointed out that the "Ingalls observer"—meaning me—had been driven out of Cimarron and that the Cimarron leaders had stuffed their ballot boxes with seven hundred votes and had concealed the boxes until it became known how many votes were needed. Then they had produced enough of the fraudulent votes to carry the election by forty votes.

Though the minority opinion was that the entire election should be declared void, the majority opinion was that there were plenty of honest voters in southwestern Kansas who had not been "tampered with by Soule's patronage or by Cimarron's threats" and that therefore the decision designating Ingalls as county seat of Gray County should stand.

Tin Stars

WHILE THE courts were lengthily debating the county seat issue I took a trip back home to Indiana, primarily to see my mother and Adda, but also to avoid being shot at. After the Cimarron incident I didn't go anywhere without a gun. Some friends in Cimarron sent me a warning that Charlie Dixon and the others were bragging about what they were going to do to me. I knew Dixon was a braggart, but a fool with a gun, and that Jake Shoup was still a friend of mine underneath all this nonsense. But there were a few rough characters who might take it into their heads to bushwhack me. Later I heard that Charlie had told everyone he had run me out of the county. He would soon have his mouth shut—by me.

Mother, I noticed, had not changed much. Father said quietly that things were about the same. Dan, when we were alone, said Adda was still seeing Tom Devers.

I was all set to ride to Portland when he told me that.

"Don't be a fool, George," Dan said.

"Maybe she prefers bankers to surveyors."

"George, are you coming back?" Dan asked suddenly. His

question took me by surprise, more than if Father or Mother had asked me.

"I don't know, Dan," I said. "Honestly, I don't know."

"If you stay out there another six months, you'd better start looking for a new girl, George," he said bluntly.

I unsaddled the mare and led her back to her stall. The next day I wandered all over the tract, examining the rail fence, which was as good as the day Dan and I had built it, tramped over familiar gulleys and gorges and spent some time in the swamp, examining the secret spots where once I had placed my traps. It was more than a nostalgic tour of scenes of happier days; it was part of a desire to find an answer.

Christmas of 1888 passed. For a time the crowded house, the gay laughter and the sight of roses again in Mother's cheeks pushed aside my personal difficulties. Then, as the year turned, a rider from Geneva came up to our place.

I was in the north part of the tract when Dan found me. "George, there's a message for you from Dodge City. It looks important."

I hurried back to the house. A man from the Geneva telegraph office handed me a small envelope. The message said simply, "Come back at once. Need you." It was signed Bill Tilghman.

"Is anything wrong, George?" Mother asked anxiously.

"I don't know," I said, "but I must leave at once."

"What is it, George?" Father persisted.

"I honestly don't know," I said, slightly testy. "Tilghman is a good friend of mine. Apparently he needs my help."

I left at four o'clock that same afternoon to catch the next train out of Portland. In a way I welcomed this diversion; perhaps Fate would take care of my decision.

Back at Ingalls, I learned that Buffalo Joe Reynolds, the sheriff of Gray County, had been shot while chasing rustlers and that Bill had been asked to take his place. His first job was to remove the county records from Cimarron to Ingalls.

"How are you going to do it?" I asked Bill.

"Just go in and take the records," Bill said casually.

"When?" I asked.

"Tomorrow," Bill said.

"Saturday?" I exclaimed.

Bill nodded.

"Don't count me in," I said.

Bill ignored me. "Newt Watson (the newly elected Ingalls county clerk) went into Cimarron to get the records and they drove him out. They said there weren't enough men with enough guts to come in and remove the records."

"So you want me to go with you and prove there are?" I said.

Bill nodded. "I'm deputizing you, Billy Ainsworth, Fred Singer, Neal Brown, Jim and Tom Masterson and Ed Brooks. Newt Watson will come along with the official order for the records. Charley Reicheldeffer will drive his wagon. Incidentally, George, your county surveying records are also there. Riley refused to give them up. Want to know what he told Newt?"

"Nothing pleasant," I said.

"A. T. said to tell you if you want the records to come and get them yourself and not to send a boy on a man's errand," Bill said, grinning.

"Riley and I will settle it when we meet," I said. "I'm not going to get shot over some old ledgers and rods."

"I'll see you in the morning at ten, George," Bill said in his nonchalant way. "We'll stop by your place."

"It's a hell of a note bringing me back fifteen hundred miles to get shot at," I said.

"I hope it rains," Bill said and walked away.

Promptly at ten o'clock a wagon driven by a two-horse team stopped in front of my place. Charley was driving and the other fellows, armed with Winchesters and six-shooters, sat in the back. Neal and Fred and the others waved.

"Come on, George," Bill said. "Get in."

I just shook my head.

"Not showing the white feather, are you, George?" Bill taunted. "Some of the records we're going after are yours. . . ."

Bill never raised his voice. Had he shouted his implications I might have shrugged them off, but I couldn't disregard that soft, inquiring voice.

I stormed back into my office, strapped on my gunbelt and came out. "I'm only going along as a witness to your ignorance of the temper of those people," I said.

"Get off your soap box, George, and get in," Neal said.

I pointed to the wagon. "That's the damnedest fool way I ever saw of going into a town where people are going to shoot at you. One horse down and we'll all be in a hell of a fix."

Billy nodded to Bill. "That's all been taken care of, George," he said.

Bill stood up in the driver's seat and said to all of us, "You are all officers of the law and I don't want any shooting—only in self-defense."

"Why is everyone carrying a gun?" I asked.

"Protection," Bill said. "Now shut up, George, and let's get going."

As we started Bill explained, "If we do get separated, Charlie Brown will have a wagon waiting at the depot and he'll bring us back to Ingalls on the south side of the river."

Charley clucked to his team and we started across the plains— toward Cimarron.

THE COUNTY SEAT WAR

KANSAS CITY, MO., Jan. 13.—The *Journal's* Wichita special says: "General Meyer telegraphed that he had arrived at Cimarron, the location of the recent county seat war, this morning. All was quiet. . . ."

ANOTHER BLOODY CONFLICT FEARED

ST. LOUIS, MO., Jan. 13.—A Topeka special to the *Republican* says J. A. Sharp, Chairman of the Board of County Commissioners of Gray County, arrived this afternoon from the seat of the trouble to lay the matter before Governor Martin. He says the militia arrived just in time to prevent another battle, as the Ingalls people were preparing to make another assault upon the town and have threatened to kill the Cimarron leaders the first time an opportunity presents. He insists that there will be more trouble and says the people of both towns seem intensely excited over the matter, and that only the presence of a strong force of militia will prevent another conflict.

—Denver Republican, January 14, 1889

Battle of Cimarron

THE STREETS were deserted that bright, cold morning of January 12, 1889, when our wagon pulled up in front of the two-story brick building in which the office of the county clerk was located.

Bill Tilghman ordered me, Jim and Tom Masterson, Billy Ainsworth and Newt Watson upstairs, while he, Fred and Neal took stations around the building, ready for any mob action. But the streets were still quiet.

Riley, the ex-county clerk, was in the main office and in his office as chairman of the county supervisors was Jake Shoup. I stepped in quickly. Jake saw me and started to go for his gun, but I outdrew him. He had his gun half out of his holster and for a long moment we stared at each other. I guess we symbolized, in a way, this whole stupid business: two old friends ready to kill each other for the honor of having his own community named county seat. I remember saying, "Jake, if you pull it, I'll wing that hand, so help me."

"I should have killed you when you were here last," Jake said.

"Maybe. Turn around." He turned and I flipped his gun out. One of the boys came in and we tied up Jake and rolled him under a chair so that he wouldn't get hit if the firing started.

Riley dived for the vault where the records were kept when he saw the Mastersons come in. Jim shouted, "Touch that vault, Riley, and I'll kill you."

Jim swung over the rail. Neal, Newt, Billy and I followed, while Tom Masterson stood at the top of the stairs with his gun in his hand, just in case someone rushed us.

We each took a load of books, while Jim got the official seal so they could not issue any more script, and we hurried downstairs and threw the stuff in the wagon. Tom remained on guard upstairs. On my second trip I found my surveyor's equipment and records which belonged to me and brought that down.

I was starting out the door when I heard the first six-shooter go off—five shots right in a row. Just as I stepped into the street there was a roar and a load of buckshot raked the building not more than two feet above me, showering me with brick and flattened pieces of lead.

I threw my stuff into the wagon and drew my gun as Bill cried, "George! Up in the window!"

I looked up and took a snap shot at a man aiming at me with a Winchester. But I'm sure I didn't hit him, although he tumbled out of the window and rolled along the small tin roof and to the street.

Then, as if they had risen out of the earth, more than a hundred men, mounted and on foot, appeared. They milled about for a few minutes, shouting. Then the bullets began to fly. One shotgun blast tore the bricks above my head and showered me with pellets. Weeks later I found some in my coat pocket.

They came toward us, dodging from door to door, firing as

they came. I almost dropped my gun when I saw two women, each armed with a rifle, rush out of a side street. Bill and I used the wagon as a fort and started to return their fire. "Get the horses, George," Bill shouted. "Don't kill them—try to scare them off."

I couldn't help but laugh. There were so many it would take an expert to miss them. One rider who seemed to be shouting orders made a prime target and much as I hated to do it, I dropped his horse. He just stood there, shouting and shaking his fist, until Bill's slug threw up dust near him. Then he dived for cover. Horses were flailing at the air with their hooves, wounded ones were screaming in pain, men were shouting, the air was heavy with gunpowder and alive as if with the frantic buzzing of angry bees.

The firing became quite heavy. Finally, one bullet tore through Charley Reicheldeffer's hip. Fortunately, the bullet did not sever any bones but came out eight inches from its entry. The ball then nicked one of the team. The horses leaped forward, throwing Charley backward inside the wagon and knocking him out.

When I saw the team start up the street, I started to head them off. But Bill shouted, "Let them go, George, and keep on firing. Hold them off."

Billy Ainsworth, puffing under a load of heavy ledgers, came down with Newt Watson. "Hurry up, Billy, we can't hold them off much longer," Bill said. "Tell Jim to hurry."

We could see the crowd—there must have been sixty guns—edging up the street. I remember that one fellow, suddenly bold, started to run across the street in a dodging, twisting run. Suddenly he spun around and went down. When he got back on his feet he was holding his shoulder. "Don't kill him," Bill shouted. "Let him go."

Far down the street we could see some horsemen beginning to gather. We were now straggling on foot and since they far outnumbered us they could easily wipe us out. Fred Singer and Billy Ainsworth had now joined us and were helping to hold back some of the Cimarron fighters. "Tell Jim to come down, Fred," Bill shouted. "We've got to get out of here." Chips of brick and mortar were flying all about us.

Fred ran upstairs, then came down. "They're coming," he shouted above the firing.

"Get back to the canal," Bill ordered. "Shoot down the horses."

The Eureka Irrigating Canal was about three hundred yards from where we were standing. Just beyond that was the bridge and the road which went to Ingalls. We started to back down the street, moving back steadily, falling on one knee, firing, then retreating a few steps. Above the crash of rifles and six-shooters came the high scream of wounded horses, a sound that tears any man's heart out. But it had to be done. Two horses down. That made them hesitate.

Suddenly it seemed as if a mule had kicked my right leg from under me. I stumbled and fell. I looked down—my leg was still there, but my right boot near the shin was shredded. I got to my feet. About ten feet farther along it seemed as if that same mule kicked both legs out from under me.

This time I crashed down, harder than before. My right leg now had no feeling. I could see the blood trailing on the ground. I managed to get to my feet and, by using the Winchester as a crutch, began to make my way toward the canal. I had not gone more than thirty feet when the world exploded in a shower of stars as something nearly tore the back of my head off.

The gunfire brought me back to consciousness. I rolled over and saw blood all over the ground where my head had been.

I knew I had been hit. I thought for a moment I was dying. The whole world was spinning as I pulled myself to my feet. Still using my Winchester as a crutch, I made the last few yards—I'll never know how—to the canal. When I crawled over the edge I slid down a few feet, then clawed my way back up to the rim.

As I looked over I could see Bill Tilghman, Fred Singer and Billy Ainsworth backing toward me, firing steadily. Billy was helping Ed Brooks, who looked to be badly wounded. Beyond them was Charlie Dixon, down on one knee. There was a crack and I was showered with dirt. Now I knew it had been Charlie who had shot me. Now he was ready to finish me off.

I was weak, but not too feeble to bring the fight to Dixon. I had a score to settle with him and now I was ready to kill him. I got a bead on Charlie and pulled the trigger. There was a roar and that's all I knew. The Winchester, clogged with dirt, had exploded in my face and had knocked me back into the ditch! That's where Tilghman found me.

By this time Charley, although bleeding badly, had managed to bring his team under control. As I came to he had driven the team back to the canal, before he again slipped into unconsciousness. He was put in the back along with Ed Brooks, now also unconscious, and seriously wounded by a bullet in the side.

I recovered consciousness as Bill was lifting me up. I heard him say to Fred Singer, "Is the kid dead?"

"No, he's too damn ornery," Fred said. Weak as I was, I had to laugh. Bill and Fred heaved me in the back of the wagon and there I lay in a spreading pool of blood. We were all bleeding as freely as a creek in a thaw.

"Did the others get out, Bill?" I asked Tilghman.

"They probably made Charlie Brooks' wagon at the depot," he said. "But I'm going back to find out."

"No, you're not," Newt Watson shouted. "Here they come."

"Get in the wagon and drive, Fred," Bill shouted. "We'll get in the back."

The wagon took off with a lurch and we started our wild ride across the prairie. From far off I could hear the distant shouts and the pounding hooves of many horses. I could see Bill hurriedly piling up ledgers at the back of the wagon to make a sort of fort.

Then a rain of bullets began to hit the wagon. Some screamed overhead. I could hear Fred shouting at the team as he cracked the whip over their heads.

There was one thought in all our minds; had the other boys escaped?

Bill, Billy and Newt kept up a steady fire at the pursuing Cimarron horsemen, knocking down some of their animals and taking the starch out of some of them.

But they still pressed us hard. Finally, Bill picked up a buffalo gun from the bottom of the wagon and shouted, "This will stop them."

He placed the heavy weapon over the edge of the pile of books, sighted and fired. The crash of the gun sounded like a small cannon. Fred, who was looking back, whooped. "That's stopping them, Bill!"

The heavy gun crashed again. As if in reply, six-shooters and Winchesters barked, slugs splintering the wagon and plunking into the heavy ledgers.

But the buffalo gun and Billy's and Newt's rifles were too much for the Cimarron riders. When two more horses went down the other riders pulled up short. They just cursed and shouted after our wagon, which rapidly disappeared in a cloud of dust.

The Battle of Cimarron was half-over.

When we reached Ingalls the bottom of the wagon looked as if we had just returned from selling a load of stuck hogs. Blood dripped from the cracks in the bottom of the wagon. There was blood on Bill and Fred. The blood-smeared books were shattered and had big holes in them and the sideboards of the wagon were pockmarked with holes.

The whole town gathered as Charley, Ed Brooks and I were brought into Doctor Clark's office. At first it appeared as if Ed would cash in his chips, but he held on, and Doc Clark said he was out of danger. Charley, although the bullet had gone clear through him was up and smoking a cigar within an hour. The bones in my shin were shattered, I had a deep bullet hole in the back of my knee and a slug in the back of my head. When he stopped the bleeding, Doc gave me a sedative. The boys carried me to my office and placed me on the cot in the rear of the place. I must have been out of my mind during the afternoon, because Fred Singer, who stayed with me, told me later he found me walking around with my hand held in front of me, as though I were holding a gun, muttering incoherently.

The long afternoon dragged on. There was still no word from Tom and Jim Masterson and Neal Brown. Bill Tilghman kept pacing up and down without saying much. We hoped the boys had reached the wagon and had perhaps gone to Dodge. Finally, about two o'clock, Charlie Brown came in with the news: Tom, Jim and Neal were beseiged in the city hall by the whole town of Cimarron.

"Sounds like a damn war is going on there," Charlie said.

This was what was happening back there. When we had started to retreat, Jim, Tom and Neal decided they would bring down the last of the record books. By the time they got downstairs we were up the street near the canal and the Cimarron mob were almost upon them. The only thing they *could* do was go back upstairs. In a few minutes they were cut off.

More than two hundred armed men had gathered. Some tried to rush upstairs, but Jim's snap shot took off one fellow's hat and they just turned and rushed back down. For a time there were no more heroes. Then someone put a ladder up against the building to the second-story window, hoping to trick the Mastersons into thinking that some of the Ingalls people were in town. But that didn't work. Jim kicked the ladder back into the street.

The Cimarron people had another trick. They entered the grocery store below and started to riddle the floor. Jim, Tom, and Neal then climbed to the top of the iron safe. "Treed on a safe," is the way Tom described it.

After splintering the floorboards, the men below shouted up the stairs. "If you don't come out in fifteen minutes with your hands up, we're going to blow up the building."

Jim and Tom Masterson wrote out a message to Jake Shoup, who had managed to untie himself and was standing in the street below. The message went something like this: "We have guns and plenty of ammunition. If you try to dynamite this building we'll kill the first man who enters. We are sworn officers of the law and we don't want to kill any Cimarron men, but you are preventing us from doing our sworn duty."

Just then Neal, who was peering out the window, called across the room, "Here they come, Jim."

As Tom told me later, "Jim and I leaped off the top of the safe and ran to the window. I saw a man starting across the street with a bundle of what looked like sticks under his arm. He was carrying dynamite, and once he got across the street and could hug the sides of the building, it would have been difficult to get him. And if he got in, it meant only that we would have to rush them, and we didn't know how many would have been killed or wounded. I doubt if we would have got out of the town alive."

The man who was carrying the dynamite dived into a doorway. Jim and Tom waited for ten minutes and there was complete silence in the town. Then Jake Shoup came out with a white rag tied on the end of a stick.

"Masterson," he shouted, "I want to talk."

"Come on and talk, Jake," Jim shouted.

Jake came up to the front of the building and shouted up to the Mastersons that if they would promise to stop firing they would be escorted to the depot and put on a train to Ingalls.

"We're not going to surrender our guns," Jim replied.

"No need to, Jim," Jake said. "We don't want any more shooting. Billy English is dead and we have some wounded. There's been enough blood spilled already."

"You should have thought of that before you fired on peace officers, Jake," Jim said. "Did the others get away?"

"I think George Bolds is in a bad way," he said. "And some of the other boys were hit. It was a bad morning all around."

Jim and Tom talked it over and decided it wasn't a trap, so they came down into the street with their guns drawn and ready for any bushwhacking. But there wasn't any. The men began to collect behind Jake.

Jim nodded in the direction of the depot. "Let's go, Jake," he said.

The Cimarron men drifted on both sides of the Mastersons and the strange procession began to move up the street: Jake Shoup in front, the Cimarron men grim and dusty, carrying their Winchesters; the tips of their holsters sagging just under their overcoats, their hats pulled down on their faces; then the Mastersons, Jim, his face cold and impassive, and Tom, slightly stouter, with Neal walking between them. They had put their guns back in their holsters, but they kept their hands on them. "We weren't out of town by any means," Jim told me.

The tension must have been electric at the depot, because, as Jim said, there was some grumbling in the ranks, but Jake was the boss. He just growled to them to shut up or they'd all be killed. His men gave Jim, Tom and Neal some hard looks, but they didn't draw on them. If they had, the Cimarron depot would have made the O. K. Corral fight look like only a prelude to a real massacre.

Eventually, the train arrived. When they reached Ingalls they found out why Jake and the Cimarron men had let them go. When the press reports flashed across the press wires from the Kansas City *Star,* who had the story from the *Jacksonian,* a rival to the *Union,* in Ingalls, a friend told Bat Masterson, who was then operating a gambling house in Denver. Bat wired Jake, "If you don't allow my brothers, both law officers, to leave your town peacefully, I'll hire a train and come in with enough men to blow Cimarron off the face of Kansas."

That night, wrapped in bandages like a mummy, I lay on my cot while a steady stream of visitors came in and out, all promising to join up and go in and finish the job in Cimarron. It took a lot of talking by Tilghman to calm the hot-heads.

The second day after the battle there was a commotion outside my office and the door was flung open. Standing there was Ben Daniels, the deputy whose life I had saved in Dodge some years before. Behind him were two men. From their expressionless eyes and the way they wore their gunbelts, gunfighter style, with the ends tied around their thighs I knew their profession—hired guns.

Ben looked surprised when he saw me. "Bat Masterson said he

heard you were dead. I thought I'd look up a few people in Cimarron for you and pay them a visit."

"No need to, Ben," I said. "The doc says I'll pull through and I guess there's been enough killing already over those damn records."

"Sure glad you pulled through, George," he said. "I'll chin for a while and we'll have a meal and I'll head back to my saloon in Denver. Those damn bartenders are probably robbing me clean right now."

The two men behind him didn't say a word. Ben told me they were two killers he had working for him in his gambling place in Denver to discourage the rough element, as he called it, from holding him up.

Later my old friend, Prairie Dog Morrow showed up to see how I was. He and Ben stowed away some food and whiskey.

"Be sure to look us up, George," they both said. I shook hands and watched them ride out of town. I never saw either of them again.

"Outlaw?"

GRAY COUNTY was a powder keg for days following the Battle of Cimarron, as the newspapers called our shooting affair. The Cimarron *Jacksonian* commented: "Six of the Ingalls gang, including Bolds, were shot and badly wounded. But to our utter disappointment, all the hellions will recover. If ever we longed to see the business of an undertaker boom and lots of deep-eyed demons laid to rest beneath the soil, it is now."

J. W. "Will" English and A. J. Bliss of Cimarron were dead. Several men were wounded, none very seriously, but Cimarron was ready to continue the war.

The afternoon following the shooting, riders began to form in the square at Cimarron. Every man had a six-shooter or a Winchester. They were going to burn Ingalls to the ground.

Someone sent word to Ingalls, where the townspeople quickly piled bales of hay as roadblocks at the entrances of the streets and put sandbags on roofs to make forts. Guarding them were men with rifles.

A posse of Dodge City men—all men who could handle a gun—rode into Ingalls. They made my office their headquarters.

They didn't do much talking, but it was evident what they were in town for. Some of the New York newspapers and big western dailies reported that we sent out scouts as far as the Texas border to recruit a small army of hired killers to protect the town. They were not paid or recruited; they had come because they were friends of mine and the Mastersons.

Jake Shoup rushed to Topeka and Governor Martin sent in General Myers and his troops. They surrounded Cimarron and set up pickets a mile outside their lines to warn the main body if the Ingalls men started to ride in. Meanwhile, the troops had a devil of a time with the Cimarron boys. They were out for blood and the sight of two of their citizens lying in state added fuel to their rage. As many as two hundred horsemen, as well as wagons and buckboards, loaded with armed men, were milling about Cimarron's square, ready to invade Ingalls.

However, the fuse fizzled out. General Myers ordered the mob not to leave the town limits. He told them he would shoot down the first man to leave. This was blunt talk, but it took some of the fire out of them.

But the county was still restless. Rumors sprouted everywhere. The curious came to gape at me and the bullet-shattered wagon. I didn't care. I just lay there wondering if I would ever walk properly again. Doc Clark had managed to get the slug out of my shin and fix up the wound, but he couldn't get at the ball in the back of my knee and he was afraid to probe for the slug in the nape of my neck. Both began to pain me and the leg wound began to fester. Doc Clark called in the doctor from Dodge, but he couldn't do much good.

"George," he said, "you had better go to a Kansas City hospital."

"Hell, I'm all right," I said.

"Well," Doc said, "you'll be a hell of a sight to your mother with a wooden peg for a leg."

That scared the devil out of me. Two weeks after the battle I went to a small hospital he recommended near Kansas City. But the physician he had known had died and some others had taken over the place. It was a shabby old frame building, but I was so sick I didn't care. They put me to bed after I had placed my money, about five hundred dollars, in their safekeeping. They gave me an elaborate receipt. That night the head nurse came in and we struck it off just fine when she learned that I came from Gray County. It seemed that an aunt of hers lived in Caldwell and another of her kin in Liberal, so it was like "old home week."

But as we talked, I sensed she was worried. When I asked her why, she just changed the subject. I forgot about it and went to sleep. That night I awoke with a start when I heard a noise and went for my gun under the pillow by instinct. It was only the nurse. She whispered that I had better get out and fast. The two so-called doctors were really two shady abortionists and they had already taken my money and were planning to dispose of me. However, she said, she had the combination of the safe. She had already opened it and had taken out my money. She pressed the envelope in my hand. I didn't need any more urging. I dressed and hobbled out, first pressing a hundred dollars on the nurse, who didn't want to take it.

I wasn't too steady on my legs and it was difficult to climb down the flight of stairs. The nurse said she couldn't help me because if we were found together it would mean not only her job but she would be in for a terrible beating.

I took each step carefully, with my hand on my six-shooter. I was determined I would kill the first one of them who came toward me. The pain I was suffering was terrific, and I think I was feverish and not too accountable. But what I *did* know was that I had my money and no one was going to take it away.

The place was like a tomb. Each creaking step was like the sound of raw pine lumber being ripped apart. But nothing stirred. I left the building and took off as fast as I could. A man in a wagon gave me a lift and I managed to get to the depot.

As I recall, it was about four o'clock when the train arrived at the deserted depot. I hobbled aboard, so doubled up with pain that I could hardly stand. I was just on the top step when I heard a carriage come up at a gallop. I turned and there were the two doctors. They started shouting for me to come back, that I was a sick man. The conductor looked at me with a queer expression.

"What's the matter, Mister?" he asked.

"They're a couple of thieves," I said. "They run what they call a hospital, but it's just a place where they rob people. . . ."

The conductor just waved his hand, jumped up the steps and slammed the door.

The train started with such a jerk I flopped on my back. I could hear the shouts of the two butchers, but they were soon lost in the grinding and clicking of the wheels. The conductor helped me to a seat and he cared for me until I got to Dodge. They virtually carried me off the train.

Three days later I was on my way to Fort Wayne, where Father and Dan were waiting to take me to a clinic there.

Both Dan and Father stayed with me while the doctors removed both slugs. I had a wonderful constitution and in ten days I was myself again. One of the first things I asked Dan about was Adda. He avoided my looks and said he guessed I should forget her.

"Why, Dan?" I asked.

Dan sighed. "Adda's father has given her orders never to see you again."

"My God, what have I done?" I cried.

Dan studied me. "Nothing, George, nothing except being called a leader of an outlaw gang which raided Cimarron." He leaned closer. "Father didn't want to tell you, but Mother was packing to go to Ingalls to claim your body when the message came that you were alive."

I was stunned. Outlaw . . . ?

I hurriedly described the political picture in Gray County for Dan and gave him a glowing account of the high caliber of the men with whom I had ridden into Cimarron. "Bill Tilghman is one of the most honorable men in the West," I said. "All of us were deputized as officers of the law."

Dan shrugged. "I've heard that there's a thin line separating some of the marshals in those towns and killers." He looked at me. "George, did you kill two men in Santa Fe? The papers said you did."

"They tried to rob me," I said. "Both needed killing."

Dan looked shocked. "Needed killing?" he asked. "Were you after them as a deputy?"

I was forced to shake my head. Dan looked at me in a strange way. Then, without saying anything more, he changed the subject. When he left I lay there in the dark for a long time. I hadn't known before that I had been reported killed. I cursed myself when I thought of what a shock it must have been to Mother and Adda.

I didn't get much sleep that night. I was twenty-seven now, and Adda was gone. I told myself that it served me right. Could I expect a girl to wait for me while I roamed around the country? The miracle was that Adda had waited this long.

But there was always another hill to climb. . . .

The Last Hill

WHEN I returned to Ingalls in the winter of 1889, Gray County seemed to have settled down. The Battle of Cimarron was still talked about, but life was going on; men had more important things on their minds, spring planting and the next roundup.

The Garden City Land Office didn't have much surveying to be done now. Most of the folks were moving toward the frontier of Oklahoma. I packed up, locked my office, and with most of my stuff wrapped up in a slicker and a blanket, took the Santa Fe for Arkansas City, Kansas.

They were going to open the Unassigned Lands in Oklahoma. There was going to be a Run for it—this was the last of the open lands. The camps were stretched along the prairie from Caldwell to Arkansas City. Thousands of men, women and children had been camped along the banks of the Arkansas River, some of them for years. Most of them were the original "boomers" who had invaded the Indian Territory illegally several years before with Captain David Payne. It had been Payne's arrest which focused national attention on the Unassigned Lands, which the government finally opened to the public.

President Harrison proclaimed that on April 22, 1889, any American citizen over twenty-one could stake out a claim for one hundred and sixty acres of land, or a quarter-section, as they called it.

The procedure agreed upon was very simple: it was the case of first come, first served. The settlers could ride a horse, a buckboard, surrey or dray—or they could walk. The idea was to get your stake down first and register your claim at the land office in Guthrie.

The Gladston House in Arkansas City was full, so I bedded down in a stable and was glad to get space. The place was full of life. Men, four-deep, stood at the bars in the hidden "liquor joints," bootleggers peddled their wares openly, gamblers ran their games in tents, gay ladies plied their moonlight trade and the whole place had the flavor of the gold camps at their peak and the cow towns when the herds were driving north. This was before the settlers were permitted to cross the Cherokee Outlet to the line on the 19th.

I wandered from camp to camp. I was like a tumbleweed; I went where the restless winds blew me. I met a number of men whom I had known in Dodge, Caldwell and towns in northern Kansas counties. Inevitably they asked me about the Cimarron fight, but I shut them off fast. I had had all I wanted of that episode. My wounds had barely healed and were still vivid reminders.

On the 19th the Cherokee Outlet was opened and the wagons moved to the Oklahoma line.

At night the camps along the line were something to see; campfires winked like the yellow eyes of a multitude of cats crouching in a line along the black prairie. Fiddles scraped, Jew's harps twanged and husky voices lifted in both bawdy songs and spirituals.

The cavalry, under Captain Hays constantly patrolled the land searching out "Sooners"—those men who tried to hide out in the Unassigned Lands "too soon'—and bringing them back to Arkansas City.

I looked for Bill Tilghman and although I heard he was around, I always seemed to miss him. But I did catch up with Eat-Em-Up-Jake, a part-time hired gun, rustler and outlaw whom I had known in Dodge City.

"My God, Jake," I said, "are you aiming to settle down?"

"Hell, no," he grunted. "I came to rob somebody."

I didn't see Jake until I returned to Arkansas City from a trip across the Strip to the line. In the afternoon he hailed me as I was crossing a street to the Gladston House. Jake, who was getting drunk, held up a wad of bills. It seemed he had made a killing at cards and didn't have to rob anyone—at least for a time.

"The hell with this place Bolds," he said, "come on over to my camp."

I was tired of riding around and one place was as good as another, so we rode to the banks of the river where he was bunking down with a Missouri family. The farmer was dirt-poor with a scrawny, toil-worn wife and a passel of kids. I wondered how this rickety wagon would ever make the run. Jake said they came from Russia, Missouri, where he had some kin and that sort of made him part of the family.

It was a meager meal of cornpone and sowbelly. Jake kept nursing that keg of bottled lightning he'd bought and putting on the brag. I just let what he said go in one ear and out the other. Jake didn't seem much like the deadly gunfighter talk had made him out to be. To me he seemed to be an old drunk. In a way, it was pathetic. The lanky farmer wasn't impressed either. He continued with his chores, while his wife corraled the children into the wagon.

After Jake had told all the lies he knew, he settled down to steady drinking. I just sat and stared into the fire. I was lonely.

Jake's voice startled me. When I looked up he was handing me the jug.

"Dammit," he growled, "are you deaf? I asked you what the hell you were thinking about?"

I shrugged and told him not to rile me. To satisfy him I accepted a swallow. God, I can still taste that raw whiskey.

"Where you from, Bolds?" he asked.

I told him. He rubbed his beard and told me his earliest memory was of stealing a neighbor's horse. He said it with a trace of pride in his voice. Then he went on to tell me how he had traveled around, punching cows, rustling, horse-stealing— he said he once ran a herd of stolen horses almost a thousand miles—and some road agent work. Just rambling talk. As he talked I looked at him across the fire; looked at the dirty, bearded face, red-veined by poor whiskey, the glazed old eyes, the rotted teeth.

Suddenly I remembered what my mother had done once, when Dan and I were small. She had been telling us about the seasons and, to help us understand, she drew an ugly old man's face and told us it was "Winter." I looked at Jake. He was "Winter." I was "Summer." But soon I would be "Autumn."

Jake's startled voice was at my back as I walked away. It kept asking in a plaintive way where I was going. I said over my shoulder that I was going home.

No Wedding for Tom Devers

I NEVER made the Run. Physically, I wasn't up to it. I guess I had left the hospital sooner than was good for me.

I was listless and just sat in my office back in Ingalls and watched the town move past. I wrote to Dan and Father and told them how I was getting on and somehow, merely writing a letter to Indiana seemed to link me closer with home.

I think it was in May, 1889, about a month after the run, when Bill Tilghman sent me a letter asking me to come to Guthrie and visit him and Neal. One place was as good as another, and I took the Santa Fe to Arkansas City, hired a horse—a jug-head if I ever rode one—and headed across the Cherokee Outlet. Settlers were still coming back from what they had thought was paradise and some were even staked out in the Outlet. They stayed there until 1893, when the cavalry cleared them out for the biggest of the several runs into Oklahoma.

I arrived in Guthrie and saw Bill and Neal and for a time rode with them. As I recall, Bill had a couple of racehorses and a small track. But as the weeks went by, it all seemed as if everything had happened before. I told Bill I'd bet if I stayed there a few more years some damn fool would be asking me to get some county records for him.

One big reason the frontier had paled on me was the specter of Adda marrying someone else. It hadn't been as easy to clear her from my mind as I had thought. She was constantly in my thoughts, along with my folks and the farm.

One morning, after a long, restless night, I saddled up.

"Back to Ingalls, George?" Bill asked.

"Indiana this time, Bill," I said.

I can remember how he squinted up at me.

"Home, eh, George?"

I nodded. Neal came up and I leaned down and shook his hand.

"George is going to Mee-rage, Neal," Bill said seriously.

We all laughed and then I rode off. I never saw Bill or Neal again. I had climbed my last hill. I was going home.

I stopped first at the Merchants' Hotel in Portland to see Adda. With a thousand doubts in my heart, I sent my name up by a bellboy. He came down in a few moments and told me to come up. I knocked on the door and a man's voice asked me to come in.

Mr. Weldon studied me when I entered. "Just passing through, George?" he asked not unkindly.

"No, sir," I said. "I'm on my way home."

"You look thinner," he said. "How is your wound?"

"It was just a nick, Mr. Weldon," I said. Then I took a deep breath and talked. I guess I talked for more than an hour. He just sat there, nodding and listening. Maybe he was a mite envious. There are few men who have lived the exemplary life, the quiet life, who don't hanker at one time or another for a taste of the wanderer's role.

No Wedding for Tom Devers

When I had finished, my mouth was as dry as a sun-bleached buffalo bone. If Mr. Weldon had been a drinking man I would have asked him to come down to the bar. He tapped his desk for a few minutes, then shrugged his shoulders.

"As you know, George, Adda has been seeing some other young men and I don't like to interfere in her life. But if you wish, I'll leave her a message that you'll be here this evening."

"Thank you, sir," I said. We shook hands and I left.

"Seven sharp, George," he said.

I had a shave and the Negro porter in the barber shop brushed me down as though I were a prize mare. The dust rose in clouds. He shined my boots and at least I looked presentable. I was so jittery I could barely eat supper. At seven I was knocking on her door.

"Come in." My heart jumped like a winged buck. I knew whose voice that was.

"Good evening, George."

There she was in the sitting room, looking as pretty as a rose after the dew. I guess she knew it. I stumbled in and she waved me to a chair.

"You're looking thinner, George," she said.

"I rode up to Arkansas City for the Run," I said.

I tried to tell her how it was: the long line of canvas schooners, the home-seekers, the cowpunchers. She nodded politely.

"What were they looking for, George?" she asked softly.

"A new start," I said. "A new home."

"I don't need a new start, George," she said. "I have a home in Indiana and I love it."

"I have a home here, too, Adda," I said. "In Indiana."

"Are you through wandering, George?" she asked.

"Yes, Adda," I said. "I'm going back to Adams County tonight. I'm home."

"For how long, George?" she asked. "For a day and maybe a month this time?" She was still talking softly. "Then where will you go next time? You've tried Oklahoma."

"I'm home now."

I walked across the room and sat down beside her. "I'm home, Adda . . . I've come home to you."

"Why, George?" she asked. "Why—this time . . . ?"

"I saw myself in a man's face," I said. I tried to tell her what I had seen in Jake's face across the fire in the Cherokee Outlet that night.

She shook her head. "It's too late, George," she said. "It's too late—I'm engaged to be married."

I could only look at her. I was too stunned to speak. I should have been ready to accept the inevitable, but somehow I always thought that Adda would wait.

I asked her with dry lips, "Who is he?"

"Tom Devers," she said. "He asked Mother and Father last week and they approved."

"And you?" I insisted. "And you, Adda?"

She was fighting to hold back the tears. "I couldn't keep waiting, George," she said. "I couldn't keep waiting while every restless wind blew you from town to town. Half the time I didn't even know whether you were alive or not. Even your own mother and father didn't know. And then when Dan came that day and said you were dead. . . ."

"But it was a mistake," I said.

"I know—Dan came back the next day and told us you were still alive but wounded." She shook her head. "George, I just couldn't go on that way any longer."

"When are you and Tom getting married?" I asked.

My voice seemed to belong to someone else. I was almost

startled that it could sound so calm when I asked her that question.

"The arrangements for the wedding haven't been made," she said in a small voice.

Then I started to talk. I talked and talked and talked. Adda just sat, silent and stony-faced. Nothing I could say seemed to move her. Suddenly I felt so empty, so sick at heart that I couldn't go on. I cursed every day I had been away from Adda. I cursed the years and the places that had called me.

Then I stood up and walked across the room to where I had placed my coat on a chair. In those few seconds the dam inside Adda broke and she began to weep. I went back to her and took her in my arms.

That was the moment I knew there would be no wedding for Tom Devers.

She let me kiss her, but the moment our lips touched, she pushed me back, her eyes on fire.

"George Bolds," she cried, "you take off that damn gun!"

I was so amazed I said, "Yes, ma'am," and unbuckled my gunbelt and put it aside. It was the only time in our long life together that I ever heard Adda use a curse word.

We were married that September and I hung up that six-shooter.

But I was still quick on the trigger. We had just come back from our honeymoon—we had been married only ten days—and I was upstairs shaving, preparing to welcome some folks coming to our housewarming.

I heard a man's voice and curious, I went downstairs. There was a good-looking, well-dressed fellow, with some flowers, talking to Adda as if he owned her. I just walked to the bedroom, yanked that six-shooter from the holster and stormed down-stairs.

"Who in the hell are you?" I shouted.

He looked and gulped. Then he murmured something to Adda and ran out of that house. It seemed he was one of the fellows who had been seeing Adda and hadn't known she was married. He must have figured I was about to gun him where he stood.

I must have been a sight in my undershirt, lather on my face and a gun in my hand. . . .

Mr. and Mrs. George W. Bolds,

At Home,

After October 1, 1891.

West Line Street,

Geneva   *Indiana.*

George Bolds.   *Adda Weldon.*

Epilogue

So George and Adda were finally united on September 21, 1891—Adda's way. Their wedding, according to the yellowing newspaper clippings, was one of Portland's "biggest social events." It took place in the lobby of the Merchants' Hotel and was attended by many of the town's first families. George just growled whenever he spoke of it, but smiled when he recalled how pretty Adda had looked.

"I would have been a damn fool to have stayed back there and lost her," he said to me. "I'm glad I knew when I had enough . . . I sort of ate my cake and had it too . . . I had my years of freedom and wandering and I married the girl I loved. And we've had a rich life together with children I'm proud of. . . ."

George brushed lightly over his post-frontier years. But for the record, he and Adda left Portland for Geneva, where George was in the mercantile and oil business, then later moved to Bearcreek Township when oil was struck there. It was then that Adda found herself living frontier-style. The oil boom brought a rough element to the community, but Adda demonstrated she could match any of the women who broke sod on the Kansas frontier.

Once when George was away and a man tried to break in their front door, Adda ran into the bedroom and came out with a small pearl-handled revolver. She aimed it at the man's head. "If you don't leave immediately I'll kill you," she shouted.

The intruder stared through the glass. Adda walked to the door. "I'll count three," she said. "One . . . two. . . ."

By three he was gone.

"I was shaking so much after he left I could barely hold a glass of water," she said later.

After Indiana, where George won and lost a small fortune, he and Adda moved to Hammond, Louisiana, where he operated the Morris Retreat Farm with William and Gilbert Houlton. The Retreat was surrounded by 60,000 acres of land and Bolds and the Houltons established it as one of the largest livestock farms in the South. To this great farm came breeders from as far north as Iowa and as far east as Kentucky. It became the head-quarters of the Louisiana Swine Breeders' Association. George served one term as President.

By 1910 river sidewheelers were moving up and down the river with the name "Bolds' Livestock Farm" on their sides. Bolds' pure-blooded Duroc hogs were known throughout Europe and Central and South America.

Happiness was mixed with sorrow. One son, Herbert, died after ten months of a fatal and painful disease. During the long nights George and Adda never left the infant's crib. But there were other children—five in all—and their farm prospered.

But shortly after World War I, disaster struck. A hog plague wiped out the farm. After the debts were paid, Bolds became city construction engineer and inspector of improvements of Selma, Alabama. He served in this capacity until 1930, when all construction was ended in that community, then moved to New York City with his sons.

When Adda died George said, "I guess part of me went with her."

In 1954 George joined her. George's sister, now eighty-seven, is still living on the home place in Adams County, Indiana, and her grandson is farming another eighty acres as well as the original tract.